THIS COPY OF

**LAGONDA
2, 3 & 3½ LITRE
IN DETAIL**

IS SIGNED BY THE AUTHOR

Arnold Davey

ARNOLD DAVEY

H&S

LAGONDA
2, 3 & 3½ Litre

In Detail

LAGONDA
2, 3 & 3½ Litre

In Detail

BY ARNOLD DAVEY

Herridge & Sons

Published in 2007 by
Herridge & Sons Ltd
Lower Forda, Shebbear,
Beaworthy, Devon EX21 5SY

© Copyright Arnold Davey 2007

Designed by Ray Leaning,
MUSE Fine Art & Design Ltd.

Special photography
by Simon Clay

ISBN 978-0-9549981-8-9
Printed in China

Picture acknowledgements
Unless otherwise attributed, all black and white
photographs come from the Lagonda Club
Heritage Trust or from the author's collection.

Contents

Foreword

The public's conception of "Lagonda" varies from vague thoughts of funny lopsided boats in Venice to a recently introduced family hatchback from Renault (the Laguna). Only the enthusiast will have heard of the Lagonda car make, even though it is one of the longest lived in the industry. It was founded in 1899 by Wilbur Gunn to make steam engines for Thames river boats. He made his first motorcycle for sale in 1900 and grew steadily more ambitious. From motorcycles, Gunn progressed to tricars and eventually four-wheeled cars, which grew steadily bigger until in 1913 he decided to tackle the "cars for everyman", market which was abruptly stopped by the 1914-18 war. After peace was restored the company steadily took its products upmarket since it couldn't compete on volume with the likes of Ford or Morris. In 1925 the introduction of the 14/60 saw a quantum jump in the nature of the product and Lagonda made its re-entry to the quality car market.

During the period 1920-40 the nature of the car industry underwent a huge amount of change, not only in the products themselves but also in the way they were made. Lagonda was not rich enough, being perpetually short of money, to invest heavily in the expensive plant needed to mass-produce cars, and anyway the number of likely customers for so upmarket a vehicle was not enough to justify a change in the traditional way of making a car: a separate steel chassis on which was mounted a wood-framed, metal-panelled body. But the nature of the cars so produced did change to meet the growing demand for more comfort and refinement, coupled with less maintenance - and all without any loss of performance. The same period also saw the decline of the open tourer body in favour of closed cars that did not require special clothing. Each of the models of Lagonda covered here has its own character and we will trace the development of each in turn.

Considering the limited funds available, Lagonda had a continuing and successful involvement in competition at the highest level, and indubitably its finest hour was to win the Le Mans 24-hour race in 1935, one of only four British makes to do so. That the company was in receivership at the time and due to be auctioned the following day makes the story seem more like fiction, where the author is pouring on the drama. Yet that is what happened. The early essays at international motor racing were rewarded with mixed results, but some of the more lurid adventures, such as the 1928 crash at Le Mans, gained enormous publicity for the firm, even if it was not exactly what the management would have wished for. When the factory was instructed by the Society of Motor Manufacturers and Traders to stop entering trials and rallies the cause was taken up by private owners, some, but not all, with surreptitious factory support, but the minor events of the period tended to be sketchily reported and are frequently vague, as they

Wilbur Gunn. The only proper portrait of him, taken towards the end of his life and after he had trimmed his waxed "Kaiser Bill" moustache.

relied on outsiders supplying the information to the motoring magazines.

The models covered in this book were all dropped in 1935 when the newly re-formed company under Alan Good and W O Bentley decided to concentrate entirely on the 4½ Litre and, later, V12 models. These and the history from 1935 to 1940 are all covered in the companion volume in this series, *Lagonda 4½ Litre and V12 in Detail*.

Arnold Davey
June 2007

Chapter One

The Background

We must start by apologising to any readers who also have the companion 4½ Litre volume for covering the same background story of the beginnings of Lagonda's hundred-year history. But it is important to do so for the benefit of others who have not read the earlier book and who will need the whole story.

First we must explain the strange, Italian-sounding name. The company was founded by an expatriate American, Wilbur Adams Gunn, who was born in Troy, Ohio, in 1860 but brought up in Springfield, where his father, James Wynn Gunn, was postmaster, clergyman and ran a bookstore. Wilbur was apprenticed to Singer's, the sewing machine company and eventually set up as a sewing machine repairer in Springfield. In 1885 he married Bertha Myers, a neighbour, and in 1888 they moved to New York, where a daughter, Marjorie, was born. Wilbur's brother-in-law, Horatio Bradley, ran a company called the Lagonda Manufacturing Company which made cleaning equipment for boiler tubes and in April 1891 Wilbur left America, alone, to come to Britain to represent the company here. Lagonda was the name of a district in Springfield, so called after a corruption of the Native American name for a stream now known as Buck Creek.

Once here, Wilbur also took on consulting engineering work, specialising in hydraulic power plants, then very popular for things like lifts and theatre safety curtains. As a hobby he got interested in steam engines, and having settled in Staines, Middlesex, found there a demand for small steam engines for steam launches. His second hobby was opera singing, and it is believed that through this he came to meet Constance Grey, living with her husband Charles at The Cottage in Thorpe Road, Egham. The Greys were well connected, Charles being the brother of Lord Grey and Constance the daughter of a senior cavalry officer. Charles died in 1896 and by the beginning of 1898 Wilbur had divorced Bertha (or been divorced by her) and married Constance. On the marriage certificate Wilbur said he was a widower, which may have been true since Marjorie had been adopted by Wilbur's sister Nannie. But he also said he was 35 when he was 38 and gave his profession as "vocalist", probably to avoid offending Connie's family by revealing he was in "trade".

At about this time, he was visiting a site in connection with his hydraulics consultancy and found the cycling very hard work as the winter roads were "heavy", Victorian code for several inches of mud and horse droppings. So he made himself a little petrol motor and fixed it to his bicycle, driving the front wheel through a train of gears, later replaced by a belt. In this, Gunn was undoubtedly a pioneer

The first Lagonda motorcycle of 1900. Gunn had made one for himself before that but this one was for sale. Motorcycles were produced for about four years, getting steadily more powerful, until overtaken by the popularity of Tricars.

in motorcycling.

Once installed in The Cottage, Gunn took over the greenhouse and converted it into a workshop for his steam engines, demand for which was growing to such an extent that in 1899 he set up a private company called the Lagonda Engineering Company, and the following year he made his first motorcycle for sale, photographs of which survive. He only made and fixed the engine, the cycle parts coming from a Staines cycle maker called Knights. Cycling clubs were popular and fashionable and at this time did not distinguish between powered and non-powered machines, largely because there was little difference in speed between them. Gunn's motorcycles were only advertised locally, by word of mouth, but in November 1902 he registered "Lagonda" as a trademark and the following year he became a founder member of the Autocycle Club, later the ACU.

The big event of 1903 in the motorcycle world was the 1000 Miles Trial. Gunn took part and for the first time got some national publicity, for the event dominated the motorcycling press for weeks. He got a second class award and enough orders to begin to hire permanent staff. Alfie Cranmer, late of the Staines Linoleum factory, had been associated with Gunn since 1899 at least, but now became a paid employee, together with Bert Hammond, recruited from Knights. Not long after, Bill Amiss and George Wise joined, all

these four staying with the company for 30 years or more.

Motorcyclists wanting to carry a passenger at this time usually had to tow a trailer, an unpopular device, for the unfortunate occupant got bombarded with mud and stones from the back wheel while breathing in copious lungfuls of exhaust gas. There were stories, too, of them getting left behind when the towing hook broke and the driver didn't notice. From about 1904 the tricar idea began to take hold, with the passenger in the front

Wilbur Gunn in his workshop about 1899. He is on the left and Alfie Cranmer in the background.

Wilbur Gunn in the June 1906 Land's End to John O'Groats Trial on a water-cooled Tricar. The passenger is Alfie Cranmer. They got a Gold Medal.

Bert Hammond in the special lightweight 18hp racer at Brooklands in 1909. They won the Summer Handicap.

seat, nearer the accident but at least able to breathe. Gunn was a pioneer and sold his first tricar to a friend, G W Manning, who was both secretary of the Thames Valley Motor Cycling Club and also, by profession, Engineer and Surveyor to Staines Rural District Council. Manning was responsible a few years later for the first trials of tarmacadam as a solution to the dust and mud problems of roads. This first machine started out with a 3½hp motorcycle engine and a single-speed belt drive, but Manning found the performance so poor that Gunn had it back and rebuilt it with a 5hp engine, chain drive and a two-speed gearbox.

By now Gunn had rather lost interest in his other sidelines and set about building a

proper workshop by roofing over ever greater parts of the garden at The Cottage. He extended the brick wall along the Thorpe Road frontage up to roof height and cut a larger door in it to allow the tricars in and out. In the spring of 1904 he went public and set up the Lagonda Motor Company Limited on 18 May, with seven directors who bought the earlier private company off Gunn and issued debenture shares.

From 1904 to 1907 the tricars got bigger and heavier, finishing with 12hp watercooled engines and wheel steering. Gunn was always keen to promote his make by entering competitions and Lagonda tricars were extremely successful at trials and hillclimbs. Eventually there were teams of entrants who had some form of factory support, even if they owned the machines themselves. In the motorcycle era Gunn had provided a special machine for Harry Rignold to ride to represent Great Britain in the 1904 International Trophy race, held in France. To begin with, Gunn tended to conscript his wife to occupy the tricar's front seat but later friends of members of staff were expected to sit there. However, the tricar boom suddenly collapsed in 1907 with the advent of motorcycle sidecars, easier to drive and offering the flexibility of being detachable. Gunn's company went into Receivership in the spring, having built 69 tricars.

It is not quite clear what happened next, since he went on producing vehicles somehow. It is believed an "angel" came to his rescue in the form of a financial backer, C H Clapham, who paid the wages and generally kept the concern afloat. With tricars unsaleable, it was fairly simple to add a fourth wheel and some bodywork to produce a 10/12hp car. The first one was ready for Gunn to drive in the 1908 London-Edinburgh Trial. It was registered P 3856. One assumes its V-twin engine would have been turned through 90 degrees to get a simpler drive train, but not even a photograph of this car survives.

After building a very few 10/12hp cars, Gunn must have begun to feel that more performance was required. The tricars had been among the largest and fastest of their kind, but adding the fourth wheel and proper coachwork meant that the car was only adequate in this department. I doubt if the

funding was available to develop a larger Lagonda-built engine, and even if it had been, the time taken would have imperilled the company, so Gunn did the obvious thing and bought in an engine for his next design, the 14/16hp. This engine came from Coventry-Simplex and was a sidevalve four-cylinder, the cylinders cast as two pairs, with magneto ignition and a water pump. A JAP carburettor was fitted, and the three-speed gearbox with gate change was of Lagonda's own make. The engine size is unknown but can be estimated as under 2 litres. Not content with this, later in 1909 Gunn produced a 16/18hp model using a larger 2140cc Coventry-Simplex engine. This car had heavier axles, detachable wheels and a full four-seater body, compared with the 2/3 seater body of the earlier car. Provision was made for a dynamo, so clearly electric lighting was also possible. Gunn had always provided positive location of his driving wheels, even on the tricars, so it was no surprise to find the rear axle located by pairs of long radius arms which gave truly vertical movement, the springs having shackles at both ends.

There was a brief flurry of racing at Brooklands in 1909, where Bert Hammond drove a lightweight 18hp two-seater , winning the first Summer Handicap he entered and perhaps catching the handicapper unawares. In later meetings that year the Lagonda was handi-capped more severely and could do no better than second, even when Wilbur Gunn took over the driving.

The British motor industry before the First World War was more concerned with domestic sales than exports, and when it did export it was normally to the Empire. Wilbur Gunn, as an expatriate himself, looked further afield and perceived Russia to be a likely market, with little home industry and a large moneyed class as potential customers. So he set up a Russian branch in 1910 and attempted to gain publicity by entering the 1910 St Petersburg to Moscow Reliability Trial,

To follow up his successful rally, Gunn took a stand at the St Petersburg Motor Show in 1910. The long radius arms that controlled the rear suspension are very evident. For no clear reason the furled flag on the windscreen pillar is the Red Ensign.

An 11.1hp two-seater of 1914, photographed at Hammersmith. The two-seater had more primitive weather equipment than the coupé, no external door handles and very little visibility for the driver if it rained.

which covered over 2000 miles of unmade roads under official military observation. The organisers had so over-regulated the event that at the finish a large number of entrants had equal marks, so to produce a winner a high speed return to St Petersburg was added, for which Gunn was the only entrant. He achieved the set schedule and was awarded a special gold medal and certificate by the Tsar, presented personally at Tsarskoe Selo, the summer palace. This success produced sales in Russia and most of Lagonda's small 1910/11 production went there.

Gunn had a passion for making everything he could in-house, even nuts and bolts, so it was not surprising that he had been working on designs for his own engines, both four- and six-cylinder, to go into a beefed-up version of the 16/18hp chassis. These models were only publicly announced at the time of the 1911 Motor Show in October but we have good evidence that some were supplied to Russian customers earlier that year and the announcement only coincided with UK sales. To enable him to concentrate on production, Gunn appointed a sales agent, The Burlington Motor Company of Piccadilly, who had a depot in Addison Bridge Place, opposite the Olympia site of the Motor Show, saving Gunn the trouble and expense of a stand.

The new Lagonda-made engines shared a cylinder size of 90x120mm, giving 3054cc and 58bhp for the four and 4580cc and 80bhp for the six. The 90mm bore size was the same as the tricars had used and was the limit the

Lagonda machine shop could accommodate. Prices ranged from £485 for a two-seater on the 20hp chassis up to £750 for a 30hp limousine. These were expensive cars, the limousine being the equivalent of £60,000 today, and the prices had to be reduced in 1912 when Burlington set off on a sales tour covering the country, pushing the 20hp more than its bigger brother. Burlington was one of the first firms to offer part-exchanges and made a lot in their publicity of this new facility. Hitherto, old cars had been left to rot.

By leaving the sales effort to Burlington, Gunn had been able to concentrate on his works at Staines (actually across the river in Egham). The profits coming in from his expensive cars had enabled him to buy up his neighbours, principally Warmingtons, a coachbuilder, and Heads, undertakers and furniture makers, along with a small public house. By the end of this series of purchases he had acquired the whole corner site between Thorpe Road and The Causeway, and on it he set his employees to work building a much enlarged factory for his exciting new project.

Gunn was an admirer of Henry Ford and shared his view that the future of the motor industry lay in catering for a mass market rather than only for the wealthy. To attract this market, with its limited budget, the cars were going to have to be very simple, easy to make and straightforward to service. Accordingly, in 1912 Gunn and Cranmer designed the 11.1hp, Lagonda's version of a "People's Car". To finance production, which, to make significant profit, was going to have to be in hundreds rather than Gunn's current handful a year, he set up a new company, Lagonda Limited, in March 1913. This was the end result of a series of complicated financial manoeuvres involving Henry Tollemache and Harry Griffin, who owned a cab company and repair business in Hammersmith. The deal was that Lagonda Ltd would make the new 11.1hp cars and Tollemache & Griffin Ltd, another new company, would sell them. At about the same time, the Burlington Motor Company, who had been selling the big Lagondas, were bought by Siddeley-Deasy and relocated to Coventry.

The new finance got Gunn out of debt and he now had, by 1913 standards, a large site to build his new factory on. There wasn't enough to spend on fancy architecture; the corrugated iron northlight roof, timber frames and earth floor were workmanlike rather than impressive, but were fairly normal for the period.

The 11.1hp, on the other hand, was anything but normal for its time, for it had no chassis frame in the then accepted sense. Instead there was a "hull" made of tinned steel sheet riveted to angle steel strips which formed the main structure, and to this were attached several large sub-assemblies. These were: the power unit, comprising engine, clutch and gearbox with the transmission brake and pedals attached; and the "road unit" which was the transmission, rear axle with its locating A-frame and the front axle assembly with its radius arms. Each of these sub-assemblies could be built up simultaneously in different parts of the works and they all came together at a late stage of production, with the main body already painted and trimmed. By the same token, for ease of servicing large chunks of the Lagonda could easily be detached and dealt with away from the car. Another advantage, to Wilbur Gunn's way of thinking, was that he no longer had to rely on others for pressed-steel work as the whole hull could be made up in the Lagonda factory using only semi-skilled labour.

The engine, clutch and gearbox were all one unit and the aluminium sump, far from being merely an oil container, stiffened the whole structure, with the block and non-detachable head bolted to it at one end and the gearbox attached to the other. In this, as in several other design features, it followed Ford's lead. The engine had four cylinders, each 67x77.8mm, giving 1099cc, with overhead inlet and side exhaust valves (ioe). The inlet valves were opened by pushrods and rockers, the latter unusual in that they were longitudinal and not transverse. The original design was faulty; the rockers were too short and tended to lock up, so an early modification was to substitute much longer ones that overlapped, so that number 1 rod operated number 2 valve and so on. This called for a change in firing order.

A three-speed. gearbox with centre change drove the worm-drive rear axle, which was suspended on quarter-elliptic springs controlled by an A-frame pivoted on the rear of the gearbox.. The front axle had a transverse half-elliptic spring which was shackled at both ends and located by another A-frame. As was conventional then, the brake pedal worked a transmission brake and the handbrake operated iron shoes in drums on the rear axle.

Only one body style was offered, a cheeky 2-seater coupé, and only one colour, green. The car was quite tiny, only 10ft 3in (310cm) long, and it weighed only 9cwt (457kg). Even the radiator was "home made", using 3 rows of vertical tubes joining the top and bottom tanks, with the Lagonda script badge pressed into the top one. Cost and weight saving dodges abounded. For example, there was no steering box. Instead, a short arm was bolted to the steering column and this operated the drag link directly, giving one-to-one steering, like a bicycle. Cranmer cut the bevel gears for the rear axle directly into upsets on the half-shafts and contrived a gearbox that used only three sizes of cog. After not very successful experiments with an SU carburettor, a Zenith instrument was standardised, and the engine's 6:1 compression ratio, aided by the car's light weight, gave a respectable performance for the period, with fuel consumption of 51 miles per gallon and a top speed of 48mph (the factory claimed 50mph).

Although the firm's publicity had been

Bill Oates built himself a specially tuned 11.1 two-seater for trials in 1914. He is shown in the process of winning a Gold Medal in the Colmore Cup Trial. His passenger is Wilfred Denison, a director of Lagonda Limited.

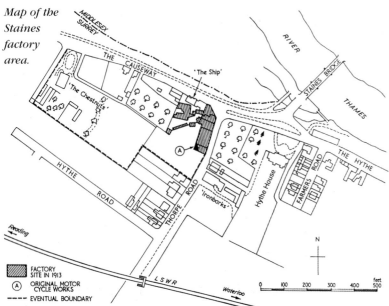
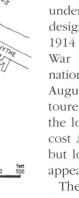

Map of the Staines factory area.

An 11.9hp coupé in the yard at Hammersmith Road, December 1920. The two men are holding up a white sheet and waving it about so that it goes out of focus. This made life easier for magazine photo editors by removing the background. Over the years this sheet became greyer.

promising cars in late 1912, it was the autumn of 1913 before one was available for road test by the motoring press, all of whom were initially very suspicious of having to change gear with the left hand, though graciously conceding that one soon grew used to it. *The Cyclecar* was very enthusiastic, entitling their test "A wonderful proposition in miniature cars".

It has always been assumed that Lagonda Ltd, the 1913 company, only ever produced the 11.1, but the recent discovery of a 1914 brochure shows that it continued to publicise the 20hp and 30hp cars, even though they cost from three to five times as much and

were aimed at a totally different market. How many were sold is a moot point. Throughout its life Lagonda never threw anything away and one suspects these larger models were unsold products of the earlier firm.

In June 1914 a second model, a more primitive 2-seater without the glass side windows, undercut the coupé's £150 by £3. Two more designs followed swiftly: a van in September 1914 to take advantage of the fact that the War Office had commandeered all the nation's carthorses on the outbreak of war in August, and then in November a 4-seater tourer which used a longer wheelbase and the lower gearing introduced for the van. It cost £7 10s (£7.50) more than the 2-seaters but looked very lumpy beside their cheeky appearance

The government prohibited car manufacture, other than for the War Office, in November 1916, but by then Gunn and Lagonda were well into munitions work, where the firm's reputation for precision machining paid dividends. The factory expanded further to fill its site and was re-equipped for the new work. At its peak the company employed 800 women in the main machine shop alone, out of a 1600-strong workforce, and was almost certainly the biggest employer in the Staines/Egham area. Gunn was working a 24-hour day, seven days a week, and the company went heavily into debt at first to pay for the masses of new machinery needed to turn out the millions of shells demanded by the forces. In the middle of 1917 Tollemache & Griffin Ltd was wound up, having existed solely to sell Lagonda cars, but there seems to have been some sort of merger, never officially recorded, since most T & M shareholders later appear as Lagonda ones.

The new enlarged works had swallowed Gunn's house, and he and Connie moved in 1917 into Hythe House, a fairly grand residence only yards from the factory and facing Staines Bridge.. It was owned by Osman Goring, the local butcher, who also owned "Ironbarks", a neighbouring estate that eventually became part of Lagonda property in the Second World War.

All munitions work stopped overnight in November 1918 and Wilbur Gunn, now 59 and in failing health, faced the task of

converting a factory reconfigured to produce millions of shells back to car production. Fortunately his key staff had been exempted from conscription and could set about the conversion at once, while the army of women were mostly laid off. The 11.1 was to be re-introduced, but the days when you could sell a car with no electrics had passed, so a starter motor, dynamo and electric lighting now featured, together with geared steering and a Panhard rod on the front axle to counteract the vagueness that followed from the transverse spring having shackles at both ends. At the end of this the car's weight had crept up to 12.7cwt (647kg), and the coupé was offered at 275 guineas (£288.75), with the 4-seater ten guineas more. The van did not reappear. Lagonda took a stand at the 1919 Motor Show and on it showed a new flat-fronted honeycomb radiator on the coupé, while the 4-seater had to make do with the vertical-tubed bullnose variety. Galloping inflation raised the prices to £351.15 and £372.15.

Wilbur Gunn's health deteriorated rapidly in 1920, and although he was well enough to take part in major reliability trials, including the London-Edinburgh at Whitsun, he died on 27 September of lymph gland cancer. His going left the company rather rudderless, for he was both engineer and businessman. The solution was to split the functions, with Colin Parbury taking on the management and Alfie Cranmer the engineering. To facilitate this, Parbury moved into "The Chestnuts", a large house immediately adjacent to the factory in The Causeway. Meanwhile Connie Gunn found Hythe House a burden without Wilbur's salary and moved to a hotel in Weybridge. Eventually, her eyesight failing, she became a boarder in a private house near Wimborne in Dorset, where she died in

Bert Hammond and Glen Logan in the second "works" 11.9 two-seater, ready for the October 1921 JCC 200 Mile Race at Brooklands.

The factory in 1921. On the original print you can make out "Lagonda Motor Co., Motor Cycles and Tricars" on the wall at the extreme left, which was part of Wilbur Gunn's original roofed-over garden. The Ship Inn on the extreme right is surrounded on three sides by the Lagonda works, with secret entrances through the fence.

August 1930.

The Motor Show of 1920 saw the introduction of a new model, the 11.9hp. This was an enlargement of the 11.1 and was aimed at the same market, which had grown more demanding since 1913. The engine was enlarged to 69x95 mm, giving a capacity of 1420cc. It looked similar outwardly, still with exposed valve gear, but the construction had changed in that the block and crankcase were now two separate items, the latter being of aluminium. A stiffer crankshaft reflected the longer stroke and the auxiliary drives were all modernised. Aluminium pistons replaced cast iron and the bullnose tube radiator vanished, all models now having the flat honeycomb one, which Lagonda made in-house. The chassisless construction was retained, but the short-wheelbase version did not carry on, all cars now having the 9ft (274cm) wheelbase. This had little effect on the appearance of the 4-seater but added a long sloping tail containing the dickey seat to the coupé, rather unbalancing its profile.

Prices were still creeping up in a seller's market; Lagonda sold 15 cars a week in 1920, and the coupé was retailed at £495. But this boom was soon to collapse and by the following winter discounts were easily obtainable. The upheaval that Wilbur Gunn's death had caused led to a complete overhaul of the firm's finances, at the conclusion of which, in January 1921, Barclay's Bank took over all the various accumulated debts in return for a mortgage on the whole company. This was

an attractive idea at the time but was to lead to disaster in 1935.

We must now mention W H (Bill) Oates. A tricar owner in 1905, he was taken on the staff to run the service department in 1910. During the war he had risen to the rank of Major and been awarded the OBE, returning to the company in 1919. In 1915, before joining up, he had built himself a special lightweight tuned 11.1 for competition use and had some success in the limited number of events held in wartime. Now, in 1921, he decided to have a go at track racing and constructed a tiny single-seater 11.9. With a body built on the same principles of angle steel and sheet metal as the production car but only 28in (711mm) wide, the racer was startlingly quick, producing lap times in the middle 80s at Brooklands where the standard 11.9 would have been pressed to reach 50mph. By October 1921 Oates had worked his racer up to the point that he took a whole string of 1½-litre records at Brooklands, ranging from the flying mile at 86.91mph to 100 miles at 80.19mph. The company's advertising at the time rather naughtily implied that Oates's car was a standard 11.9 by stating, truthfully, that he was a private owner, but it is doubtful if anyone really believed this.

Inspired perhaps by Oates's successes and possibly also by its new-found freedom from debt, the firm decided to enter the track competition world as well as continuing its long-standing participation in trials and rallies, where the 11.9 was to gain a very distinguished record. The event chosen was the Junior Car Club's 200 Mile Race of 1921, the first long-distance race in Britain for 1½-litre cars. The concept had generated enormous excitement and practice was permitted for three weeks before the actual race date of 22 October 22. The factory built a pair of two-seater racing cars very similar in appearance to Oates's single-seater and very nearly as fast. They had special long-stroke engines of 1496cc, and enormous fuel tanks to enable them to run the whole race non-stop. Oates was to be one driver and Bert Hammond the other, both cars carrying riding mechanics. We know Hammond's man to have been Glen Logan but the other hero is not known. In the race, which was uneventful but much faster than expected, Hammond finished 11th at 76.9mph to Oates's 13th at 73.8mph. Oates was rather miffed at this as he was supposed to be the team leader and Hammond didn't get another "works" drive until 1928, and then only as reserve driver. The winner was the Talbot-Darracq of Segrave, averaging 88.8mph. Lagonda's publicity stressed how reliable the cars had been, with a non-stop run and tyres still in perfect condition at the end.

The Motor Show followed, but only minor changes to the engine were noticeable, namely removing the studs that went through the exhaust manifold. In a quest for more sales prices had been reduced, the "green only" paint policy was relaxed, and a minimally equipped K model was introduced early in 1922 at £294.

Oates's track records didn't stand for long, and by the end of 1921 Kaye Don had pushed the 1½-litre hour record to 94.7mph, but Oates continued to campaign his single-seater, with modified bodywork this year, probably intended to provide better cooling. He also added hillclimbs to his programme, with mixed success and a gallingly long series of second places. By the end of 1922 he had increased his best lap speed at Brooklands to 88.6mph. The factory-backed trials team continued to get good results, gold medals being the norm.

For 1922 the JCC 200 Mile Race was re-scheduled for August, and this year only one car was entered, for Oates to drive. He added more positive lubrication of the valve gear by rigging up a hand pump for the mechanic to operate, and since that individual could not also pump up the petrol at the same time, an engine driven air pump was fitted to pressurise the tank. The engine had also been more highly tuned after the unexpected speed of last year's race and the car was significantly faster, but he must have overdone this, for the engine blew up on lap 17

Final Assembly and Testing, 1921. Bert Hammond, on the right in a jacket, is in charge.

A 1924 12/24 tourer. The long arm of the law is here represented by Miss Clara Perkins of the Somerset Constabulary. Photo by Dick Gilbert of his great-aunt.

and the car retired.

The 1923 models again had only minor changes at the Motor Show of 1922. A larger fuel tank with a reserve supply and gaitered springs (although not on the cheap K model) more or less sums them up. *The Motor* visited the works in April 1923 when the spring buying rush was on and output had risen to 25 cars a week from a workforce of 500. The writer commented on the chassisless construction and remarked that "a famous Italian make" (must be Lancia) was just about to follow suit. In fact, unknown to the journalist, Lagonda were about to compromise it to some extent. The 12/24 model, which came out without a lot of fuss in the latter half of 1923, although built in the same way, featured longitudinal "chassis" members only a few inches apart which lent themselves much more readily to a conventional coach-built body, opening the way to saloon bodies, an increasingly important part of the market and one which Lagonda had not catered for since 1913.

The 12/24 engine was a development of the 11.9, with, at last, enclosed valve gear and the auxiliary drives rearranged to give better accessibility. Power output was increased but no figures were issued. The transmission brake, very prone to filling the cockpit with smoke, was dropped and in its place a second set of shoes in widened rear brake drums was operated by the brake pedal. To the surprise of some commentators Lagonda

did not alter the fly-off nature of the hand-brake, whereby the button on the lever had to be depressed to set the brake, release involving merely tugging at the lever. This arrangement was to become common for sporting cars and had the advantage of allowing simultaneous hand and foot application in emergencies without any danger of the brake locking on.

The 12/24 body styles were, to begin with, exactly the same as the 11.9's, with prices only slightly higher. It was proposed to sell the two models side by side, a policy unlikely to work if they looked the same. Soon minor differences began to appear, domed section wings at first and then, by the end of 1923 a taller, more rounded radiator (bought in from Gallay, a crack in the "everything made in-house" policy). A more elaborate enamel radiator badge also arrived, still featuring Wilbur Gunn's "Lagonda" script. A new body style called an "All-weather saloon" (the R-type) appeared in the autumn, this being a four-door four-seater with a folding hood and glass side windows. It turned the scales at 16cwt (819kg) according to the factory, but 17.25cwt (883kg) was recorded at the RAC Six Day Light Car Trial of 1924, which also disclosed a compression ratio of 4.76:1, well down on Gunn's 6:1 of 1913. Performance was unaffected, with a top speed of 50mph, but some of the acceleration had been produced by lowering the gearing, so that the engine's ability to rev in the 4000s was called for to get the most from it. That these gears were too low is borne out by the yarns related by journalists as to the incredible gradients upon which they had been able to start from rest in top gear.

The "All-weather" was followed by a tourer version, the LC, which had celluloid sidescreens instead of glass windows. This appeared on the Wembley Exhibition stand in the spring of 1924. It also pioneered low-pressure tyres (4.95 x 28) and front wheel brakes, both only options at extra cost. Finally, at the 1924 Motor Show, a full saloon body (the S type) was announced on the 12/24. It was a six-light four-door of extremely rectangular appearance, four inches (100mm) wider than the all-weather and, as expected, heavier at 18cwt (914kg). The car was, however, extremely well equipped for its class and this was clearly going to be the company's new policy. They were never going to be able to compete with Austin or Morris on price but they could out-luxury them to justify a higher price. This S type model pioneered a feature to be found on all Lagonda saloons up to the introduction of trafficators, the quick-drop driver's window. This window was controlled by a long lever and the glass was spring-loaded downwards but could be locked in any position by the lever. The thinking was that, in the days of hand signals, the driver might frequently wish to drop the glass in a hurry but usually had plenty of time to raise it, which was done by reversing the action of the lever against very considerable spring pressure. Other makers were to copy this as they already had copied the fly-off hand-brake, a 1913 innovation on the 11.1.

The 1925 models had a number of new features: a plate clutch replaced the now outmoded cone, and a larger steering wheel had four spokes instead of three, possibly to keep the steering weight the same when the wider low-pressure tyres were fitted. The bench front seat, if specified, could be reclined to line up with the rear one to make a bed, and saloons had an interior light and a silk rear blind. Despite all this opulence, prices had to be kept competitive and the saloon sold for £370 against the R-type's £360.

The saloon was definitely in the upright or Perpendicular mode of design, 5ft 10in high (177.8cm) but only 12ft 3in (373.4cm) long. It looks to be a large and commodious saloon but is actually 2ft shorter than the Ford Focus of today. The absence of any luggage boot has a lot to do with this. But all these fittings added weight, and to keep some semblance of acceleration there either had to be more power or lower gearing. The 12/24 engine was still basically the Edwardian 11.1 and a radical redesign would probably have cost as much as a wholly new engine, so the alternative was taken and saloons had a distinctly unenterprising 5:1 axle ratio. Top speed remained at the 48mph that all the Elevens and Twelves seemed to reach, but whereas the 0 to 30mph time was 18 seconds, 0 to 40 took 33 seconds, so the engine was clearly running out of breath above 30mph. The wide-ratio 3-speed gearbox continued unchanged, of course, but first was now so low that one owner, in a testimonial letter, claimed that in the unspecified number of years he had owned the car he had only ever used first once, on the hairpin of Sutton Bank, near Thirsk, a feared Trials hill. First gear represented 4.7mph per 1000rpm.

Clearly, something had to be done to replace the 12/24. What it was we will reserve for the next chapter.

A 1925 12/24 saloon, Type S. Lagonda had to pile on the luxury (for the period) to distance themselves from the mass-market cars. The owner has fitted his RAC badge immediately in front of the Motometer temperature gauge, making it difficult to read. Perhaps he would rather not know.

Chapter Two

The 14/60

*Rear view of the
14/60 saloon with
period trunk in
place. Back windows
in 1926-28 were
reasonably large on
saloons, the letter-
box-like slits came
later. The demands of
modern motoring
have led to the
fitment of flashing
indicators for safety
reasons.*

Lagonda changed its models so infrequently that until the late 1930s it neither needed nor could justify the expense of permanent design staff. So, early in 1925, to supplant the 12/24, the company hired freelance consultants to design a totally new replacement. This really was to be a "clean sheet of paper" job, with no parts carried over from the earlier cars. For the chassis they hired Eddie Masters and for the engine Arthur Davidson, formerly at Calthorpe and Lea-Francis. All the Gunn/Cranmer derivations of Ford ideas were abandoned and so was the "chassisless" concept. Masters went for a totally conventional ladder-type chassis frame with channel-section pressed-steel side-members, with a mixture of tubular and pressed-steel cross-members. Beam axles front and rear suspended the car on semi-elliptic leaf springs, and four-wheel brakes figured from the outset. In plan the chassis frame resembled a wine bottle, with a narrow section at the front holding the engine and giving a good clearance for the steering lock, widening abruptly at the clutch to accommodate the bodywork to the rear. There were seven cross-members: tubes at both ends and tubes to carry the fuel tank and rear springs, and pressed-steel sections to cater for the radiator, the flywheel and the gearbox. The wheelbase was 10ft (304.8cm) and track 4ft 6in (137.2cm). Steering was by a Marles box with a column adjustable for rake but not for reach. The engine dimensions were 72x120mm, giving 1954cc.

Davidson's engine was a complete departure from previous Lagonda practice, too. A four-cylinder with a five-bearing crankshaft, it had a unique twin-camshaft layout where the camshafts were situated in the block but above the head/block joint face. When the head was lifted they stayed in place, so the timing was not disturbed. The valves were operated by rockers mounted on eccentric fulcrum pins to adjust clearances. These rockers protruded through the bottom of the head to engage with the cams. The combustion chambers were hemispherical, with the valves inclined at 90 degrees to each other

and well cooled by water passages. Crankcase and block were a single casting which reached down to the centre line of the crankshaft and had internal cross-members to support the 2-inch (50mm) diameter main bearings of the massive crankshaft, which was machined all over. The rear main bearing was wider than the others, requiring a four-bolt cap, and oil sealing was by a slinger and return thread. Right at the rear end was an extended spigot on which the clutch driving plate ran, and this was axially drilled for an oil supply with a wick to the clutch withdrawal bearing. These early crankshafts were totally solid with ³⁄₁₆in (5mm) holes drilled diagonally from the main bearings to the big ends to convey the oil. This got to the main bearings via a series of external pipes fed from number 2 main. These early arrangements were to change as time went on.

The camshafts ran submerged in oil in tunnels which were sideways extensions of the block, adding to its already excellent stiffness. Holes in the tops of these tunnels allowed the rockers to contact the cams. The detachable cylinder heads were Lagonda's

Peter Jones's 1928 14/60 demonstrates that a roomy saloon could be accommodated on this chassis and still provide reasonable performance. Earlier versions had more elaborate waistline panelling.

The prototype 14/60 chassis, as shown to the press in August 1925. There were lots of changes before production started: a cover for the flywheel, for a start, and proper universal joints in the propeller shaft. The U-shaped chassis cross-members became straight and the brake drums lost their ribs.

Detail of the 1925 prototype. By production time the clutch mechanism became much more complicated but the brake layout was simplified.

Cross-section drawing of the 14/60 2 Litre engine, showing the unique camshaft positions in extensions of the block above the block/head joint line. This later drawing actually shows the supercharged engine with bolt-on balance weights on the crankshaft and a mechanical fuel pump.

first and gave rise to the factory code OH for the engine and, eventually, the whole car. Pistons were aluminium alloy with three rings, all above the gudgeon pin, and drilled skirts. The gudgeon pins were locked to the small end of the connecting rod by a pinned setscrew, so the pin turned in the piston on bearings provided for it. The big ends were 2 inches (50 mm) in diameter, matching the main bearings

One can deduce that the designers of Lagonda's first detachable cylinder head were determined that it should not have gasket

problems. So the distribution of studs and passages is textbook perfect, with four large holes for the combustion chambers flanked by five smaller holes for the ports and 37 small holes for 21 studs and water transfer passages, all disposed exactly symmetrically. So symmetrical in fact that it is possible to fit the gasket the wrong way round, but the presence of two inlet ports on one side and three exhaust ports on the other will make itself felt when attempting to start the engine.

The camshafts were driven by chains from the front of the crankshaft in a two-stage arrangement. The lower one drove the dynamo and water pump shafts, passing under a half-time idler sprocket which also drove the upper chain and hence the camshafts; these as a result revolved in the opposite direction to the crankshaft. The magneto, set across the engine to bring its contacts to an accessible position, was driven by a "Fabroil" skew gear off the exhaust camshaft. Both camshaft sprockets were keyed to their shafts and could be timed very accurately with an elaborate vernier spider arrangement. The BTH magneto had a conventional vernier coupling for accurate timing, and the idler sprockets of the whole drive could be adjusted up or down to control chain tension. Timing a 14/60 engine can while away a long period if undertaken enthusiastically.

Carburation was by a single side-draught Zenith 30HZ instrument mounted on a water heated manifold fed from the rear 12-gallon tank by Autovac. The 11s and 12s had had scuttle-mounted tanks which fed by gravity and the owner had been expected to peer in to judge fuel contents, but the 14/60's upmarket credentials led to a proper fuel gauge, albeit mounted on the tank, not the dashboard.

The oil pump was by Rotoplunge, connected directly to an oil junction box, from whence external copper pipes led oil to the main bearings and the camshafts, the inlet side directly, the exhaust side via another external pipe across the back of the engine. Pressure was claimed to be 15psi (about 1 Bar) at 30mph..

For no obvious reason, unless it was better weight distribution, the starter motor was not attached to the engine but was strapped to

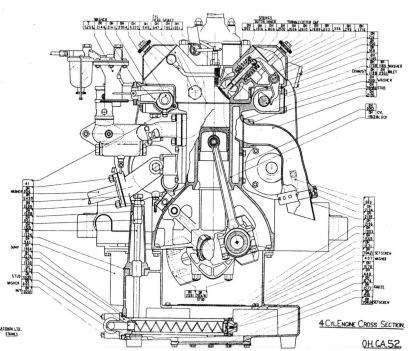

LAGONDA LTD.
STAINES.

4 CYL ENGINE CROSS SECTION.

OH.GA.52.

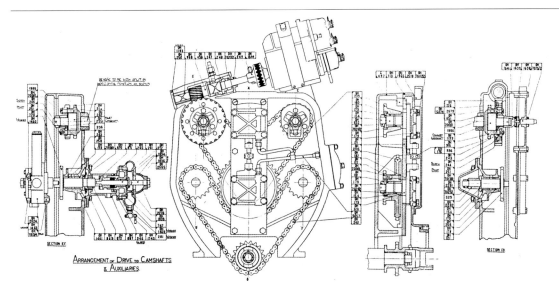

Layout of the normal 2 Litre timing drive. The first batch of low-chassis engines were built with the dynamo drive sprocket (at the middle left) omitted, which reversed the direction of rotation of the camshafts. It soon re-appeared.

the chassis cross-member just to the rear of the clutch. Its Bendix was driven by a short shaft with a fabric universal joint forward to the flywheel, which, on the prototype, was exposed. Engine cooling was by water pump, driven off the nearside timing chain. No fan was normally fitted, but one could be fitted following a special request, driven off the offside jockey wheel by extending the shaft forwards. One presumes this would have had a pulley fitted to it so as to drive the fan by Whittle belt, but no car so fitted survives so we cannot be certain.

Everything about the engine, in fact about the whole car, shows a great deal of thought given to accessibility, sometimes even to the detriment of performance. The ability to lift the cylinder head without disturbing the timing appealed to the potential owner, who could expect to be doing this twice a year to decarbonise. Unfortunately, putting the camshafts in that position meant that they were exactly where the inlet and exhaust ports should have been, and as a consequence the passages within the cylinder head are full of right-angle bends which consider-

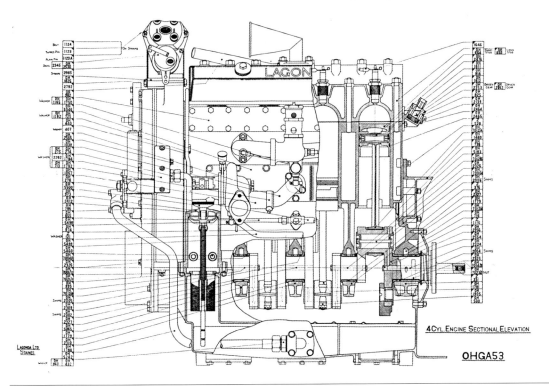

Longitudinal section of the 2 Litre engine. The combustion chambers are true hemispheres and compression ratio changes were normally achieved by piston shape alterations. Five main bearings were rare for a non-racing engine in 1925. Again this is the supercharged engine but shown without that addition.

Prototype 14/60 engine with no name on the camshaft covers and only six bolts holding the side plates. Owners of later 2 Litres can have endless fun comparing this with their later engines.

Upside down 14/60 engine lower half. Instruction Manual illustration. The pipework feeding oil to the main bearings was later replaced by internal drillings.

ably stifle the performance. The reasoning for this emphasis on maintenance demonstrates a change in ownership patterns in Great Britain. When Lagondas had last made big, expensive cars before the First World War it was assumed that anyone rich enough to buy one would employ a chauffeur, and as the typical employer of a chauffeur always believed that he would be lazing about when not actually driving, he wasn't a bit bothered by demanding maintenance schedules or by cars where large chunks had to be dismantled to service them. But now, in aiming upmarket 12 years later, Lagonda were faced with a different kind of owner, one who definitely didn't have paid help and would have to do it all himself. A car, even an expensive one, where work was simplified, with the minimum need to crawl underneath, was bound to be an attractive sales proposition.

So we find, as a selling point, that the filter container by which oil was added to the engine was large enough to take a quart can (1.14 litres), so that the owner could dump it in and go off to do something else while it drained. There were access holes all over the engine, some only really needed to clear scale from the cooling system and two just to allow a finger to test the tension on the timing chains. In fact a legend has grown up in the Lagonda Club that there is little point in removing a component to attend to it as it is just as accessible where it is. Pursuing that point, the sump drain valve had a rod

attached to it so that it could be opened from above, and all the chassis lubrication points were connected by little copper pipes to a row of grease nipples on both sides of the car underneath the front doors, hidden on the first models behind little detachable flaps. The nearside one also carried the grease gun, clipped in place.

The gearbox, Lagonda's first four-speed one, was carried separately from the engine, and the plate clutch, of Lagonda's own make, drove a short shaft with fabric universal joints to connect the two. The clutch, 11 inches in diameter (279mm), operated somewhat unusually in that the driving plate was a machined and slotted plain steel disc with an oil slinger and driving shaft attached to it. The friction material was attached to a floating plate next to the flywheel and to a cover plate. When the pedal was depressed. a pressure plate pushed the floating plate towards the engine by means of six driving pins around the circumference, freeing the driving plate and disconnecting the drive. The driving pins were supposed to be lubricated by oil passages in the flywheel, but this didn't always work and an early modification, covered by a sticker in the instruction book, saw screw-in greasers added to the driving pins, and later still, phosphor bronze bushes for them as well.

The clutch is a good, simple and reliable device which survived for 10 years in successive models, but it has a distinct aversion to being slipped, which can rapidly overheat and distort the steel disc. It has the merit that the average owner can dismantle and re-assemble it without injuring himself when the

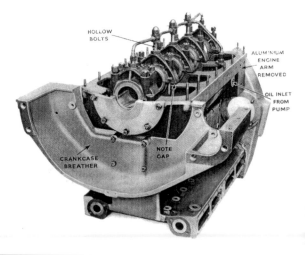

spring pressure is released.

The gearbox sat on a sub-frame with two legs on one side and one on the other to give a non-rocking three-point suspension. Fabric pads under each arm offered some noise insulation, later to be replaced by rubber hemispheres. The 'box was a conventional three-shaft sliding mesh design with the same internal ratios for all models, the saloon having lower overall gearing by virtue of a 5.44:1 (9 x 49) rear axle in contrast to the 4.66:1 (9 x 42) ratio of the open cars. The input and output shafts had ball bearings but the layshaft ran in plain phosphor bronze bushes. Internal ratios were 1.6:1 (third), 2.5:1 (second) and 4:1 (first and reverse). This became known later as the "wide ratio" set when other, more sporting, alternatives were produced. In Lagonda's economical way, all the sets used the same first- and second-gear cogs, the variation being achieved by a different pair of constant-mesh gears and a different third gear set. This gearbox, known as the OH, can be distinguished from its later cousins by its L-shaped top cover, initially an

aluminium casting, later a plain steel sheet.

Between the engine and gearbox were two aids to clean gear changing, an ejector stop and a clutch stop. The purpose of the former was to make sure the driving plate actually stopped when the pedal was pressed and didn't stick to the floating plate. The latter slowed down the rotation of the intermediate shaft between engine and gearbox by means of a Ferodo-faced arm acting on a disc attached to the universal joint spider. It was separately adjustable as to how hard it came on and when. If set both fierce and early, the

Nearside view of the engine of KO 6393. A single horizontal Zenith carburettor was standard, with a "strangler" for cold starting. Fuel supply is by Autovac (upper right). Later 14/60 engines, like this one, incorporated many of the improvements brought in with the Speed Model.

The number stamped on the timing case of the engine reveals that it came from, originally, a 1929 Speed Model. Normal 14/60 engine numbers are much more complicated.

The strangler simply shuts off the air supply to give a richer mixture for starting a cold engine. It is controlled from the dashboard by a Bowden cable.

sporting driver could get instantaneous upward changes, at the expense of more care needed on double-declutched downward ones.

The drive to the rear axle, in the prototype, was by an improbably slender propeller shaft which featured two-arm spiders to its fabric universals. By the time the model was in production, proper roller-bearing universal joints had arrived, just one of the many changes that early development produced. The rear axle, too, gained very considerably in bulk and strength between the prototype's (which looks uncommonly like a wider 12/24 item) and eventual production.

Continuing this theme, the pressed-steel chassis cross-members in front of and behind the gearbox originally curved down below

Close-up of the 14/60 carburettor. Keen owners would acquire boxes of different jets and do their own tuning.

the propeller shaft, allowing it to be installed as an entity. By production, this alarmingly wobbly arrangement had gone and straight cross-members with holes in them look a lot stronger, but of course meant more work for the fitters as the shaft passed through them. These straight members forced a move for the starter motor, which now had to sit on the gearbox sub-frame with a longer drive shaft The rear axle was a conventional spiral bevel and was mounted underslung on the rear half-elliptic springs. The first two years of production were to see several versions of the rear axle, with a variety of filling arrangements and fixing bolts, each version stronger (and heavier) than the last.

As this new model was going to be hugely faster than the rather pedestrian 12/24, enormous attention was given to the brakes. At the front, the Rubery system was employed, with Perrot shafts mounted on the underside of the axle. The operating system was by rods and cables with quite elaborate compensation between front and rear and also from side to

Until 1929 Lagonda identity plates were small with only space for one or two letters under "Type". In this case "S" stands for saloon. From 1929 on a more complicated system led to larger plates with more room.

Offside of the 14/60 engine. The dynamo is just visible between the steering box and the crankcase, one of the few components not easy to reach.

side. Use in practice showed that not all these complications were necessary and progressive simplifications followed. 14-inch (366 mm) ribbed drums all round offered extraordinarily good retardation, and at the rear the 12/24 idea of four shoes in each drum was retained, with the handbrake operating one pair and the pedal the other. Presumably as an economy measure, the ribs were dropped from the drums for production.

The 1925 cars had a pedal of amazingly serpentine shape mounted freely on a cross-shaft, itself mounted on self-aligning ball bearings. The rear brake cable was attached to a chain at the pedal end and this chain passed over a pair of sprockets, one fixed to the pedal and the other free to rotate on a short arm, so as to give a running adjustment. The other end of the chain was fastened to a bell crank which worked the front brakes via the cross-shaft. Thus there was compensation between front and rear brakes. A second chain ran from the adjustable pulley through the pedal arm and up to a handwheel adjuster. The cable to the rear brakes led to a compensator box with four sprockets and two chains mounted just aft of the gearbox. The handbrake cable led here too, and from

the exit side of the compensator box four cables led, via large enclosed pulleys, to the rear brakes. On the way they were connected to a relay lever by means of which the leverage was reduced to give the rear brakes less bite than the fronts. This also gave a means of cable length adjustment. The compensator box balanced the rear brakes against each other. Thus the only non-compensated movement was between the front brakes.

The absence of compensation between the

Lagonda went to great lengths to make maintenance easier. The grease gun lived in this little cupboard under the nearside front door, sharing it with three of the eight "grouped" grease nipples. The other five were in a similar place on the other side of the car.

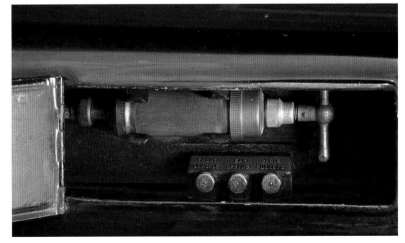

Rear seat occupants got acres of room, at the expense of no luggage accommodation. The fold-down rack on the tail was strong enough for several suitcases.

Mounting the spare wheel in the front wing gave clear space at the rear for luggage.

front brakes was deliberate, not an oversight. In these early days of front-wheel brakes, still regarded with some suspicion, there was a phobia about the supposed ill effects of a driver braking hard when on steering lock and ploughing straight on. So the geometry of the front brakes was such that with steering lock applied the inner front brake came on harder than the outer one and this was alleged to help the car round the bend. Obviously, compensation from side to side would nullify this effect. Curiously, there is nothing in the Lagonda instruction manual to refer to this, nor any guide to adjustment to ensure it works. *The Motor*, describing the prototype in its issue of 22 September 1925, stated that the front brakes were cable operated, but the photographs taken at the time show rods, and all production cars had rods at the front.

In keeping with the change to right-hand operation of the gearbox, the handbrake lever moved to the right as well and retained the fly-off action. Over the next few years this arrangement became common on sporting cars but a few road testers of the period disliked it intensely for some reason and said so. The handbrake lever was very long and at its lower end was just as serpentine as the pedal lever. This was done to provide easier access past it for the driver, but it resulted in the lever being rather far away in the off position.

Lagonda took out a patent on the whole braking system but nevertheless started to change it almost at once. Rather than list these changes the reader is referred to the diagram covering the major versions, each simpler than the last. It is a moot point whether the changes were brought in after usage showed the complications were unnecessary or just to simplify production and hence save money.

As the 14/60 was new from stem to stern, a new radiator badge was inevitable. This was the first one not to use Wilbur Gunn's signature script and it is only found on 14/60s and 16/65s. The radiator was designed by Arthur Thatcher and the nickel plated outer shell was attached to a true honeycomb matrix.

Windscreen wipers were a new concept in 1928 and only the driver got one. Some early ones were driven off the gearbox, which meant that wiping speed was proportional to road speed.

Fortunately the performance of the system remained excellent and the 14/60 had some of the best brakes of its era.

The company was well aware that this more expensive chassis would attract more demanding customers, some of whose requirements could best be met by outside coachbuilders. To assist these firms the bulkhead panel of cast aluminium, which was to become a standard Lagonda feature, carried extension brackets which supported the centre part of the dashboard, also cast aluminium, carrying the instruments. Thus the latter could be fixed in place and wired on the bare chassis, and the bodywork could be erected without interfering with them. The instrumentation was comprehensive,

Grouped grease nipples for chassis lubrication on a 14/60 saloon. This is the offside set. There were only three on the nearside, plus the grease gun in its clip.

consisting of rev-counter, speedometer, ammeter, oil pressure and water temperature gauges, and a large clock. There was no fuel gauge, as remarked above; this was on the tank. There was, however, a two-way tap to provide a reserve supply of fuel. Hand throttle and ignition timing levers were on the

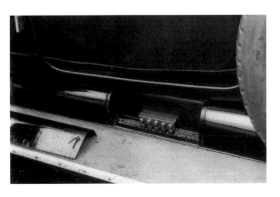

Lighting by C.A. Vandervell (CAV). Black enamel finish was the norm at the time; bright plating came later.

Vintage saloons carry period fittings of great charm. Here the wooden "smoker's companion" has in front of it an electric cigar lighter, where one presses the red button to activate it.

steering column and an 18-inch (457mm) dished three-spoke steering wheel had the horn button in the centre. The magneto switch had a key, not all that common in 1925, and when this was removed the lamps switch was locked in whichever position it had been left. The same switch controlled whether the dynamo was on or off charge, the choice in those days being the driver's. There was a single fuse mounted in the ammeter panel.

When *The Motor* first featured the car in September 1925 only a running chassis was available for them to describe and photograph. It was bodiless and only the offside front wing was in place to demonstrate the side-mounted spare wheel position. But since

the spring of that year Bert Hammond's Experimental Department had been testing the five prototypes. Fitted with makeshift tourer bodies and an anonymous radiator, these cars had started with a number of modified 12/24 parts, slowly replaced as pukka 14/60 items became available. The testers set about what would now be called "comparative performance trials" but which actually consisted of roaming the main roads of the Home Counties taking on all comers. Bert's summary of these travels was that "there was nothing to touch it in its class".

For the new engine practically every carburettor on the market was tested, even the controversial Degory floatless one. Its devotees claimed it gave enormous power at thousands of miles per gallon, whereas its detractors said wouldn't even start the engine. Lagonda engineers joined the latter camp

The offside door has plainer trim with no envelope The nearside door carries a capacious container for travel documents, instruction books and the like. The door lock release is the small metal lever visible in the window.

Woodwork surrounding the dash panel was superb, with contrasting inlays. Many customers specified this in great detail. The aluminium panel carrying the instruments was independent of the bodywork, enabling a bare chassis to be driven legally for testing before the body was fitted.

An ignition key was rare in 1928. This one originally had the feeler gauge for the magneto points attached to it, but, as usual, it has snapped off.

when even Degory's man couldn't get it to fire all four cylinders consistently.

The 12/24 had been steadily raising its standard of interior fittings and trim from the rather homespun 11.9 but, given the price range anticipated for the new model, a further improvement was called for and achieved. Walter Buckingham, in charge of body design and construction, decided on two open cars called the "Touring" and the "Semi-sports" (a refreshingly honest title) and a full six-light four-door saloon. The two open cars were quite similar in appearance but the full tourer was 11 inches (279 mm) wider at the rear and seated three abreast there, where the Semi-sports only took two. It was originally the

A 1927 Semi-sports tourer 14/60 in its most sporty form with wire wheels and a vee windscreen. The rear passengers have the luxury of their own Auster windscreen, which could only be fitted if the front seat was a one-piece bench. The "full" tourer was wider and seated three in the rear.

A 14/60 full tourer, noticeably wider at the rear. This photo dates from 1965, by which time an owner has fitted Stephen Grebel headlamps and a Speed Model radiator.

intention that the tourer would have a flat windscreen and artillery wheels, while in contrast the Semi-sports would have a vee-screen and wire wheels. But as the choice lay with the customer we find all permutations of these options in practice. The Semi-sports did have a slightly different design of front wing and this does seem to be only found on this model.

A brand new radiator design by Arthur Thatcher, Buckingham's second in command, bore some resemblance to the later domed top 12/24 item but was wider and tapered in width. It was nickel plated and carried a new badge, the first to get away from Wilbur

Gunn's script "Lagonda". The new one used a circle with a bar extending either side, rather like the London Underground sign, with "Lagonda" in an elliptical form across the middle, "Staines" above it and "England" below. This was to prove a short-lived emblem.

The full title given to the new model was "14/60 Two Litre". We nowadays drop the latter bit as most surviving Two Litres are Speed Models and using the 14/60 alone distinguishes the earlier cars. The convention of the time was that the 14 represented the RAC horsepower rating and the 60 the actual brake horsepower. But the car was actually rated at 12.9 horsepower and so was taxed at 13hp. No manufacturer was ever going to sell a "thirteen", hence the 14 part. An output of 60 bhp was claimed for the new engine, at least double what the 12/24 could offer, and this was probably about correct.

By October the company was ready to show the new car on Stand 104 at the Motor Show, alongside the 12/24, which continued in limited production and thereby continued the hallowed Lagonda tradition of using up the boxfull. The prices fixed for the 14/60 were £430 for the chassis, £570 for both open models and £720 for the saloon. In contrast the 12/24 now sold for £230 for the chassis, £295 for the tourer and £370 for the saloon. With such a radical change in construction methods it was obviously going to take time to get the 14/60 into full production and continuing sales of the 12/24 were going to be needed to pay the wages. The advertisement copywriters went overboard about the performance of the new model, saying it would do 80mph, probably making the false assumption that doubling the power would automatically double the top speed. So it was rather an anticlimax when *The Autocar* published a road test only a fortnight after the Motor Show of a saloon 14/60, PE 6459, to discover its top speed to be only 64.8mph. Apart from that, though, the testers were very impressed with the car's comfort, smoothness and handling. The presence of four gears and a right-hand change confirmed the Lagonda's place in the upper bracket of motoring, and the attention given to ease of maintenance was commented upon and appreciated. The speeds reached in the intermediate gears were 17, 26 and 43mph respectively, each representing roughly 4000rpm, while the top speed was reached at 3800rpm.

Early catalogues survive for the late 1925 production and show details of the seating, normally a bench front and rear, the front one reclineable so that it lined up with the rear to make a bed and, on the open cars, a rear compartment windscreen attached to it. If two separate front seats were ordered, this rear windscreen option was not available. All cars

Interior of a 14/60 saloon. Rear passengers get a footrest as they are too far back to use the squabs of the front seats to steady themselves. If a division was ordered, folding occasional seats were an option and the driver lost a bit of legroom.

had black chassis, wheels and wings; body colours were fawn, maroon or blue as standard but any colour was possible for a small extra charge. Safety glass was an extra, as was a division on the saloon. If this was fitted, small sideways-facing folding occasional seats were fixed to it and the front seat did not adjust. There was ample room for the occasional seats in the 31 inches (787 mm) between the front and rear seats. All models were the same length at 13ft 6in (4115mm) and overall width 5ft 4½in (1638mm).

The black parts noted above were stove enamelled for durability and black enamel chassis were to survive at Staines until the

When re-trimming the car, Peter Jones was able to re-use much of the original leather. Carpets and headlining had to be replaced.

Second World War. Having only one colour meant it was never necessary to clean out the equipment for a different colour. In later years when customers demanded body-colour wings and/or wheels, they were sprayed over the black.

The first catalogue showed the saloon with a flat windscreen and on artillery wheels with 5.25 x 31 tyres. The Semi-sports had the vee-screen, wire wheels and 4.75 x 30 tyres. The full five-seater "Touring" car seems to have been a bit of an afterthought, meriting only four lines of description and no photograph.

It is widely held that the 14/60 represented an enormous change in Lagonda's model range and this is undoubtedly true as far as the engineering goes, but less so of the appearance. Later commentators tend to compare the 11.9 with the Speed Model, and there is certainly a world of difference between these, but in between came the 12/24 and 14/60 and in body design there is a clear evolution, so much so that a late 12/24 saloon and an early 14/60 one are remarkably alike and quite difficult to distinguish, especially in a photograph where the scale may not be clear.

One change that Lagonda did not publicise was the adoption of a cellulose finish. Up to 1925 all cars had been finished with traditional brush-applied oil paint and a final clear varnish. Each body took an age to dry and was vulnerable to mouse footprints and pigeon droppings while it did so. Sprayed cellulose was touch-dry in minutes and even though it was always left to air-dry overnight the final finish was harder, brighter and less prone to damage. The paint supplier was Cellon Ltd, and it was only the appearance of their advertisements claiming the credit for the much-admired finish on the new Lagondas that revealed the change. Initially only two cellulose sprayers were taken on, Harold Guy and Ted Bibby, but others were added as the 12/24 line ran down and the 14/60 took over. The reason Lagonda were so reticent was the feeling among upper-crust car purchasers that cellulose was a bit American and OK for mass-produced cars but not for cars costing in the seven hundreds. Cellon provided Lagonda's paint right up to the 1935 bankruptcy, by which time they were owed

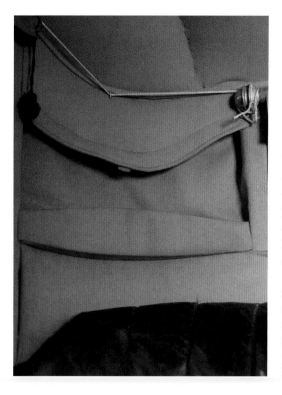

an enormous amount of money. Cellon's boss, A J A Wallace Barr, settled for an M45 Rapide saloon in lieu of payment.

In keeping with having such an important new model, Lagonda revised their system of numbering. The Car Number series had started with the tricars and had reached about 7500 by the middle of 1925. Engine numbers were of course higher and bore no relationship to the car number. By the same time they had reached about 9200. For the new design it was decided to carry on the car numbers but restart the engine numbers with the added prefix OH. We don't know if there was an OH 1 - more probably they started with OH 100 - but a simple relationship began by which the engine numbers were always about 8250 less than the car number. We must presume that it was envisaged that the run-out of 12/24 production would fill in the 7500 to 8250 range. For 1925/6 this relationship is very shaky, but it settled down later, although there are occasional blips of chaos - frequently, in the author's opinion, immediately after the summer holiday shutdown period.

Lagonda had always refrained from actually stamping the engine with its number, merely putting it on the identity plate riveted to the bulkhead. This had advantages if the car was returned to the works for serious engine work in the warranty period, since a quick engine swap got the car back to the customer quickly and the repairs could be done at leisure. The warranty period was only 12 months at this time, although it was to increase substantially later.

By January 1926, when *Automotor Journal* got their hands on PE 6459, it had covered 20,000 miles, but the writer, Edgar Duffield, said that it still felt like a new car. Road tests at this time only occupied one day and Major Oates would be present throughout, even at Brooklands for the stopwatch stuff. The photographs accompanying this article show some of the changes that were occurring since the prototype description. Most are minor: the access plates to the camshafts, originally held on by six bolts, now had ten, and there was a completely different design of water offtake from the top of the cylinder head. Detailed development of this kind continued throughout the life of the 14/60 and gives rise to the generally accepted

saying "They never made two alike".

For the spring selling season of 1926 prices were raised to £450 for the chassis and £590 for the open cars. The 80mph claim was quietly dropped in favour of emphasis on smoothness. The previous claim that the car was as smooth as any "six" now increased to any "eight". As very few people had actually driven an eight-cylinder car, this was pretty safe. *The Motor* tested a Semi-sports tourer in July (on artillery wheels, just to confuse) and although speeds in the indirect gears were higher as a consequence of the taller rear axle ratio, the top speed of 65mph was almost exactly the same as the saloon's. The speeds claimed in the gears look a touch optimistic. Thus 24mph claimed in first is equivalent to 5200rpm, 36mph in second is 4865 rpm and 53mph in third is 4570rpm. Either they thrashed the car unmercifully (as *The Motor* testers were inclined to) or the speedo was reading fast. They commented, as everyone did, on the thought that had gone into making things accessible and on the comfort. A slightly vague reference to the windscreen wiper being "positively driven" meant little to the reader and actually describes a cable drive from the rear of the gearbox, found on these early cars. It was assumed that a wiper which went faster when the car did made sense, and the fact that the wiping stopped when the car

Early electric windscreen wipers were not conspicuously reliable, so an external knob enabled the driver to see something if they failed. You would only discover this in wet weather.

Charlie Gray, Chief Tester, with a 14/60 Doctor's Coupé in the grounds of "The Chestnuts", next to the factory. Note the ear-less hub nuts, removed with a special spanner.

did was of no consequence.

On the open cars the sidescreens, when not erected, were stored behind the squab of the back seat in numbered places. You departed from the numbered order at your peril, likely to have one left over when the locker was full. It was noted that Hartford friction dampers were fitted all round, with the rear ones mounted transversely to resist roll. It is in fact probable that all production cars were so equipped, but the prototype made do with "snubbers". *The Motor* only got 25 miles per gallon, which is a touch high and may reflect very hard driving. Perhaps Major Oates looked the other way while they had a real go.

Once production got going the car sold well. Not in the volume that the 11s and 12s had reached, but at a substantially higher price. Based on the Car Numbers of survivors it is estimated that about 250 14/60s were sold in 1926 and about 400 in 1927. This compares with the 700 a year estimated for the earlier models. The performance, which was nothing special for a 2-litre car, escaped adverse comment, whereas the excellent handling and brakes, plus a comfortable and well-equipped body, came in for praise. Considering how basic the K Model 11.9 had been, Lagonda had performed quite a *volte face*. But all that extra equipment added weight, the 14/60 chassis turning the scales at 18cwt (914kg) and the saloon on the road at 28.75cwt (1463kg).

In considering the sales figures it must be remembered that selling cars at this time was a viciously seasonal occupation. Sales really

only took place from Easter to Ascot Week, after which "everyone" departed to the country. By August the whole clientele was either on the Riviera or on the grouse moors. The Motor Show in October, at which next year's models were displayed, was cunningly timed and produced a flurry of sales from what would now be called "early adopters", folk who *must* have the very latest thing. This boost only lasted about six weeks, after which the company would go into hibernation until the following spring. Only key personnel were kept on, the rest laid off until the next year.

By the Olympia Show of 1926 the 14/60 was well established, but nevertheless a number of small changes were brought in. The brake layout at the pedal was simplified and screwed adjusters were added to the rear operating arms, so that slack in the cables could be taken up. The gearbox now sat on hemispherical rubber pads instead of the fabric ones. Bodywork changes were equally modest. Open car windscreens grew a 4-inch (100mm) long support extending down the side of the scuttle and all doors were made a little bigger. Saloons lost the double mouldings around the windows, these being replaced by single ones, and the radius of the roof panel where it curved down to meet the rear window was increased. The new catalogue had a photograph of a rather smart 2-door "Doctor's Coupé", but gave no details of it or a price. Arthur Thatcher recalled making them in small numbers, so it was a Staines product, but none has survived.

Outside coachbuilders had taken up the chance of performing on the Lagonda chassis and at the Show five of them exhibited. Great Western Motors had a very large saloon, as did Caffyns (also finished in cellulose), while James Young had an elegant 2-seater tourer in cream. Lagonda's own exhibits were a tourer in black with red wings and trim, a semi-sports in "Suede" with "Nutria" trim and a saloon. Sharing the stand was the new six-cylinder car, as will be described in the next chapter. Prices were unchanged, but a new model, the "Saloon de Luxe" appeared at £30 extra and also a "Saloon Landaulette" at £770. No details of either have survived.

Unremarked at the time but of great significance later, in the autumn of 1926 a schoolboy of 14 called Frank Feeley joined the firm and entered the bodyshop under Arthur Thatcher. His father already worked in the chassis erecting shop. Frank made remarkable progress and by 1935 was in charge of bodywork design. He was immensely helpful to the author in researching Lagonda history in the 1970s and, as a man in a position of authority when very young, was still young enough to have clear memories of the company and the personalities involved.

14/60 SUMMARY STATISTICS

Engine

Configuration	4 cylinders in line, overhead valves, two "underhead" camshafts
Capacity	1954cc
Bore & stroke	72 x 120mm
RAC rating	12.9hp
Compression ratio	5.9:1
Firing order	1,2,4,3
Valve timing	io 5° ATDC, ic 50° ABDC, inlet open 225° eo 48° BBDC, ec 8° ATDC, exhaust open 236°, overlap 3°
Tappet clearance	Inlet & exhaust 0.004in(0.10mm) hot or cold
Brake horsepower	60 @ 4200rpm
Main bearings	5
Main bearing diameter	2in (50.8mm)
Big end diameter	2in (50.8mm)
Oil capacity	2 gallons (9.1 litres)
Cooling system	Water pump, thermostat (no fan). Capacity 4 gallons (18.2 litres)
Ignition system	BTH magneto
Ignition timing	36° BTDC fully advanced
Contact breaker gap	0.012in (0.30mm)
Sparking plugs	18mm Champion 16. Gap 0.018in (0.46mm)
Carburettor	Zenith 30HZ
Fuel supply	Autovac from 12-gallon (54.5 litres) tank
Dynamo	Rotax/CAV
Starter motor	Rotax/CAV
Clutch	Single dry plate by Lagonda, 11in diameter (279mm)

Chassis

Wheelbase	10ft (3048mm)
Track	4ft 6in front & rear (1372mm)
Overall length	Tourer 13ft 6in (4115mm)
Kerb weight	Chassis 23.5cwt (1194kg) Tourer 30.75cwt (1562kg) Semi-sports 30.25cwt (1537kg) Saloon 32cwt (1626kg)
Turning circle	41ft 10in (12.75m)
Wheels & tyres	4.75 x 30 tyres on 21in rims
Tyre pressures	32psi front, 30 psi rear (2.2/2.07 bar)
Brake drums	13.75 x 2.5in front, 14 x 3in rear (349 x 63.5mm/356 x 76.2mm)
Steering	Marles worm and roller
Propeller shaft	Timken taper roller in early cars, Hardy Spicer plain bearing later
Rear axle	Semi-floating spiral bevel by Lagonda
Rear axle ratios	4.67:1 (9 x 42) Tourer & Semi-sports 5:11 (9 x 45) Saloon 5.44:1 (9 x 49) & 5.33:1 (9 x 48) alternatives in saloons
Mph/1000rpm in top gear	18.6 (4.67 axle), 17.3 (5.0 axle), 16.3 (5.33 axle) & 16.0 (5.44 axle)
Rear axle oil capacity	3 pints (1.7 litres)
Dampers	Friction by Hartford, transverse at rear
Battery	12 volt negative earth 11-plate tall

Gearbox

Type	Four-speed sliding mesh by Lagonda. Code OH
Internal ratios	Top direct, third 1.6, second 2.5, first & reverse 4.0
Overall ratios	4.67, 7.47, 11.67, 18.67 or 5.0, 8.0, 12.5, 20.0

Prices	1926	1927
Chassis	£450	£495
Tourer	£590	£650
Semi-sports	£590	£650
Saloon	£720	£785
Weymann Saloon	£770	

Chapter Three

The 16/65

Prototype 16/65 engine with one tiny SU carburettor feeding split inlet ports. For production cars a better design, water heated, fed a rake-type manifold, and a single updraught Zenith was fitted. The suction oil filter, seen here vertically below the carburettor, was moved forward on production engines to give access to the oil pump.

It was not at all surprising that Lagonda should bring out a six-cylinder car a year later to accompany the 14/60. What was surprising was how different the engine was to its four-cylinder brother, when the chassis was so alike. Six-cylinder engines were becoming very fashionable: in fact *The Motor* headlined one issue with "1926 — The Year of the Sixes". The new model was called the 16/65, the 16 representing the RAC rating of 15.7hp, on which the road tax was based, and the 65 may have been the power output or the cylinder bore.

The chassis was clearly a cousin of the 14/60's but with an extra nine inches (229mm) in the wheelbase, all of it at the

front end to accommodate the longer engine. Although not immediately apparent, the side members were deeper in section and made of thicker metal. The cross-members were much the same, too, except for the one under the radiator. This took on a very deep U-shape to make room for the dynamo, which was mounted on the front end of the crankshaft, so that it lived underneath the radiator. Its end cover, behind which the brushes lurked, poked out for easy access. The starting handle had to go into this cover, so to keep the electrics dry a plated cap screwed on to the handle access hole. Mounting the dynamo, with its considerable revolving mass, in this position produced some of the effects of a torsional crankshaft damper, a feature with which the engine was not otherwise fitted.

Everything else on the chassis looked just like the 14/60's including the brakes and axles, although the rear track was 2 inches wider at 4ft 8in, this being the introduction of the Lagonda "heavy" axle, distinguished by a different method of filling. Gearbox, transmission and lubrication arrangements were all as on the 14/60. But the engine, which one could reasonably expect to be one and a half 14/60s, was utterly different. Instead of the twin "underhead" camshafts there was only one, set low down and working the valves through pushrods. While the 14/60 had a water pump but no fan, the 16/65 had the

A 16/65 saloon of 1927. Definitely on the stately side, this car is fitted with a division and, probably, fold-up occasional seats in the rear.

reverse. The 14/60 had hemispherical combustion chambers with valves at 90 degrees to each other, the 16/65 had valves all in line, vertical and operating in combustion chambers which were more or less a rhombus with rounded ends. Above all, where the 14/60 engine was a mass of intriguing shapes and was set about with ancillaries, the 16/65 was a very plain rectangular lump with one tiny carburettor bolted straight on to the head, the porting being internal.

Nevertheless, this engine was by the same Davidson and detailed similarities were there if you hunted for them. Once again the oil filler held a whole quart can while it drained away, actually a half-gallon this time, as befits a larger engine. The oil pump used a similar system but was turned through 90 degrees and the magneto was again set across the engine so that access to the business end was easy, but on the opposite side this time. Everything about the engine was massive. The crankshaft ran in seven main bearings

and drove the camshaft by a simple two-sprocket arrangement, unlike the 14/60's complexities. Instead of roller chains an inverted tooth type was substituted. The camshaft was carried in four bearings and ran submerged in oil. Its tunnel was closed by three light alloy castings and removing these covers revealed one of the more unusual features of the engine, a set of rockers interposed between the cams and the pushrods. These rockers were carried on three short

Offside of a 16/65 engine. A plain rectangular lump, the sort of thing Monsieur Bugatti would admire, were it not so heavy. (Instruction Book illustration).

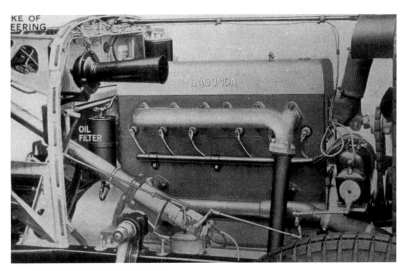

Dashboard of a 1927 16/65. Note that the chassis cross-members have become straight, with the drive shaft threaded through a hole. The 16/65 owner didn't get a rev counter, so the layout of the dials differs from the 14/60.

shafts supported by horizontal studs screwed into the block at the upper edge of the camshaft tunnel opening. In the centre of the camshaft a skew gear drove the oil pump via a short shaft The oil pump was by Roto-plunge again, but this time had "Lagonda" cast on its lid and had been turned round so that the relief valve housing was horizontal.. At the upper end of the pushrods the rockers had an adjustable ball-ended tappet screw at one end and a captive roller on the end which engaged the valve via a thimble over the end of the stem. The valves had double springs but the heads were tiny compared with the 14/60's 1½-inch ones. The rocker shaft was split in two and oil was fed under pressure to each half by a pair of external oil pipes. On the way, the front pipe also supplied oil to the timing case where a skew gear concentric with the larger chain wheel drove the magneto via the conventional vernier coupling. The horizontal BTH magneto ran at three-quarters engine speed, which was unusual but not unique.

On the prototype a suction oil filter, similar to that fitted to the 14/60, was mounted centrally on the near side of the engine adjacent to the oil pump and vertically above the bulge in the sump which held the famous half-gallon of oil you could tip in and leave without worrying — a point frequently made

in road tests. But in this position the filter completely blocked access to the pump and for production cars it was moved further forward, at the expense of having to provide two extra external oil pipes. Oil pressure was expected to be 16psi, compared with 15psi for the four-cylinder car. As well as the suction filter, a bypass pressure filter was provided which lived alongside the Autovac and looked remarkably like it. Perhaps to avoid mistakes, for production it was moved lower down. It was designed to fail safe; oil would just avoid it if it got blocked. One benefit of these changes from 1925 was that the oil pump would lubricate from the first revolution of the engine when it fired, doing away with the perceptible delay found in the earlier engine.

The cooling being by thermo-syphon, water passages were very generous, with large-diameter hoses and water around each bore. There was no thermostat but the fan was a beautiful two-bladed propeller-like affair of cast aluminium, driven by a link vee-belt from a pulley on the half-time shaft. It ran at three-quarters engine speed and adjustment was by an eccentric mounting at the fan end. Although the radiator looked like the 14/60 one, it was taller and the top tank extended several inches further back, so that the hose entered from below rather than from behind. There was a provision, in the catalogue at least, for a water pump to be fitted "for hot climates".

An example of Davidson's attention to detail was the provision of a starting handle with three dogs at 120 degrees, which meant that it was always possible to find a position for a pull-up when starting by hand, a situation which can cause trouble with a six-cylinder engine and only two dogs.

The clutch used was exactly the same as the 14/60 one and the pistons and connecting rods all bore the family resemblance. The aluminium ribbed sump held 3½ gallons, compared with 2 gallons in the 14/60, and the crankcase/sump joint face was on the crankshaft centre line.

The block and head were remarkably simple externally and the prototype car exhibited at the show was fitted with a single dual-choke Cox-Atmos carburettor bolted directly to the head, except for an interposed distance piece which provided vacuum outlets for the Autovac and the windscreen wiper. The inlet ports were unbelievably tiny, at a guess less than an inch each, and passed through the pushrod gallery before splitting to feed three cylinders each. In contrast, there were six quite large exhaust ports on the opposite side of the head, each close to its valve and leading to a cast, ribbed manifold that swept forward to outlet by number 1 cylinder. This inlet port arrangement didn't go into production, however,. One suspects that the emphasis on low-speed torque that these gave completely strangled the engine at higher speeds. There may have been icing troubles too, since production cars had a water-jacketed manifold and the head coring was changed completely. New, larger inlet ports were made between numbers 2 and 3 and numbers 4 and 5 cylinders, and a D-shaped water transfer port replaced the original inlets in the centre of the head. A new fabricated manifold and an updraught Zenith carburettor. were fitted, after experiments with an SU on a Y-shaped manifold had been abandoned. There is reason to believe, too, that the compression ratio was raised by machining the head between proto-type and early production cars as the sparking plug recesses break through the head face on the early engines, whereas the prototype had clean head faces. This doesn't

occur with later cars, leading to the supposi-tion that a revised casting was used.

The dimensions of the new engine were 65 x 120mm, giving 2389cc, only 435cc bigger than the 14/60, in a car weighing 5cwt (254kg) more. Although the 14/60 was not, at this time, regarded as particularly sporting, the valve timing of the 16/65 was even more conservative and there was not even the 3 degrees of overlap found on the earlier design. Everything, in fact, pointed towards the design being angled towards low-speed torque and smoothness to the exclusion of all other factors. In this also it was in contrast to the 14/60, where use of the gearbox paid dividends if the owner wanted the most out of the car, even though Lagonda's advertising paid great attention to the low-speed pulling powers. Having produced an engine with all this torque, so that gear changing would hardly ever be necessary, Lagonda then continued to use a transmission with wide ratios for no very obvious reason. The gearbox was the OH one with ratios of 5:1 (top), 7.99, 12.5 and 20:1, giving speeds of 56mph maximum, with 40mph and 27mph in third and second. Comparable figures for the 14/60 were 4.67, 7.46, 11.65 and 18.64:1 and 65, 43 and 26mph. A bit of arithmetic shows that the gearbox internal ratios were the same, only the rear axle ratio changed. So the overall performance was no better, possibly

A 16/65 tourer of 1927, quite similar to the 14/60 Semi-sports but with a more staid front wing line. This car has a bench front seat which not only reclined but could be lined up with the rear one to make a bed. An Auster rear windscreen was commonly specified with the bench seat.

A rare picture of Brigadier-General Metcalfe, taken in 1933 at the Lagonda Car Club's Hanworth Rally.

slightly worse, than the 14/60's, any extra power being offset by extra weight.

The standard body was a six-light saloon which was an obvious relative of the 14/60, but taller. The windscreen was either flat or vee, to customer's choice, and wire wheels were standard, but the hubcaps had no ears, being removed when needed by a special spanner supplied in the comprehensive toolkit. At the rear, hydraulic lever-arm dampers replaced the Hartfords used on the 14/60. Inside the car the equipment was lavish for the day, with folding footrests in the rear, pile carpet over sorbo rubber, a clock, pneumatic seat squabs with spring cushions, folding occasional seats, two cigar lighters and so on. One surprising omission was a rev counter, although otherwise the dashboard was similar to the 14/60's. The owner still had to walk to the rear of the car to check fuel level. The greater headroom increased the sense of spaciousness in a car actually only 14ft 7½in long, which nowadays would be regarded as only medium sized, but then there was no boot to add several feet in length as now. The prices fixed were certainly higher than the 14/60's at £570 for a chassis and £795 for the saloon, raised to £860 the following spring. More expensive options were a Saloon de Luxe at £870 and a Landaulette at £890. The buyer, for his extra £120, got refinement and luxury fittings for which he paid extra road tax and more for his petrol, although we don't know how much, since contemporary road tests ignored petrol

consumption unless it was very good. If it wasn't, there was no mention.

By the end of 1926 the 14/60 was selling well and the company had cleared the 12/24s out, but customers for the 16/65 seemed to be elusive. Judging by the number surviving (one), the model seems to have been rather a Cinderella, but all Lagonda's early records have been destroyed and we shall never know for sure how many were built. Even though the 3 Litre should have superseded it in 1928 - it was meant to - the 16/65 was a listed model until 1930.

When it came to numbering the 16/65s a very odd thing happened. We saw in the last chapter that 14/60s had begun at Car Number around 8250, with the engine numbers starting again. It must have been assumed that the 12/24 would go on selling, since it was so much cheaper, and Car Numbers from where they had got to in October 1925, around 7500, had been left blank for this purpose. In the event 12/24 sales dropped rapidly, 1926 sales only amounting to about 200 vehicles. So the early 16/65s were given Car Numbers starting at 7901 with a prefix of Z and engine numbers starting at 1001, also with a prefix of Z (for the last word?). For the first time there was some correlation between car and engine numbers, so that car Z7913 had engine Z1013, Z7931 had Z1031 and so on. This anomaly lasted until the end of 1927, perhaps coinciding with the introduction of the larger engine, when 16/65s began to appear with Car Numbers in the same series as the 14/60 and engine numbers in the sequence started by the first 14/60. So we have the odd situation that engine Z1031 in Z7931 of July 1927 is earlier than engine Z771 in Z9028 of June 1928. It isn't at all clear what happened when the engine numbers in the 14/60 and 2 Litre sequence reached the numbers already issued to early 16/65s. This would have happened in late 1928.

The whole issue of identifying cars at this time was slightly muddled. The car's identity plate had three lines: "Type", "Engine Number", and "Car Number". When only the one type was being made "Type" merely said T for tourer, S for saloon or R for Allweather. With the advent of the 14/60, "SS" for Semi-sports was added. Adding the 16/65 to the range meant some differentiation, so a Z was added to its engine number and an OH to the four-cylinder cars. But whoever at the factory had the job of stamping these plates didn't always remember to add the prefix and there are a number of cars from the late 1920s with none. If such a car falls into the hands of a Lagonda novice he will have no way of knowing what he has from the ID plate, although counting the cylinders will give a clue.

An important change at the factory in 1926 was the appointment of a new Managing Director, Brigadier-General Francis Metcalfe. He joined the existing directors, Messrs Parbury, Denison, Tollemache and Cranmer, and within a few months changed radically not only the way the cars were sold but also the nature of the cars themselves. Francis Edward Metcalfe was born in 1878 and was a professional soldier before coming to Lagonda, being awarded the CMG and DSO in the First World War and the CB in 1919. He was every inch what was then regarded as a "sportsman", given to wearing blinding check suits, tweed caps and a monocle. We will come to his influence on the cars later, since that took time, but immediate changes were the closing down of the London Depot at 195 Hammersmith Road (the old Tollemache & Griffin site) and the transfer of all service work to the factory at Staines. Shortly afterwards Bill Oates took a lease on the Depot and opened a dealership in Lagondas and Standards. This marked his departure from Staines, where his job as Sales Manager was taken by Frank King, whose first task was to re-organise the dealerships. At the end of this it is interesting that only three of the eleven dealers were outside London. Bill Oates's new set-up left him less time for competitions and he was never as happy with the larger cars as he had been with the "Elevens". Added to which, the SMMT in 1927 decided to withdraw recognition from most of the big trials, which meant that factory teams weren't to compete. So 14/60s were much scarcer in competitions of this type than the 11.9 and 12/24 had been.

Despite Lagonda's heavy involvement in trials and rallies, it had never produced a production sports car; all the competitions, apart from Oates's single-seater and the 200 Mile Race cars, had been conducted in prosaic tourers or saloons. But from the beginning of 1927, probably as a result of General Metcalfe's influence, a low-key factory participation in racing started. On 7 May the Essex MC held a Six Hour Race for standard touring cars, during which the first ten laps had to be completed with the hood up. Probably reasoning that the delay involved in stopping to put it down again offset the advantage of lower weight, Lagonda entered a 14/60 saloon to be driven by Frank King and E Davidson. They did well, lying fifth early on, and averaged 58.7mph for the first three hours. But a piston broke and ended their effort.

Then on 24 May the factory was back at Brooklands with a special lightweight fabric covered 14/60 saloon (Car No. OH 8626) for some RAC-observed runs which resulted in the issue of RAC Certificate No. 650. Bert Hammond was the driver. The standing-start mile was covered at 49.61mph, the flying half-mile at 67.34mph and the Test Hill was climbed at 15.67mph from a standing start. The 0-50mph time was 24 seconds and the fuel consumption at a steady 40mph was 24.22mpg. Brake tests then ensued, with stopping distances of 22ft 7in (6.9m), 55ft (16.7m), 98ft 7in (30m) and 159ft 8in (48.7m) from 20, 30, 40 and 50mph respectively. There is a photograph of the car on the certificate and it

Weymann fabric saloon on the 16/65 chassis, as shown in the 1927 catalogue. The weight saved must have improved performance markedly but unfortunately no magazine seems to have tested an example.

The 16/65 h.p. Six - Cylinder "Weymann" Saloon - £845

has a non-standard body with only four lights and an extended boot. It had the 4.67:1 axle and weighed 29.5cwt (1499kg) unladen and 35.25cwt (1791kg) with four occupants, who were in place for all of the tests. This car, or its twin, features largely in the 1927 Lagonda Fete at Brooklands.

The purpose of these tests is obscure. They were never mentioned in advertising and are not particularly impressive, even allowing for them being conducted four-up. The original claim of 80mph looks rather daft if a top speed of only 67mph is all that can be verified. It is just possible that the tests acted as a base from which tuning improvements could be compared, although one wouldn't expect to go to an RAC Certificate to achieve these. Within a month Frank King was driving a 14/60 Semi-sports at the BARC Whitsun meeting and lapped Brooklands at 81.37mph in the 90 Long Handicap. This was way beyond what any ordinary 14/60 could do and it is clear that sporting performance was being sought and gained.

The next idea for selling cars was the Lagonda Brooklands Fete, first held on 18 August 1927. The idea was to hire Brooklands on a weekday, lay on competitions ranging from real races to gymkhana-type frolics, and invite the world to attend for free. All dealers were charged with contacting past, present and potential customers and were leaned on heavily to provide prizes. As an added teaser, the company took whole-page adverts in the motoring papers promising the debut of an exciting new model, featuring a speedometer dial registering over 80mph, but rather spoiled the impact by the dreadful drawing used to illustrate the car concerned. You can understand that the company wouldn't want to break the embargo on the actual appearance of the secret new model, but this drawing would put off all potential buyers.

The exciting new model was the 2 Litre Speed Model, a sporting four-seater tourer version of the 14/60, with considerable changes to the engine to reflect the harder driving it was likely to get, and clothed in an extremely handsome body which owed something to the Vauxhall 30/98 and the Vanden Plas Bentleys but was smaller and lighter in concept and appearance even if not in actual weight. The first announcement was

very low-key, just a paragraph and a photo in *The Autocar* of 26 July 1927, the same issue containing a road test of a 16/65 saloon and the advert with the awful drawing. We will delay the description of the new model until the next chapter and pursue the 16/65 story.

The road test was of a saloon, PH 1599, finished in two tones of grey. It had leather upholstery, leather loose cushions, two cigar lighters, ladies and gent's companions with the expected goodies inside them, armrests and footrests, a parcel net and a spring-loaded rear window blind. One suspects this was the de luxe version. A great deal of space was devoted to descriptions of the fixtures and fittings and the general impression given is of an extremely luxurious large car, easy to handle because of light steering and excellent brakes, but with rather pedestrian performance, 10-60mph occupying 54.6 seconds. Admittedly this was in top gear, which could be held down to 5mph. The car could be started from rest on the Brooklands Test Hill in second gear, causing one to wonder what first was for. The brakes were excellent, stopping the car from 40mph in 90ft (27.4m). The testers remarked that the demonstrator had already done 17,000 miles and that perhaps these figures could be improved upon - ie the car was a touch worn. The general convenience and outstanding ease of maintenance were remarked on, with the grouped greasers and the accessible magneto, helped by the well-stocked toolkit kept in a roll clipped to the side of the car by the passenger's feet, so that you didn't have to shift your luggage to get to it. *The Autocar* and *The Motor* both got an indicated 65mph as the top speed. New features were a 2-gallon (9-litre) reserve in the petrol tank and the oil filter referred to above.

At about the same time, the summer of 1927, a tourer version of the 16/65 was quietly introduced. It was clearly a cousin of the 14/60 one, was 9 inches longer and looked taller, perhaps because of larger tyres. It was priced at £725 and a new feature was the addition of elaborate side pieces to the front bucket seats to hold the occupants in place in rapid cornering. Unfortunately, they also made access and egress very difficult and were soon dropped as being out of place in such a dignified car.

16/65 SUMMARY STATISTICS

Engine

Configuration	6 cylinders in line, pushrod overhead valves
Capacity	2389cc (1926), 2692cc (1927)
Bore	65mm (1926), 69mm (1927)
Stroke	120mm
RAC rating	15.7hp (1926), 17.75hp (1927)
Compression ratio	Not known
Firing order	1,5,3,6,2,4
Valve timing	io 10° ATDC, ic 50° ABDC, inlet open 220° eo 42° BBDC, ec 10° ATDC, exhaust open 232°. Overlap nil
Tappet clearance	Inlet 0.004in (0.10mm) hot Exhaust 0.006in (0.15mm) hot
Brake horsepower	Not published
Main bearings	7
Main bearing diameter	2.25in (57.15mm)
Big end diameter	2in (50.8mm)
Oil capacity	3.5 gallons (announcement), 2 gallons (instruction book) (15.6 & 9.1 litres)
Cooling system	Thermo-syphon, fan assisted. Capacity 6 gallons (27.3 litres)
Ignition system	BTH magneto
Ignition timing	36° BTDC fully advanced
Contact breaker gap	0.012in (0.30mm)
Sparking plugs	18 mm Champion 16, gap 0.018in (0.46mm)
Carburettor	Zenith updraught
Fuel supply	Autovac
Tank capacity	1926: 12 gallons (54.5 litres) 1927-on: 14-gallons (63.6 litres)
Dynamo	CAV/Rotax AT 124
Starter	CAV/Rotax SC78
Clutch	Lagonda 11in (279mm) single dry plate

Chassis

Wheelbase	10ft 9in (3277mm)
Track, front	4ft 6in (1372mm)
Track, rear	4ft 8in (1422mm)
Overall length	Tourer 14ft (4267mm) Saloon 14ft 7½in (4458mm)
Kerb weight	Chassis 23.5cwt (1194kg) Saloon 33.75cwt (1715kg) Tourer not known
Turning circle	Not measured
Wheels & tyres	5.25 x 21 tyres on 4.5in rims
Tyre pressures	40psi front, 38psi rear (2.76, 2.62 bar)
Brake drums	as 14/60
Brake linings	as 14/60
Steering	as 14/60
Propeller shaft	Hardy Spicer plain bearing
Rear axle	Semi-floating spiral bevel by Lagonda
Rear axle ratio	1926 5:1 (9 x 45) 1927 5.3:1 (9 x 48)
Mph/1000rpm in top gear	18.74 (5:1 axle), 17.7 (5.3:1 axle)
Rear axle oil capacity	3 pints (1.7 litres)
Dampers	Hartford friction at front, hydraulic at rear
Battery	12 volt negative earth, 11-plate tall

Gearbox

Type	Four-speed sliding mesh by Lagonda, Code OH
Internal ratios	As 14/60
Overall ratios	1926 top 5.0:1, third 8.0:1, second 12.5:1, first & reverse 20.0:1 1927 top 5.3:1, third 8.48:1, second 13.3:1, first & reverse 21.2:1

Prices	1928
Chassis	£570
Tourer	£740
Saloon	£860
Weymann saloon	£845

Chapter Four

Speed Model

Bill Oates (centre) on the Finishing Straight at the 1927 Lagonda Fete at Brooklands.

The factory's efforts to stage the Brooklands Fete resulted in about 1500 people turning up, not bad for a Thursday. The morning was given over to exhibiting the model range and demonstration runs on the track in all of them, with the emphasis naturally on the new Speed Model. There was no nonsense about Competition Licences, you just showed up and entered. After lunch there was an Appearance Contest, won by Major King with a tourer, either a

14/60 (*The Motor*) or a 16/65 (*The Autocar*). Next came two heats and a final for the one-lap race for 14/60s, with a Le Mans start. "Mac" McCallum in a fabric saloon won the first at a canter. This may have been the RAC Certificate car, since it was perceptibly faster than the other cars in the heat. The second heat was won by Fletcher in a tourer. In the final, Reise's tourer lapped somewhere in the 70s and beat both heat winners. The next race was for 12/24s, won by Ellis. Mrs Church's car was slow to start and, treading hard on the throttle pedal in an attempt to catch up, she pushed it through the floorboards, where it stuck, making fact of what had been a Brooklands joke. There followed a slow-running contest in which observers were carried to ensure no clutch slipping. Last past the post and hence the winner was Grimaldi, a dealer from St Albans in a 14/60. The final event was a timed climb of the Test Hill, won by Nicholls in a 14/60 Semi-sports in 14.9 seconds from Benson in 15.6 seconds. Benson later became a prolific Trials entrant in 2 Litres and one suspects that "Nicholls" was actually Bob Nicholl of Fox & Nicholl. Actually, Benson and McCallum did identical times and tossed a coin to decide second and third places. All in all it was a very enjoyable day out; the Speed Model demonstrators had had a good airing in front of their potential customers and on the whole the event had been a good bit of salesmanship.

*Peter Minett's 1928 high
chassis Speed Model tourer.*

Nearside of high chassis Speed Model 2 Litre engine. The original Zenith has been replaced by an SU, a common change. The SU is thought to give extra power and is certainly much easier to understand.

Ancilliaries on the nearside of the engine. From left to right: the oil pump; the oil junction box; the oil filler and the water pump driven by one of the sprockets on the lower timing chain.

On the face of it the Speed Model could have been just a sporting new body on the 14/60 chassis, but in fact the company was much more thorough and some very important changes to both chassis and engine accompanied the new model, many of them applied to the later 14/60s as well, in due course. The new model was likely to be driven much harder and at higher revs than its touring predecessors, so considerable

thought had been given to the lubrication arrangements. On the 14/60 the oil pump drew its lubricant from the sump via three pipes, each with two unions. The first pipe connected the sump outlet to the suction filter mounted vertically beside the crankcase. The second pipe led from there to a housing on the engine bearer and the third pipe from that to the oil pump. For the Speed Model the oil suction filter was relocated to lie horizontally

Forty years of research have failed to find any significance in the numbers stamped on high chassis engines, apart from the "S" for Speed Model. This is not engine number 1750 nor 497.

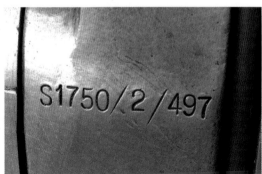

Offside of the high chassis Speed Model 2 Litre engine.

within the sump and a single longer pipe connected it to the pump, still made by Roto-plunge but a more modern type with Lagonda's name on it. Less visibly, the series of pipes and unions that fed oil to the main bearings inside the crankcase were all replaced by drilled passages through the crankcase itself and its webs. Big ends were supplied, as before, by diagonal drillings from the main bearings. To reduce the mass of

metal whirling around, the crankshaft, hitherto totally solid, now had quite large holes drilled through the big end journals, oil tightness being achieved by little aluminium end plugs secured with a through bolt. To maintain balance, the extended arms of numbers 1 and 4 cylinder crank throws, which acted as balance weights, were drilled also, but had no little plugs since there was no oil there. One suspects that the drilling operation was done

The steering box is by Marles. Rod controls adjacent to it operate the ignition advance and the hand throttle, both located on the other side of the engine and requiring fairly complicated control rod runs.

Spare sparking plugs are carried in a special housing on the bulkhead. Modern plugs are rarely changed between services but that was not the case in 1928.

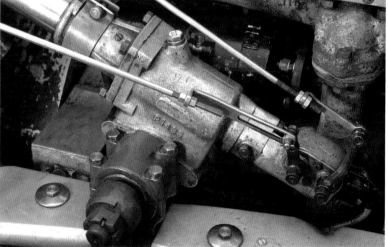

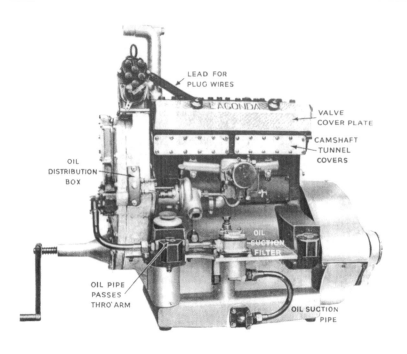

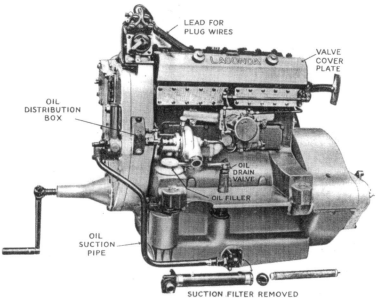

In this shot of the offside of the engine you can see the closely spaced cylinder head studs. Davidson was determined there should be no gasket problems, a policy which paid off handsomely when superchargers were added.

External changes to the 14/60 engine, top, compared with the Speed Model (Instruction Book illustration).

on a line boring machine since the crankshaft flange to which the flywheel was attached also acquired part-circle cutouts that serve no useful purpose. The hollow journals allowed the maximum permitted revs to be raised, but have a downside in that should a big end run, the molten white metal is likely to get in there; although it is no great task to remove the end plugs to clear it out, commercial repairers can be relied on not to do it, with a strong chance of a further bearing failure in due course.

Another feature of the Speed Model engine reflecting higher revs was a simplification of the small end of the connecting rods. The set screw and bushes were abandoned and the gudgeon pins were now fully floating with aluminium end pads. New pistons by BHB adopted the principle pioneered by Bentley, where the top surface of the piston was connected to the gudgeon pin boss by two angled struts and not by the periphery of the piston. Thus the pressure of the combustion stroke tended to produce an outward pressure on the skirts, reducing blow-by but permitting a slacker fit when not under load, good for reducing wear. The compression ratio was raised from the 14/60's 5.9:1 to 6.8:1, regarded as very high at the time, and two exhaust camshafts were fitted, giving 236° of opening for the inlet cam instead of the 14/60's 225°.

The high chassis front axle has the brake operating rods attached to its underside. Lowering the chassis in 1929 involved a new axle beam with these rods passing through it.

A similar Zenith Triple Diffuser carburettor was used but with a 26 choke tube instead of 22, a 115 main jet instead of 105, and a compensator jet of 95. Soon after the introduction of the Speed Model, Lagonda gave up printing jet sizes in the instruction book, probably recognising that carburettor tuning was regarded as a black art at the time and owners — well, some owners — loved to fiddle and wouldn't take much notice of recommendations anyway.

More attention was given to engine ventilation, with perforated plugs in each rocker cover and a crankcase breather connected to the hollow offside rear engine bearer. The instruction book was revised to cover both the 14/60, now called the Standard OH, and the Speed Model. It had a subtle change. On page 14, H P McConnell, the author, is seen testing the timing chain tension with his little finger and not the forefinger he used in 1925.

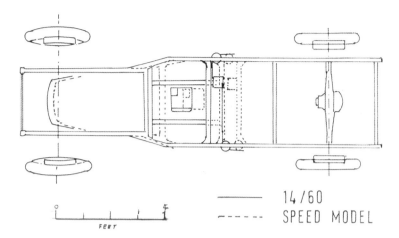

14/60
SPEED MODEL

Sketch of the changes to the chassis frame to turn the 14/60 (shown solid) to the Speed Model (dotted).

Perhaps he had ignored his own advice in the earlier book not to do this with the engine running.

Turning to the chassis, the most obvious change was the re-positioning of the engine and radiator, the latter now directly above the front axle. To do this the engine had been moved back about 6 inches (150mm). But the changes were more radical than just moving the engine. New chassis frame side members were employed, on which the point where they diverged from each other was also moved rearwards by about 6 inches, and all the cross-members around the gearbox and

Brake system layout for the Speed Model. This drawing, from the Instruction Book, shows the extra cross-member behind the rear brake compensator box. Impecunious owners soon discovered that when the outer brake shoes at the rear wore out their linings you could swap the cables over with the hand brake ones and delay paying for a re-line.

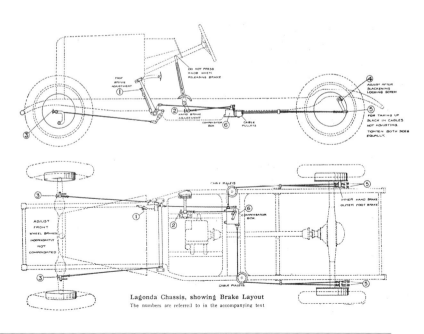

Lagonda Chassis, showing Brake Layout
The numbers are referred to in the accompanying text

Walter Buckingham, Lagonda's body designer, distrusted large doors because they could overload the pillars. The two provided on the Speed Model were the smallest he could get away with.

braking system moved a similar amount. There must have been a problem with the rear brake cables, where they ran transverse to the chassis, distorting the frame when tension was on the cables, for an extra cross-member was inserted immediately to the rear of the brake compensator box, which would resist the pull on the cables more effectively. This additional cross-member was applied to the standard 14/60 chassis from this point on. As the cross-members had moved back, the

brake cables were now shorter, as was the propeller shaft, which had acquired enclosed Hardy plain-bearing universals instead of the earlier taper roller variety. Another unseen modification affected the front hubs, whose taper roller bearings now had their larger diameter at the outer ends instead of the inner ends of the axle.

The continuing changes to the brake layout carried on, with the removal of front-to-rear compensation and the substitution of a rod

The three designs of brake pedal layout from 1925 to 1927, when it settled down.

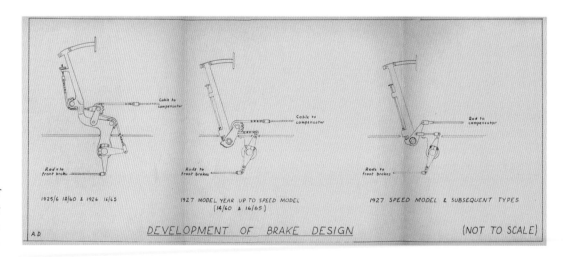

for the cable from the pedal to the rear compensator box. To relieve some twisting loads, the bearings of the front cross-shaft were re-positioned outboard of the brake rods, and inside the brake drums the rear shoes were pierced with a lattice pattern to save unsprung weight.

The account of the varieties of rear axle fitted to 14/60s becomes rather confused here. The 1926 instruction book illustrates a very lightweight (for Lagonda) rear axle, with no visible nuts on the front of the differential housing for the bearing housings, and a filler neck attached to the front lower section. The 1928 book depicts two different rear axles, neither the same as the 1926 one. It makes it clear that the Speed Model axle,

High chassis Speed Model tourer, chassis OH 8985, photographed in a London square before the war. Note the fabric-covered bonnet, achieved by the Buckingham method described in this chapter. Black headlamps were cheaper than plated ones and very common then. There was a theory to justify them which said that reflections in plated headlamps from following cars distracted the driver at night.

although different in appearance to the 1926 axle and with visible nuts holding the bearing housings, still has the same filling method. It goes on to illustrate the Standard OH axle, i.e. that fitted to 14/60s at this time. This has a filling aperture right on top, but to avoid overfilling, you can't pour anything into it without twisting to one side a handle which, when turned, opens a valve lower down so that excess oil would just escape through it. Now this design is normally only

There are no doors on the offside of the Speed Model tourer. That rear wing line can only be described as "cheeky" and must have led to clinching sales to the sporting owner.

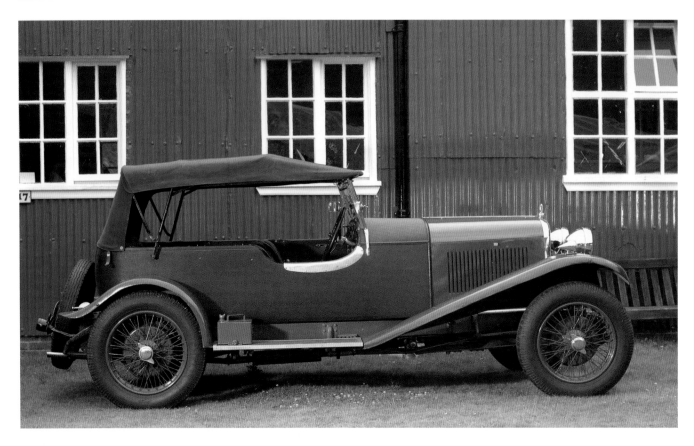

The 'goalpost' frame that supports the headlamps and wings is normally painted body colour but an owner has plated this one to match the radiator.

The hood mechanism is quite complicated but the result is an erected hood that does not spoil the car's appearance. Sidescreens are added in serious rain.

The hood bag has acquired a nice patina. It would originally have been black to match the more recent tonneau cover.

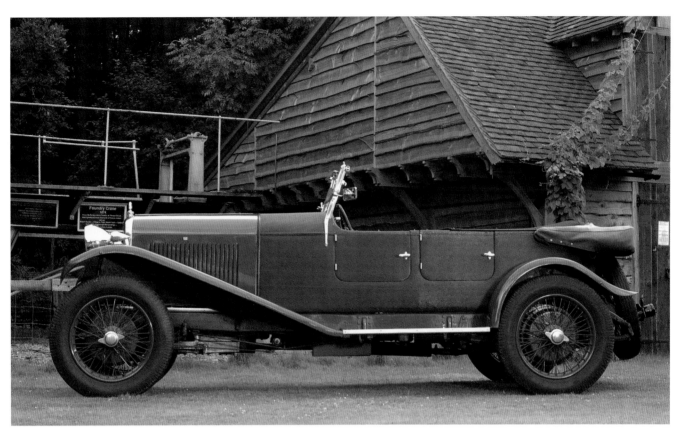

The Speed Model tourer body design did not have room for any little cupboards for the grease gun and it retreated to the tool roll under the scuttle.

A new radiator badge was designed for the Speed Model. Quite expensive to make, in champlevé enamel, it was appropriate for an expensive car.

The water temperature gauge is attached to the radiator filler cap, possibly a retrograde step from the 14/60's dashboard instrument. It may have been felt that in that position the driver couldn't help noticing it. Fortunately, a 2 Litre in good condition rarely overheats.

Interior of the Speed Model tourer. The tools hid in a roll, carried in the little locker in front of the front passenger's door.

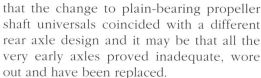

Having no boot allowed enormous leg room for rear passengers. No centre armrest on this early version.

found on the "heavy" axle, introduced with the 16/65, whose instruction book shows exactly the same pictures, but labelled for the six cylinder car. It is a moot point whether any "light" axles ever had this filler, as all existing ones seem to have the Speed Model version with the low-set filler. As befits a sporting model, the taller rear axle ratio was set at 4.2:1 (10 x 42). It is possible

that the change to plain-bearing propeller shaft universals coincided with a different rear axle design and it may be that all the very early axles proved inadequate, wore out and have been replaced.

Apart from an additional oiling point, no changes were made to the clutch, and the gearbox was unchanged except for a closer set of ratios. The 14/60 indirects had been 1.6, 2.5 and 4:1, with reverse the same as first. The new set were 1.26, 1.96 and 3.14:1. The battery was moved to live under the front passenger seat. The solenoid was omitted and a heavy-duty switch on the dashboard substituted.

One of the features of the 14/60 had been the cast aluminium dashboard, which was outrigged from the bulkhead and formed part of the chassis rather than being attached to the body. The Speed Model having its steering column set more nearly horizontal and the driver's seat consequently further back, this became rather impractical and was abandoned. Instead there was a conventional wooden dashboard which contained in its centre an oblong metal panel for the switches and some of the instruments.

A speedometer reading to 100 mph might impress small boys but was not really necessary. The miles recorded only went up to 9999.9, a Lagonda habit that persisted until 1935.

Central instrument panel by CAV. The rev counter is separate, directly in front of the driver. The oil pressure gauge reads to 100psi. (about 7 bar), but 20 to 30 is a more normal pressure.

The Smith's rev. counter reads to 5000 rpm with no red line. The 2 Litre's rather strangled breathing meant that it rarely could rev high enough to harm itself.

High chassis Speed Model dashboard. The tall thin gauge to the left is the Hobson petrol gauge.

Offside view of a high chassis Speed Model tourer, taken in London in 1929. The "double diamond" pattern embossed on the trim of the nearside front door was a Lagonda favourite and featured on tourers for many years.

The 14/60 tourer had been a good-looking car in an unremarkable way but the Speed Model tourer was a real head-turner. To this day it remains one of the best proportioned and most handsome cars of its era, and although on the heavy side for a 2 litre it still was two hundredweight (102kg) lighter than a Bentley 3 Litre. The re-siting of both the engine and the driver had resulted in a much longer bonnet and scuttle panel to accommo-date the driver's legs now that the seats were mounted directly on the floor, in the sporting tradition. Two bodies were offered, a fabric-covered saloon built to Weymann patents in addition to the tourer. The tourer body was no wider than the chassis at its bottom and had two narrow doors on the near side. The prototype had also had a door at the rear on the offside, but this did not feature on production cars. The driver had no door but there was a slight cutout in the side which eased entry and gave elbow clearance. The aluminium panels were covered in "Zapon" fabric over kapok filling, a very fashionable finish at the time, and Lagonda even managed to cover the bonnet in matching fabric. To do this Walter Buckingham evolved a secret method which required accurate cutting and lightning speed. The fabric used was a thick woven wool, covered with canvas and thickly cellulosed. As you can imagine, getting a wrinkle-free finish on the tighter radii of the body presented considerable problems and any double curvatures a real headache. What Buckingham devised was a method by which the cut-to-shape fabric panels were briefly soaked in cellulose thinners, which enabled

Although the Speed Model had a perfectly good starter motor, the starting handle was kept in place ready for use, spring loaded out of engagement.

The Speed Model windscreen is in three pieces, with the upper panel opening about top hinges. Originally a rubber sealing strip joined upper to lower and was inevitably right in the eyeline of drivers of any height. Now very rare.

Fuel tank contents gauge by Rotherhams. The Speed Model normally had the Hobson's Telegauge on the dashboard. Perhaps that has given up; they can be extremely difficult to repair.

Speed model Weymann saloon. We have no idea who these gentlemen are or the occasion, but the car still has its fabric finish to the bonnet and, most unusual for a pre-1939 photograph, there is still tread on the spare tyre.

the rest of the bodywork.

Exactly the same techniques were applied to the Weymann-bodies Speed Model saloons. Charles Terres Weymann was born in Haiti in 1889 and was either French, American or British, according to whom you believe. He was a fighter pilot in the First World War and after it invented his patented form of body construction. Coachbuilt bodies of the 1920s had problems accommodating the twisting and bending of the flexible chassis of the period, and after quite a short time developed a chorus of squeaks and groans on even quite good roads. This was one reason why tourers retained their popularity. Weymann's main idea was not to allow adjoining pieces of timber to touch each other by interposing steel tongues, frequently L- or T-shaped, leaving the timbers a quarter of an inch (6mm) apart. The seats were fixed to the floor, which was load-bearing, allowing the bodywork to be much lighter as its only function was to keep out the weather. The frames surrounding the doors had no bottom rail, although the doors themselves did, of course, and the doors were a very loose fit in the frames, the gaps being sealed with leather-cloth flaps. Some of the larger panels were strengthened with diagonal wire braces.

the canvas plus cellulose layers to be separated from the wool. This was then much more pliable and could be tightly wrapped around the metal panelling. One particular finish, much in demand, had the canvas woven with red strands in one direction and black in the other, giving a kind of "light black" appearance. This called for extreme care on curved sections; if it was stretched unevenly one colour would predominate over the other and ruin the effect.

For the bonnet, liable to get quite hot, a further refinement was to remove the canvas too, by a second dip in the thinners, leaving only the cellulose layer with its canvas-like texture. This called for enormous confidence and great speed. No one has ever been able since to reproduce it and all cars now have shiny bonnets. In 1927 the bonnet matched

Weymann set up a coachbuilding company in Paris in 1922 and a British subsidiary in 1923, which built a factory in Weybridge in 1927. Lagonda struck a deal whereby they built their saloon bodies to Weymann's patent ideas but to Lagonda's designs, and paid a royalty on each one sold. The French Weymann firm went into aircraft production in 1929 and the British one diversified into bus and train bodies in the 1930s, eventually becoming Metro-Cammell-Weymann, builder of London's Routemasters.

A full-size Weymann body was amazingly light, something in the region of 4cwt (203kg), which includes wings and glass. The timbers were generally only about 1½ inches square (37mm) and there was no metal panelling, the exterior covering being leather-cloth over cotton wool, the latter helping with sound deadening. The scuttle panel was a double layer of Zapon with cotton wool in between the layers. Fixed glasses were held in split rubber tubing, while the moveable ones ran in felt-lined channels. Where it was

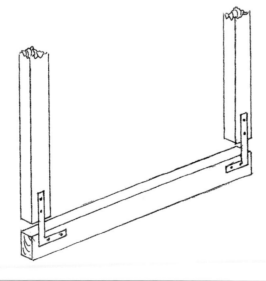

The principle of the joints in the Weymann body. The gap has been exaggerated for clarity.

unavoidable for two pieces of wood to touch, a canvas or leather gasket was placed between them.

Both the Speed Model tourers and saloons shared the same elegant sporting wing line, the rear one stopping well above the wheel's centre line and ending with a saucy tweaked up tip, the very personification of "a clean pair of heels". The windscreen had just the right angle of rake and the headlamps were carried higher than before, so that their centres lined up with the sidelamps. A dipping option was made available, the Barker dipper being a mechanical device which physically tilted the whole lamp assembly. Its operating lever looked confusingly like the gear lever and was also mounted conveniently near the driver's right hand, just like the gear lever.

The dash panel contained the speedometer, clock, ammeter and oil pressure gauge. The revcounter was mounted separately directly in front of the driver, while a Boyce Motometer was attached to the radiator cap and measured water temperature. The cap itself grew two long operating arms, nowadays being called a "dog bone" cap, kinder to fingers if touched when hot. A dashboard fuel gauge, the newly introduced Hobson Telegauge, saved the driver the chore of walking to the rear of the car to assess fuel contents. The horn button, hand throttle and advance/retard adjustment lived on the boss of a dished three-spoke steering wheel, and a multi-start screw-thread mixture control replaced the strangler of the 14/60.

The tourer windscreen was a flat one, split into four panels, the upper pair opening; the sealing strip between upper and lower panes was cunningly contrived to be in the eye-line of a driver of any height. The saloon windscreen was a single pane, opening with top hinges.

In contrast to the elegant tourer, the Speed Model saloon was a touch gawky, with the very square-cut lines that were a normal side effect of the way Weymann saloons were built. It had four doors and four lights, with all doors front-hinged. Triplex safety glass was an option, costing £5 extra for the windscreen only, £20 for the whole car. Triplex for the more complicated tourer windscreen cost an extra £5 15s (£5.75). As virtually every

The lever for the Barker headlamp dipper (with silver knob), here shown in the main beam position, was perfectly placed to go up the trouser leg when climbing into a Speed Model.

customer specified it, it became standard the following year.

The Speed Model chassis sold for £530, the tourer for £675 and the saloon £750. This was a great deal of money in 1927. The Lagonda adverts in the early days used to boast "Not a 'cheap' car". By 1927 they meant it.

The improvements and additions to the chassis meant that the Speed Model tourer, at 26cwt (1321kg), was no lighter than the 14/60 Semi-sports, but the capability of more revolutions and extra power resulted in considerably more performance. The factory claimed, indeed guaranteed, a top speed of 80mph and 70 in third. When the first road tests of the Speed Model appeared, in *The Autocar* of 16 December 1927 and *The Motor* of 31 January 1928, they were very tactful about the 80mph

The bronze casting carries the thermostat, quite a rare piece of equipment in 1928. Its operation range is adjustable. The horizontal stay above it holds the radiator in place; its other end is fixed to the bulkhead.

claim, "guaranteed" by the makers. The test car was PH 3928 and neither paper admitted they had actually seen 80mph, *The Autocar* remarking "Naturally the last few miles per hour require time to obtain", but they did see over 70mph and 60 in third. *The Autocar* also said that 80mph corresponded to 3300rpm in top, which was not true. The 2 Litre wasn't *that* high geared. On the 4.2:1 axle 80mph represents 3650rpm. Apart from that they were very pleased with the car and could barely fault it. In particular, the comfort came in for praise, not normally the case for a sporting car. They got 24 to 26 miles to the gallon and *The Motor* tactfully curtailed their acceleration graph in at 65 seconds, by which time the car was travelling at 73mph.

As mentioned above, substantial changes were made to the 14/60 and 16/65 at or just after the introduction of the Speed Model. On the 14/60 these included the drilled crank and other modifications to the engine, the extra chassis cross-member, a revised mixture control and a new design of brake layout. The 16/65 incorporated most of the chassis revisions, including the extra cross-member, but the biggest change was to bore out the engine to 69mm, giving a capacity of 2692cc. This made it an 18hp under the RAC ratings but the name was not altered. The larger engine acquired the Speed Model type of piston and connecting rod, and its crankshaft was drilled through the journals in the same way. We have no contemporary records of

the effect of the larger engine on performance, since no magazine did a road test on it.

As befits an exciting and important new model, a new radiator badge adorned the Speed Model. The L and last A of Lagonda were much larger than the other letters, the lettering being in white enamel on a blue background. The radiator itself was unchanged.

Accompanying the new models the warranty arrangements were changed in September 1927 from 12 months to a possible 10 years. The initial guarantee was for two years. At the end of that the owner had to return the car to the works, who would say what was needed to renew it. If the owner agreed (and paid) then a further two years was issued, and so on up to 10 years. The factory did honour this but it was rarely invoked, for in a period of galloping depreciation and rapid design changes the bill for repairs after the first two years was liable to rival the value of the car and certainly would after four years. Nevertheless, it was a good sales ploy. Few people, on buying a new car, ever consider their eventual disposal of it and the rich, from whom Lagonda was now seeking custom, consider their image does not allow them to be seen in anything other than the very latest thing.

At Motor Show time in 1927 Lagonda hosted a dinner at the Trocadero for their agents, and Russell Rose, MD of Central Garage, Bradford, in his speech told how one of his customers had done 19,000 miles since Easter and had left the car with his firm for all worn parts to be replaced. The total bill had come to five shillings and threepence (26p). Lagonda had Stand 134 at the Show and showed both types of Speed Model, a 16/65 saloon and a 14/60 Semi-sports. It was announced that there would be a Weymann saloon forthcoming on the 14/60 chassis, although it wasn't in the catalogue. But a Weymann on the 16/65 was in there, priced at £845. It was a very different animal to the Speed Model Weymann, very staid and rectangular, with six lights and four doors. By the 1928 catalogue a much more sporting-looking 16/65 Weymann had followed it.

Perhaps as a means of increasing production of the new models, Lagonda sought extra capital at the end of 1927 and took a £65,000

This "dogbone" fuel filler cap is not the standard one for a Speed Model. The usual one has a castellated cap.

debenture, secured on the whole factory, from the bank. Possibly connected with this, both Henry Tollemache and Wilfred Denison resigned as directors, although they kept their shareholdings. The following March an additional director was appointed, Sir Edgar Holberton, later to be Chairman.

The Speed Model didn't take long to appear in competition, starting with the London-Exeter Trial, whose traditional Boxing Day start had to be abandoned in 1927 as the weather was so atrocious. It was eventually run off on 13-14 January 1928 and two Lagondas got Gold Medals, driven by A C Benson and P W White. Mike Couper, a member of the sales team at Staines, was also entered in a 2 Litre but actually drove a Vauxhall 30/98.

The rear mounted spare wheel is no help if an external luggage rack is intended. But the spacious rear compartment and even the running boards could be conscripted.

2 LITRE SPEED MODEL (HIGH CHASSIS) SUMMARY STATISTICS
ALL AS 14/60 EXCEPT

Engine

Compression ratio	6.8:1
Valve timing (degrees)	io 3° ATDC, ic 59° ABDC, inlet open 236° eo 44° BBDC, ec 12° ATDC, exhaust open 236°. Overlap 9°
Brake horsepower	78bhp @ 4200rpm
Oil capacity	3 gallons (13.6 litres)
Carburettor	Zenith 36 VH

The identity plate only has room for a two-letter "type".

Chassis

Kerb weight	Chassis 21cwt (1067kg)
	Tourer 27.75cwt (1410kg)
	Weymann Saloon 31cwt (1575kg)
Overall length	Tourer 13ft 7½in (4153mm)
	Saloon 14ft 4in (4369mm)
Wheels & tyres	5.25 x 31 tyres on 21in rims
Tyre pressures	35psi front, 33psi rear (2.4, 2.28 bar)
Rear axle ratio	4.2:1 (10 x 42)
Mph/1000rpm in top gear	21.9
Fuel tank capacity	From 1928, 14 gallons (63.6 litres)

Gearbox

Internal ratios	Top direct, 3rd 1.257:1, 2nd 1.964:1, 1st & reverse 3.142:1
Overall ratios	4.2:1, 5.28:1, 8.25:1, 13.2:1

Prices

Chassis	£530 (1927)
Tourer	£675 (1928)
Weymann Saloon	£750 (1928)
CCS	£795 (1929)
"Le Mans"	£965 (1928)

Chapter Five

3 Litres and a Racing Team

Practice for the 1928 Le Mans race. Photo by Francis Samuelson.

For the Monte Carlo Rally in 1928, Francis Samuelson (later Sir Francis) managed to persuade Lagonda to lend him one of the Speed Model demonstrators, PH 3928, *The Autocar*'s road test car. Navigated by his wife, he reached Monte Carlo without penalty and then had to face the regularity run round the mountains, where the couple did lose some marks, but they made up for it by winning the 2-litre class in the Mont des Mules hillclimb. They came 22nd overall in the Rally. Everyone at Staines was very pleased with this and Frank King, in charge of sales, was particularly affected, so much so that he approached the board with the project

of the company financing a racing team which, successful or not, he argued, would attract a lot of publicity if entered in high-profile events such as Le Mans. He got a qualified approval and set about raising finance, some of it from the dealer network.

The London-Lands End Trial at Easter (April 6/7) saw a team of four Speed Model tourers all gain Gold Medals, driven by Mike Couper, P W White, A C E Benson and S C H "Sammy" Davis, the last driving the faithful PH 3928, now resplendent in a two-tone paint job. In May *The Automotor Journal* finally got to test a 16/65, the 2.7-litre version of course, but they seem not to have driven it, contenting

themselves with a detailed description. The dashboard had now grown a revcounter, but still had no petrol gauge; that walk to the tank was needed, but a filter had appeared in the air intake as well as the fuel supply, and the new water-heated inlet manifold was appreciated for its contribution to smoothness. The car tested was a tourer with a vee windscreen and wire wheels. The same month saw the same magazine publish a road test of the Speed Model Weymann saloon (PH 8247). Edgar Duffield, the writer, was as outspoken as ever and decried the way the car was running rich and hence not performing properly. It turned out that he had got the car from an agent, Lagonda Distributors (London) Ltd, and their Noel Martin wouldn't let him drive, so to produce a three-page article on a car you have only ridden in, not driven, was quite an achievement. He was very impressed by the Weymann body and was under the impression that Weymann themselves had built it because of the high standard of finish. He made a sideswipe at Bentleys, comparing the 2 Litre with the 3 Litre Bentley, the performance being much the same but not the cost.

At the end of May it was A C E Benson's turn to drive PH 3928 in the London-Edinburgh Trial, gaining a Gold Medal, as did P W White in another Speed Model. Benson also gained the much coveted Triple Award, given to drivers who got Golds in all three of the

Two of the four 1928 Team Cars in the yard at Staines. These are high chassis cars with low chassis engines (the dynamos are visible under the radiator). Wire mesh windscreens are folded flat, with a grab handle for the driver to erect the screen if bombarded by stones from a car in front. The elaborate radiator filler caps contain a steam valve with an overflow to a catch tank. The personnel are, left to right, Ted Bolton (Works Manager), Walter Buckingham (body designer), A E Masters (chassis designer), Alf Cranmer (Technical Director), Bertie Kensington-Moir (racing manager) and Bert Hammond (Head of Testing and reserve driver).

Francis Samuelson and Frank King at Le Mans in a 1928 Team Car, probably in the queue for the scrutineer.

Clive Smith's 1929 high chassis 3 Litre Weymann saloon may well be the only one left. Seen here at the 2006 Lagonda Club AGM in Aldermaston.

Speed Model rear wings emphasize the sporting nature of the car.

MCC's major trials.

The racing team was beginning to take shape. Somehow Lagonda had lured Bertie Kensington-Moir away from Bentley to run it, probably by putting pressure on his boss in Hanover Square, Gaffikin Wilkinson, a Lagonda dealer. Frank King had also twisted the collective arm of the dealerships to subsidise the running cost. A team of four special Speed Model tourers was to be built, allowing one to be a reserve. The aim was principally at Le Mans, for its enormous publicity value, but other long-distance races for sports cars were scheduled in which the 2 Litre's stamina would, it was hoped, offset its considerable weight.

A great deal of work was done to the cars to make them into racers. To begin with, the engines had the dynamo mounted on the nose of the crankshaft as in the 16/65, a feature which became standard the following year with the advent of the low chassis car. To accommodate it, a special chassis cross-member, probably from a 16/65, was fitted. The engine was substantially modified, although the details are lost. Two carburettors were fitted and the compression ratio was raised to the limit that the Le Mans-issue petrol would accept without pinking. A freer-flowing exhaust system led to a tail pipe with only the most rudimentary silencer. (There were to be complaints about the noise from the Lagondas in France). Bearing in mind the Le Mans rules about replenishment, a supplementary oil tank was installed under the scuttle with a filler protruding through the dash and a control to allow more oil to be fed to the sump while on the move. In addition, the normal oil filler under the bonnet was extended several inches and protruded through the bonnet side, so that the latter did not have to be opened to add oil, saving time at pit stops. The camshafts were special, the crankshaft and flywheel were lightened and specially balanced, and everything was assembled with extra care and lock-wired. The radiator looked standard but had a very tall filler neck, a quick-action clip filler and a steam valve, to which was attached an overflow pipe leading under the bonnet, probably to a catch tank. The chassis looks standard, although the chances are that it was of thinner section steel. There were extra Hartford friction dampers at each wheel and the drop arm was longer to give quicker steering. A very tall rear axle ratio and close ratio gears in the gearbox meant that first gear was important, used twice on each lap. A special brake adjuster was placed so that the driver could reach it while on the move. The bodywork looked to be standard Speed Model except that the vertical valances inside the front wings were omitted. Inside the body, however, every non-essential panel was left out and the heavy glass windscreen was dropped and replaced by a wire-mesh affair kept folded down permanently. The driver made do with an aero screen. Bonnet catches were abandoned and the edges of the bonnet

sides fitted into aluminium channels, the whole assembly anchored by the obligatory strap. The radiator and the headlamps had mesh stoneguards and the lamps also had oilcloth covers for daylight running on the Saturday.

When finished the four cars were lined up and photographed by the same breezeblock wall in the yard that had featured in the 11.9 era, surrounded by key members of the team. The four were registered as PH 8595 and PK 1058 to 1060 inclusive. PH was the reserve car, the others the nominated team. As they would race without number plates, factory numbers 1 to 4 were painted on the chassis in the order given above, so that cars could be identified if bodies got removed. After this, all the cars were taken to Brooklands and driven over the track's awful bumps for eight hours. They were then returned to the bodyshop and all screws replaced with one size longer ones. Ballast representing passengers had to be carried at Le Mans and this took the form of square-section steel tubes filled with lead, fastened to the chassis in front of the radiator.

Le Mans had by now become the most important race of the year for a firm selling sports cars, largely as a result of Bentley successes. The final Lagonda line up for 1928 was:

Car 1 PH8595 Reserve car for Bert
                 Hammond
Car 2 PK1058 Race number 16 for Baron
                 André d'Erlanger and
                 Douglas Hawkes
Car 3 PK1059 Race number 18 for Clive
                 Gallop and Eddie Hayes
Car 4 PK1060 Race number 15 for Frank
                 King and Francis Samuelson

Before the big event, it was decided to run the reserve car in the Essex MC Six Hour Race at Brooklands on 12 May, with Frank King and Baron d'Erlanger as drivers. After a Le Mans start with cold engines, the first 10 laps had to be run with hoods erected. The Lagonda drivers did a huge mileage in practice, during which King managed to hit a sandbank without serious damage. In the race the Lagonda went out within the first 10 laps with what was given out to be a broken valve. But on stripping the engine down nothing was found to be broken and the fault was eventually discovered to be a piece of

rag in the fuel tank, possibly left from the tinning operation, which had become lodged inside the carburettor between the float chamber and the main jet. Birkin's Bentley 4½ Litre won the race at 72.27mph. Piqued at losing their Six Hour trial for such a trivial reason, Lagonda booked Brooklands for the following Wednesday and ran off a six-hour private trial at an average of 68.9mph with no recorded troubles. The Six Hour Race had also seen a non-works entry by Roland Hebeler, with Ian Hepburn as mechanic, in a Speed Model. Mike Couper was acting as pit manager. They were forced to retire at about half distance when a timing chain broke. Presumably they could have replaced it, but the time taken to retime the engine would

The oval panel dashboard was found on all Lagonda models by 1929.

Originally this car would have had only one carburettor; twin SUs came in with the Special, right at the end of 1929, but this is thought to be the original engine modified. A large Autovac (top right) takes up a lot of underbonnet space.

have ruled them out of contention. The private trial showed that the cars were reliable enough and the rag incident could be dismissed as teething trouble, unlikely to be repeated.

The team set out together for Le Mans, accompanied by General Metcalfe in his Weymann saloon PK 1030. They stopped overnight at the Samuelson's in Sussex before crossing on the Newhaven boat. In practice the cars went very well, lapping at a regular 68 mph with a best time of 9min 20sec

(68.5mph). Then, in a last-minute flurry, someone recorded over 69mph, although it is not clear who did this. The cars were obviously a force to be reckoned with in the 2-litre class, even if no threat to the Bentley favourites. Some last minute work had to be done at the Morris-Bolleé factory in Le Mans. The only obvious change was the addition of two diagonal bracing rods to the frame which supported the headlamps.

The afternoon of Saturday 16 June was showery, but the track was drying as 32 of the 33 starters roared off. The Baron's 2 Litre refused to start. He climbed out and investigated the carburettors — nothing. So he changed the plugs and found them to be wetted up. Eventually he got away nearly a lap down, just before the three Bentleys came round in the lead, pursued by a Stutz. Samuelson in the leading Lagonda was placed 10th. Two laps later he was seventh, making up for a not too good start. Gallop was close behind him, these two leading their class and mixing it with the larger Chryslers and sometimes splitting them. Baron d'Erlanger was unable to make anything up on his team-mates and although the pit had issued orders to ease off (it is a very long race) the drivers either didn't see them or chose to ignore them. Samuelson's driving was reported afterwards to have been "wild" and several times

Le Mans, 1928. Francis Samuelson struggles to free his car from the fence which it had crashed into after being rammed by his team mate.

Made it! Samuelson at last ready to resume the race, having extracted the car from the fence. But not for long.

he slid wide at Mulsanne, possibly as a result of horrible understeer caused by the 3cwt (457kg) of ballast carried so far forward. Samuelson himself later claimed that the heat had melted the tar at this corner. Anyway, by lap 12 Samuelson had caught and lapped d'Erlanger and was lying sixth overall. The Baron was furious at this and was still very close behind when Samuelson had an even bigger slide at Mulsanne, couldn't hold it, and hit the sandbank. The car then bounced back straight into the following car's path. There was nothing the Baron could do and his Lagonda shunted the other one back into the sandbank, but much harder, so that it crashed through the wooden fence meant to protect the spectators. D'Erlanger was cut about the face but his car was just about driveable, despite a twisted front axle, a cracked chassis frame and assorted damage to springs, brakes and so on. It was a very drunken-looking 2 Litre that limped back to the pits to be handed over to Douglas Hawkes. The near-side headlamp pointed to the sky, the wing that side was twisted out of shape and the radiator was nowhere near vertical. Hawkes set about first aid to the car while the Baron had his injuries looked at. Meanwhile, Samuelson's car had sustained very minor injuries but had been in gear when it was rammed and the selector for first and second gear had snapped off. He set about digging it out of the sand and prying it loose from the fence. A kindly spectator, who knew the rules about outside assistance, found a spade and threw on the ground so that Samuelson could "find" it after a decent interval. In all it took two hours before Samuelson could get his car back to the pits. Unfortunately, with only third and top gears operative, the car could never have climbed the slope away from the Pontlieue hairpin, so it had to be withdrawn. Gallop's third car had been running about 400 yards behind the other two at the incident, and although he didn't see the accident the tumult among the spectators warned him as he approached the hairpin that something dramatic had happened, and he was able to slow down enough to avoid the accident and continue on his way, now leading the class.

Having done first-aid repairs, Hawkes set out on a slow exploratory lap to see if the car was fit for racing speeds. It wasn't. During the

lap one of the front nearside dampers fell off. He also discovered that the twisted axle gave very curious braking, exacerbated by the crack in the frame. He returned to the pit where all the other front dampers were slacked right off and the front brakes disconnected. Hawkes then set off in earnest and, after he had got used to it, managed to work the ruin up to lap speeds of 65mph in the later stages of the race, when both drivers had grown accustomed to the crazy steering and the roads were a bit emptier.

Gallop and Hayes's car continued to lead its class and was in eighth place overall on the 22nd lap when the bottom of the radiator cracked round one of the bosses where it was attached to the chassis and began to lose water rapidly. The rules prevented replenishment, so the car was withdrawn. There are contradictory stories about when this happened, *The Autocar* quoting both the 24th and 64th lap in different parts of the same account and *The Motor* merely saying "before daybreak".

D'Erlanger and Hawkes had now got used to driving number 16 in its ruinous state but had to have a long stop after night fell to try to get some lighting actually showing the road ahead. As others dropped out, so they had been picking up places, going from 16th at 10pm to 11th at 4am, a position they were to hold until the end, even after the sorely tried chassis frame broke near the radiator

Le Mans 1928. The battered No. 16, with no front brakes and a broken frame, battles on to the finish.

Lagonda Fete at Brooklands, 5 July 1928. 14/60s still form the majority of cars but there is a sprinkling of Speed Models.

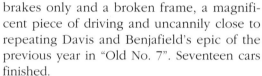

Miss Iris Monckton at the 1928 Fete, not in her beloved PH 2440 but apparently trying a Speed Model for size.

early on Sunday morning. As expected, a 4½ Litre Bentley, driven by Barnato and Rubin, won at 69.11mph, although the Stutz gave it a run for its money for 22½ hours. The Bentleys had cracked their frames too, but not in accidents. The remaining Lagonda had covered 1353 miles, averaging 56.39mph on rear brakes only and a broken frame, a magnificent piece of driving and uncannily close to repeating Davis and Benjafield's epic of the previous year in "Old No. 7". Seventeen cars finished.

The motoring press was full of the crash, of course, and both F Gordon Crosby and Bryan de Grineau drew it for their magazines, while Sammy Davis referred to it in his account of the race, as seen from the cockpit of his Alvis. The general consensus was that Lagondas had been extremely unlucky and that a single misjudgement had wrecked the chances of a team whose speed had been amazing, reaching 90mph on the Mulsanne straight. Frank King had got his publicity all right, but not quite what he wanted. It is interesting to quote in full the advertisement used by Lagonda the following week. A large slab of typescript headed "Lagonda at Le Mans", it began:

"Bad luck redeemed by heroic endeavours and mechanical endurance— that is the brief history of Lagonda's first effort at Le Mans. In the second hour of the race the first Lagonda driven by Capt. F H Samuelson was involved in a thrilling crash with the second Lagonda driven by the Baron d'Erlanger and W D Hawkes. In spite of personal injuries to the driver and the fact that the car had sustained a twisted axle, a broken frame and disabled brakes, the race was continued. The engine bonnet was never raised from start to finish and despite its enormous handicap it actually maintained an average speed of 56 mph over the whole 24 hours, i.e. in spite of one hour lost after the crash. Lagonda thus qualified for the Rudge Whitworth Cup next year — a tribute to the skill and endurance of the drivers and above all to the stamina and power of their all-British Lagonda."

Then underneath, in smaller print, "The above performance was put up by an absolutely standard Model such as can be supplied by any Lagonda agent. Specification gladly supplied on request."

Apart from the downright falsehood about the car being a "standard model", the advert is a masterpiece of the Dunkirk spirit 12 years before its time. An ingenuous reader may be forgiven for thinking that the second car may have crashed because it had two drivers at once, but one sees the copywriter had a deadline to work to and it was important to mention both drivers. Ironically, No. 15 was so little damaged after the crash that once the gear selector had been replaced it was driven home with no trouble.

Only a few weeks later the second Lagonda Fete was held at Brooklands on Thursday 5 July. As before, only the Appearance Contest was held before lunch, with a special prize for the oldest Lagonda present in running order. A late wheel-steered Tricar was present but didn't win this; perhaps it wasn't running. From one o'clock, seven further events were run off, the majority one-lap scratch races for specified models in different states of trim, i.e. stripped of wings or not. There was also the slow running race, with observers carried and timed climbs of the Test Hill. At the end of it all a Grand Aggregate Challenge Cup was awarded to Miss Iris Monckton, who had won three events in her 14/60 tourer PH 2440 (Car Number OH 8650). The scratch race for Speed Models proved so popular that heats and a final had to be run. Unfortunately no speeds were recorded. The programme's list of officials reads like a roll call of the great

1928 Lagonda Fete. Bill Oates' wife driving the Speed Model while their daughter Esmé is at the wheel of the Tricar.

and good in Lagonda affairs at the time.

Stewards	Sir Edgar Holberton, Brigadier-General F E Metcalfe, Colin Parbury, Alf Cranmer
Starter	S C H Davis
Timekeeper	Lionel Martin
Secretary	Frank King
Judges	H Kensington-Moir & R M Spring.

As a lunchtime diversion the surviving team car from Le Mans, still unrepaired, did a demonstration run on the track and was then put on display in the paddock so that people could marvel that it was driveable at all, let alone average speeds in the 60s. To capitalise on the occasion, a further, undamaged, car was available for demonstration runs. This was probably the reserve car, and one former Lagonda employee of recalls being driven round Brooklands in this car, four up, and seeing an indicated 97mph on the straight. Bert Hammond was the driver. By the end of July the factory was offering replicas of the works team cars for sale at £965, a huge increase in price over the standard Speed Model. Few, if any, seem to have been sold. Certainly none survive.

Also in July 1928 a private owner, Bob Nicholl, of whom we will hear much more later, entered four races at the BARC evening meeting and won one of them at 78.31mph. He was driving a 2 Litre Speed Model tourer, stripped of its wings and lamps. His partner,

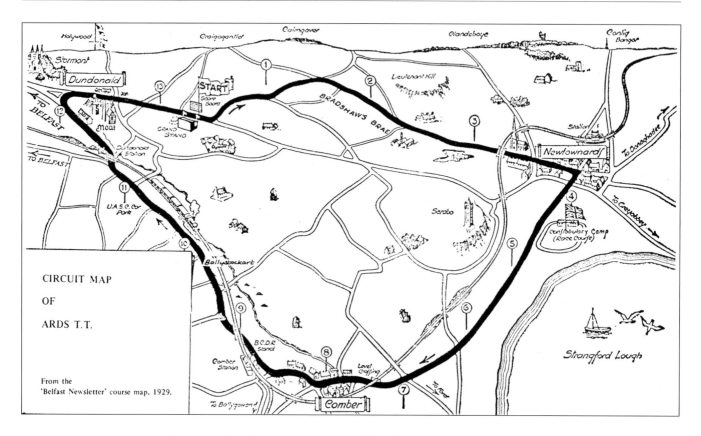

CIRCUIT MAP

OF

ARDS T.T.

From the
'Belfast Newsletter' course map, 1929.

*Circuit map of the
Ards Tourist
Trophy race.*

Arthur Fox, also drove a 2 Litre, possibly the same one, to come fourth in the 90 Long Handicap at the September BARC meeting. A month later Fox had worked his car up to a lap at 88.94mph in the October meeting. It is possible that this was one of the works cars.

During the latter half of the 1920s, the term "rally" began to be used for some very varied types of motoring events. The Monte Carlo Rally started, and remained, a tough proposition that would try any vehicle and any driver to the limit, but in England a much more decorous form of rally developed that was nearer to Ascot Week than to Amundsen. They were generally promoted by a seaside resort out of season to drum up trade and comprised little more than an amble over a set route at legal speeds prior to assembling on the "prom", a few gentle tests and a most seriously contested concours d'élegance. Some of these events attracted inordinate publicity and it was soon necessary to introduce price classes to stop Rolls-Royces winning the lot. By the mid-1930s certain near-professional entrants were having special cars built just for these curious events. The first Lagonda success in such a rally came in July 1928 when

E G Carr of Carr Twysden (a Lagonda dealer) won a prize with a 14/60 tourer in the first Bournemouth Rally, his prize being for "the outstanding open car costing between £401 and £800". The Speed Model's fabric-covered bodywork did not really lend itself to the mirror-like polish treatment and it was usually the coachbuilt cars that featured. One exception was in September when Mrs Ada Pemberton won her class in the Southport Rally with a Speed Model tourer registered VM 2. The class in question was for 10-14hp open cars entered by the trade, in her case Lagonda Distributors (Manchester) Ltd.

The racing shop at Staines was at this time hard at work rebuilding the racing team cars for the newly resurrected Tourist Trophy race. This had not been held since 1922 on the Isle of Man and it was proposed now to run it on a new course near Belfast, based on Newtownards, generally shortened to Ards. It had a long lap of 13.7 miles and was fast but desperately narrow, with twists that made overtaking difficult, combined with unruly crowds who had paid nothing for admission. The 1928 race was to be held on 18 August and a good entry had been attracted, including works Bentleys, although they withdrew when the handicaps were published.

The drivers picked for the T.T. were Baron d'Erlanger, Eddie Hayes and "R. Hall", the latter actually Eddie Hall, some years later to feature in riveting battles with the big Lagondas in his Derby Bentley. By the end of July *The Autocar* found the Lagonda team well advanced and "wonderfully impressive in their detailed approach". One aspect of this was a trip by Kensington-Moir and Hayes in an Avro Avian biplane to fly over the course and see for themselves how snaky it was and where the tricky corners might be.

The driver and car line up was

Major E Hayes	chassis 1PH8595
	Race number 43
Baron d'Erlanger	chassis 3PK1059
	Race number 42
Eddie Hall	chassis 4PK1060
	Race number 44

PK1058, the crashed Le Mans car, was not entered, presumably being either rebuilt or scrapped. The Lagondas were in Class E, given two credit laps to the Scratch cars. The only other car in their class was the OM of Oats (not our Bill Oates).

The team crossed to Belfast on 10 August and set up in Nelson & Moore's premises in Chichester Street. To minimise inconvenience to the public, practice was to start at 5.30am, and since both the race and practice were on public roads large crowds were expected. The nearest point to Belfast, Dundonald, was reachable by tram, so the adaptable Transport Department arranged to start their trams at 3.30am on practice days. Some 50,000 people took them up on the idea for the first, Wednesday, practice session.

The Lagonda team's practice times for the first day were

Major Hayes	Lap 1, 14m 20s.
	Lap 2, 13m 51s.
Baron d'Erlanger	Lap 1, 15m 9s.
	Lap 2, 14m 32s.
	Lap 3, 14m 10s.
E. R. Hall	Lap 1, 14m 46s.
	Lap 2, 14m 51s.
	Lap 3, 14m 55s.
	Lap 4, 14m 26s

By comparison, Birkin's Bentley, still in the race at this stage, lapped in 12 min. 58 sec.

Thursday's practice, at the same ungodly hour, saw Hall improve to 12min 58sec, while Lord Curzon's Bugatti got down to 11min 48sec. But since the race was run as a handicap, there was little point in thrashing the car to put up a good time; practice was really to familiarize the drivers with a new, tricky and demanding course.

The cars were not much altered from the Le Mans trim, changes being a second aero screen for the riding mechanic, the deletion of the external oil filler and a few other details. Under the rules of the race, the first two laps had to be run with hoods erected. In the scurry of lowering his, Malcolm Campbell's Bugatti caught fire and was burnt out.

The 1928 T.T. team, as recorded by the Belfast newspaper. Baron d'Erlanger is third from the left, Eddie Hayes fifth and Eddie Hall (hatless), sixth. A second aero screen for the mechanic has been added to each vehicle.

The handicap, based on credit laps, ensured that a horde of little Rileys was in the lead initially, but a large scoreboard at the start and finish point endeavoured to explain to the crowd the true position as the race progressed.

On the fifth lap d'Erlanger came into his pit to change a broken rocker, losing about 35 minutes. By 10 laps Hall was up to sixth overall with Hayes 14th to Clive Gallop's leading Riley. Half distance was 15 laps (205 miles) and Hall had dropped back to eighth but was still leading the class, albeit behind the leader of the 1½ litre cars. Hayes was 11th and d'Erlanger well down, suffering endless trouble with broken rockers, always the same one, making one suspect a lubrication blockage. His mechanic became very good at changing them, reducing the time from 35 minutes to 20 and then 12 minutes. In the end the pit told him to limit the revs to 2000, but this made the car so slow that he was "flagged off", ie made to retire for being so far behind, about seven laps in the end. His best lap was on lap 9, run off in 12min 53sec (63.62mph). Meanwhile Hall was up to fourth overall by lap 20 but began to run short of oil, with the inevitable result of a run big end. Amazing pit work repaired this and he was sent out again, but with another 2000rpm limit, leading to another retirement on lap 26 for being too slow. Hayes only survived his team-mate by one lap and then went out after his fastest lap in 12min 41sec (64.62mph) broke a rocker. So no Lagonda finished the race.

The winner was Kaye Don in a Lea Francis, but only 12 cars finished out of 44 starters, so the new course was obviously very hard on vehicles. Great things were predicted for the event. The Lagonda racing team's future was less rosy. In Ulster, Hall had been the most consistent and also the fastest Lagonda driver, with a best lap in 12min 36sec (65.05mph). But the sum total of one finisher, granted a heroic one, from a season's events wasn't very encouraging, despite the feeling that most of the team's misfortunes were no more than bad luck. This, however, was a difficult line to pursue at a board meeting with the bank's man sitting there. Nevertheless, the racing programme wasn't abandoned and a last fling was for one car to run at the Essex MC Brooklands meeting in October, coming third to Saunders Davies's Sunbeam in the 10-lap handicap. The driver was Howard Wolfe.

In August the factory issued a statement that no alteration would be made to any of the Lagonda models during the 1929 season. Detail improvements were possible, of course. They then said that as from 1 October 1928 some prices would be increased and that if a car was bought before that date it could be converted to a 1929 model later. Actually, the only two prices to change were the Speed Models, the tourer going up £20 to £695 and the Weymann increased by £45 to

1928 Tourist Trophy. D'Erlanger at the start and finish point, pursued by Kaye Don (Lea Francis), the eventual winner.

£795. For the extra money it was proposed to add a petrol filter, spotlight, fire extinguisher, plug carrier and a new four-spoke sprung steering wheel. The Weymann was to have all these, plus an opening windscreen as standard, Triplex glass throughout, special parking lamps, a parcel net and two companions (little compartments in the rear quarters for toiletries).

Once again, as in the mid-1920s, the dreaded cycle of inexorable weight gain was starting, but in the best Lagonda tradition this statement didn't tell all the story, for the major preoccupation at the works at this time was the launching of a new model, the 3 Litre. This was to be another attempt at the luxury market, with perhaps the advantage of the lessons learnt from the poor sales of the 16/65. The new model was a logical development of that car, using two chassis lengths, one at 10ft 9in (3277mm) wheelbase and identical to the 16/65, and a new longer one at 11ft 6in (3505mm) for the bulky limousines some customers required. The engine was also a development of the 16/65's but was far more than just a boring out to 72mm. The 120mm stroke was retained, so the capacity was now 2931cc, and as these cylinder dimensions were the same as the 2 Litre's it was theoretically possible to use the same pistons and connecting rods, but the two

designs were so dissimilar that this didn't work. Both block and head castings were new, although obviously descendants of the 16/65's. The valves were still pushrod operated but whereas the earlier engine had rockers both above and below its pushrods, the new engine dispensed with the lower set and with the shafts they worked on. In their place was a conventional roller tappet with a light spring around it. At the upper end of the pushrod a loose ball was fitted between the hemispherical cups on the ends of the rod and the rocker. The tappet adjusting screw on the other end of the rocker was also ball-ended and bore on the thimble on the top of the valve. The shape of the block in this area now changed and the complicated castings which had closed the access chambers were now replaced by six plain aluminium cover plates, a recognition feature of early 3 Litre engines. The cylinder head porting was revised and the central D-shaped water port on the inlet side was now squared off. Inside the rocker cover the oil pipes to the rocker shaft were replaced by drillings, and the small balance pipe which linked both halves of the inlet manifold also disappeared. For the first time a water pump was fitted, driven from the same shaft as drove the magneto, but from the opposite end. This of course led to a rearrangement of the pipework, and as a thermostat was now incorporated to give swifter warm-up a bypass had to be added for when it was closed. The water jacket around the inlet manifold was extended to its whole length and a single updraught Zenith carburettor was used. The camshaft and its timing were unchanged but there were numerous detail alterations to oil pipes, shaft diameters and so on. It is reasonable to call the 3 Litre engine a new one, despite some outward similarity to the 16/65 unit.

Apart from reverting to crosswise Hartford friction dampers at the rear, both front and rear axles and the rest of the chassis were continued unchanged, but the bodywork chosen was modernised, with a more rounded shape at the rear. Only four-door saloons were available, that on the long chassis having a winding division and occasional seats which could be set to face forwards, sideways or backwards, or folded up and slid on runners underneath the front seats. This long saloon was of six-light Weymann construction and featured a most ingenious sunshine roof, called the "SOS" (Sun or Shade). It had separate opening sections for both front and rear compartments. In effect, each section was a pair of roller blinds, set across the car amidships and at the rear, the leather outer roof rolling up clockwise round the rear one and the cloth inner lining rolling up anti-clockwise round the front one (viewed from the left hand side). It all sounds very prone to rattles and leaks and was quietly dropped after a year.

On the shorter chassis two bodies were offered, a coachbuilt six-light saloon at £940 and a Weymann saloon which could have either four or six lights at £925. The long-wheelbase limousine cost £965 and the bare chassis cost either £650 or £660, according to wheelbase.

Naturally a luxurious 3 Litre on the long chassis was featured on Stand 131 at the Motor Show, along with a blue 16/65 saloon with black wings and brown interior and a pair of Speed Models. On one coachbuilder's stand, that of John Harris of Reading, a black Speed Model with red wings was displaying Harris's special idea by which the rear of the hood could be folded up for ventilation, whilst leaving the rest erect.

Despite the August announcement there were detail changes for 1929. All the 2 Litres and the 16/65 grew larger petrol tanks, now 14 gallons (64 litres), a change visible from the rear by a change in shape, the top of the tank now no longer following the line of the chassis frame side-member. On the Speed Model Weymann, the body shape at the scuttle was changed, doing away with the little step-out and making the body more of a one-piece appearance. A tiny flap in the roof became standard to aid ventilation. On the coachbuilt 14/60 saloon all the corners were more rounded and the corner radii of the windows were increased. A slight rake to the windscreen was almost undetectable. The tyre size of all 2 Litres went up to 5.25 x 31 and the 16/65 ones became 6.00 x 33. All 16/65s were henceforth to have the rather tedious 5.3:1 rear axle ratio and this also found its way on to 14/60 saloons and tourers, although not the Semi-sports. "Cerric" finish was now admitted and was standard on all models, and the varnish shop could be disposed of at last.

With nice timing for the Motor Show headlines, the works sent a Speed Model tourer to Brooklands on 22 October and had a go at some international records. The car chosen was PK 2339 (OH 9138) and the driver W M (Mike) Couper. They were successful - the 200km record in Class E was secured at 79.55mph and the 200 miles record at 80.07mph. Once the records were in the bag, Couper put his toe down harder and did a further three laps at 84.6mph, just to show that the car had not been flat out. The company of course claimed the car was absolutely standard, but it became rather famous during the following year and it certainly wasn't standard then. While at Brooklands, Couper assisted a motorcyclist attacking the 2 x 12 hour record by driving behind him in the dark periods to show him the way, although what the rider felt about riding into his own shadow for hours isn't known.

Couper drove PK 2339 again in the 1928 London-Exeter Trial and he, Benson and White all got Gold Medals. This Exeter was regarded as the toughest ever run, not just because the MCC were tightening up the rules but due to the weather, with continuous snow and sleet storms, floods and gales.

3 LITRE (72mm bore) SUMMARY STATISTICS

Engine

Configuration	6 cylinders in line, pushrod overhead valves
Capacity	2931cc
Bore & stroke	72 x 120mm
RAC rating	19.3hp
Compression ratio	5.7:1
Firing order	1,5,3,6,2,4
Valve timing (degrees)	io 10° ATDC, ic 50° ABDC, inlet open 220° eo 42° BBDC, ec 10° ATDC, exhaust open 232°
Tappet clearance	0.008in (0.20mm) hot
Brake horsepower	not published
Main bearings	7
Main bearing diameter	2.25in (57mm)
Big end diameter	2in (51mm)
Oil capacity	2 gallons (9.1 litres); from 1932 3 gallons (13.6 litres)
Cooling system	Water pump, thermostat and fan
Capacity	6 gallons (27.3 litres)
Ignition system	Scintilla magneto MN 6 (coil by 1932)
Ignition timing	36° BTDC fully advanced
Contact breaker gap	0.012-0.016in (0.3-0.4mm)
Sparking plugs	Champion 16
Carburettor(s)	1 Zenith updraught (high chassis) 2 SU HV4 (low chassis)
Fuel supply	Autovac (early cars), AC mechanical pump (later cars) 20 gallon (9.1 litre) tank
Dynamo	CAV/Rotax
Starter	CAV/Rotax
Clutch	11in (279mm) single dry plate by Lagonda

Chassis

Wheelbase	10ft 9in (3277mm) or 11ft 6in (3505mm)
Track front & rear	4ft 8in (1422mm)
Overall length	Tourer 14ft 8in (4470mm)
Turning circle	43ft (13.1m)
Kerb weight	Chassis 25.75cwt (1300kg) Tourer 30.25cwt (1537kg) Short saloon 32.5cwt (1651kg) Long saloon 36cwt (1829kg)

Gearbox

Type		Z-type 4-speed sliding mesh by Lagonda			
Overall ratios		Top	3rd	2nd	1st & reverse
4.1:1 axle	ZC	4.1:1	6.9:1	10.8:1	17.3:1
	ZD	4.1:1	5.6:1	9.4:1	15.1:1
	ZE	4.1:1	5.15:1	8.05:1	12.88:1
4.7:1 axle	ZC	4.7:1	7.9:1	12.4:1	19.8:1
	ZD	4.7:1	6.4:1	10.8:1	17.3:1
	ZE	4.7:1	5.9:1	9.2:1	14.8:1

Rear Axle

Type	Semi-floating spiral bevel by Lagonda. Alternative ratios 4.1:1 or 4.7:11.
Mph/1000rpm in top	4.1:1 axle 23mph; 4.7:1 axle 20mph
Propeller shaft	Hardy Spicer, plain bearing universal joints
Dampers	Hartford friction, transverse at rear
Battery	12 volt, 11-plate tall
Wheels & tyres	6 x 33 tyres on 21in rims (1929) 5.25 x 31 tyres on 21in rims (1932)
Tyre pressures	Front 37psi, rear 35psi (2.55/2.41 bar)
Brakes	As Speed Model 2 Litre

Prices	**1928**	**1930**	**1931**	**1932**
Chassis	£650 & £660	£775	£752	
Tourer	£820	£945	£1000	£900
Saloon	£940	£1100	£1100	£990

Chapter Six

Low Chassis

In January 1929 a new body design for the 2 Litre was announced. On the Speed Model chassis, it was called the "Close Coupled Saloon" (CCS) and was a fixed-head coupé featuring a large external boot and folding seats in the rear that could be turned into luggage space. It had very elegant proportions and soon attracted the familiar title of the "honeymoon coupé". Only two doors were provided, but they were huge ones to allow fairly dignified access to the rear seats. Their weight must have worried Walter Buckingham, so he saved a little by having sliding window glasses instead of wind-up ones. Even so, most of these bodies broke up quite early in their lives, the weight of the doors proving too much for the A post. Later on a 3 Litre version appeared and later still one on the 4½ Litre chassis.

At the beginning of January 1929 the first published road test of a 3 Litre appeared in *The Automotor Journal*. The car tested was a

Right at the beginning of 1929 the "Close Coupled Saloon" (CCS) was introduced on the high chassis, offering either space for four or for two and a mountain of luggage. Later generations called it the "honeymoon coupé". Complete with Speed Model wings, it proved popular but short lived as the heavy doors overstressed the pillar. Variants of this design were offered until 1935.

four-light Weymann saloon, PK 4831. This car is interesting in several ways and was probably a development vehicle not representative of the eventual production. It had a Stromberg carburettor, fitted to a 16/65 inlet manifold. The camshaft cover plates were 16/65 too. A Scintilla magneto was another novelty. The dashboard was from a Speed Model and the driver's window didn't have the quick-lift mechanism. Parking lights, which had been added to the specification of the more expensive models, were little auxiliary lamps attached to the sidelamps and showed white light to the front and red to the rear. In those days, when it was compulsory to have side and tail lamps lit when parked on the highway, the saving of the drain on the battery by having only one 6-watt bulb instead of three was worth having. Lucas electrics had taken the place of CAV. Edgar Duffield did the road test again and confused readers by saying that the Lagonda factory was on the Middlesex side of the river and was one of the landmarks of the Bath Road. He can be forgiven for that last bit as Gall & Inglis road books called both the A4 and the A30 the Bath Road. However, he liked the car and said it was the nicest British car he had tried since the Motor Show the previous October. No performance figures were published, though.

Mike Couper in the trusty PK 2339 was travelling marshal in the London-Lands End Trial at Easter. Four other Lagondas were entered, for P W White, J S Hathaway, G W Gemmell and H C Parry. Only Parry got a gold. Couper, Hathaway and White failed Beggars Roost and Gemmell failed Bluehills Mine.

In March a tourer version of the 3 Litre appeared, along with the Close Coupled Saloon on this chassis. Both were really six-

Sketch showing one of the rear armchair seats down and the other packed away.

Although the revised T2 tourer body had appeared on the supercharged 2 Litre in July 1930, early low chassis 3 Litre Specials stuck with the T body style. Now owned by John Sword, this is the car road tested by The Autocar *on May 8, 1931. It was stated in the test that production cars would have the later body design.*

Extract from a 1929 Lagonda advertisement showing how one or both rear seats of the CCS folded up to increase luggage capacity. The boot came equipped with two large fitted suitcases.

Tourer bodies of this era fitted between the wheels; wheel arches came five years later. The asymmetric wing nut that secures the spare wheel was a Lagonda speciality. If it works loose, the heavy end will stop at the 6 o'clock position and it won't get any looser.

Cycle type wings had a brief period of being very fashionable, roughly from 1929 to 1933.

cylinder versions of the Speed Model with bodies exactly the same in appearance, apart from the longer bonnet needed to accommodate the larger engine. For these slightly sportier versions the engine had a higher compression ratio and revised inlet manifolding, but still the single updraft carburettor. The front of the car was made more imposing

by the adoption of the new Lucas P100 headlamps, and the radiator was protected from flying stones by a wire gauze stoneguard with a distinctive diamond-shaped bracing which was to become a Lagonda distinguishing feature. The fuel tank had been enlarged to 20 gallons (91 litres). Inside the gearbox the more sporting ratios of the Speed Model were installed and the rear wings still had the cheeky turned-up ends.

The gearbox was a new one. One presumes the steady increase in power from the first 16/65, which had used the 14/60's OH gearbox, had made the transmission rather marginal. The new gearbox used either roller or ball races throughout and was perceptibly stronger and heavier, with stouter shafts. As a recognition feature, its cover plate was square to the earlier 'box's L shape. It continued to use the reversed change pattern, with third and top to the left of first and second, and was no easier to change gear with. If anything, it was harder. This 3 Litre tourer cost £1000 and the CCS £1100, with a bare chassis available for £835. Among the luxury items aboard was a "Setalite", a device for

The diamond braced stone guard and diagonal stays to the headlamp support frame were introduced with the high chassis 3 Litre Special in 1929. The latter was probably the result of fitting the heavier P100 headlamps. A year later both features were added to the supercharged 2 Litre.

automatically switching on the parking lamps at dusk, and a spot lamp which could be mounted either on the right of the windscreen or on a bracket by the left dumbiron in foggy conditions. Wiring was in place for both locations, with a quick-release plug.

In January 1929 the Junior Car Club organised a visit to the Lagonda factory for their members, and by fortunate chance a copy of the briefing sheets issued to the factory guides has survived. Some of the statistics are a touch dubious and one suspects the press office had a hand in their production, but the given output of eight cars a week in January is believable, rising to 16 in the spring selling rush. Wilbur Gunn's gas engine which powered the line shafting driving all the machines had just been abandoned and replaced with six 42hp electric motors, but the shafting remained in place. Less believable is the assertion that there was a 50:50 mix of 4- and 6-cylinder cars in the output.

The success of the Le Mans 24 hour race had led to calls for a British version and the Junior Car Club (JCC) stepped into the breach and began to think of organising such a race

at Brooklands. They soon ran foul of the local residents, whose sensitive ears had already brought on the infamous Brooklands "can" (silencer). So a compromise was reached. There would be 24 hours of racing, but in two 12 hour chunks, with cars locked up under guard overnight. Although the spectators were not going to have the thrill of

This shot from a high vantage point shows how the front wings are attached to the brake back plates and hence turn with the steering and are unsprung.

Lucas P100DB headlamps were introduced in 1929. The main beam bulb in the centre of the lamp was at the focus of the central silvered glass mirror and gave virtually parallel rays, modified by the Fresnel lens of the front glass. The dipped bulb lay behind the bullseye lens above it and the beam could be a bit haphazard. Most early lamps were black, not plated.

summer Saturdays being spoken for. There were nine events, much as in the previous year, but with the addition of a balloon-bursting race for six-cylinder cars, mostly 16/65s. Bob Nicholl won the Speed Model races in PH 8364, with Roland Hebeler of the same firm third in one race and second in another. Eddie Masters, the 14/60 chassis designer, won the 12/24 race and a Mr Foster was second. The author now owns the cup Mr Foster won, and in the Lagonda tradition of never throwing anything away, it is hall-marked London 1906 and was quite possibly one of Wilbur Gunn's numerous prizes renovated. Iris Monckton was there again and for the second time won the hillclimb, from which Speed Models were excluded. The advertisements in the programme show the increasing importance of the event. In 1928 they were solely from Lagonda dealers, plus Dunlop. By 1929 the programmes, 12 pages longer, also carried adverts for *The Motor,* Triplex, Pratts, Cellon, *The Autocar,* Setalite, Martin Walter, Shell and Power petrol. There were excellent photos of current models, better reproduced than in the contemporary catalogues. In its report *The Automotor Journal* added some period charm by recording that the driver of the winning 12/24 in race 5, a much abused 1923 2-seater which had done 100,000 miles already as a driving school car, "threw his arms high above his head in enthusiasm as he flashed across the finishing line". A winning speed of 47mph takes some reconciling with the "flashed" bit. There was always a competition for the oldest Lagonda present and in 1929 it was won hands down by a tricar, LN 3252, dating we now know from 1907 but assumed to be much older. *The Automotor Journal* assured its readers it dated from 1897, but at the time old cars were treated as hilarious jokes.

watching night racing, they would have the sadistic pleasure of watching mechanics trying to start cold racing engines that had already done 12 hours of hard graft. The scheduled date was in May, a month before Le Mans, and entries started to roll in from January, including one from Arthur Fox of Fox & Nicholl for three 2 Litre Lagondas. *The Daily Telegraph* was persuaded to put up a £1000 prize for the winner and the SMMT agreed to present a trophy.

For 1929 the now traditional Lagonda Fete at Brooklands was brought forward to 27 April, which seems a bit early in the year, but the change to a Saturday probably forced this,

As Fox & Nicholl have finally entered the story, it will be as well to give some background. Arthur Wingrave Fox and Robert Isidore Nicholl formed a partnership in 1924 to sell and repair cars in Pall Mall, with a servicing establishment in Kensington. A year later, acting on inside information, they bought a piece of land at Tolworth on the route of the proposed Kingston By-pass. When the road was opened in 1927 they were in a splendid position to operate their Tolworth Service Station, selling several makes of petrol and with a large workshop for repair work. Nicholl was responsible for putting up the money and finding clients; Fox ran the day-to-day operations. Fox had been Service Manager for Wolseley before the Morris takeover and had been awarded the MBE for his armaments work in 1914-18. He met Nicholl at Wolseley, although the latter's upper-crust Eton and Oxford background meant that his job was really only a hobby. When Fox & Nicholl was set up they recruited a number of key personnel from Wolseley, including Donald Wilcockson, later their Chief Mechanic, and Howard Wolfe. The firm took on a Talbot agency, but when considering what to race at Brooklands, Bob Nicholl's Speed Model Lagonda PH 8364 (OH 9002) was chosen, as noted in the last chapter, frequently, but not always, driven by Howard Wolfe. Despite its considerable race-tuning, it was still tractable enough to tow Bob's powerboat on its trailer.

For the 1929 season the Lagonda management must have been in two minds about how to proceed. The 1928 racing team had generated lots of publicity but very poor results, a lot of it down to inexperience, even with Kensington-Moir's input. But help was at hand. At the end of 1928, a syndicate of Hertfordshire racing enthusiasts had decided to enter long-distance sports car racing seriously in 1929, pooling their resources. As some of them knew General Metcalfe, who lived at Cheshunt (the syndicate came from the Waltham and Hertford areas), it was natural that they should approach Lagonda for a car or cars. The syndicate, christened PERR, originally comprised Arthur Pollard, Bill Edmondson, who was the General's solicitor, George Roberts and Cecil Randall. It was soon after joined by Tim Rose Richards, whose experience at Brooklands was going to come in useful. After some negotiations with

the General, it was agreed, in February 1929, to supply the syndicate with two cars, special competition versions of the Speed Model, for £350 each - almost exactly half price - on the condition that they wouldn't be resold for less than £600. The intention was to run the cars in the Six Hours, Double Twelve, Ulster T.T. and possibly one car at Le Mans. To show how keen the factory was, the already paid-for entry at Le Mans was given to the syndicate. Further, the General approached Shell and KLG on their behalf and secured for the syndicate and for Arthur Fox the same support and money that the works team had had in 1928. Rose Richards was not party to

These radiator caps are known as "dogbone" for obvious reasons. The long arms acted to cool the end knobs so that they could be touched even with a hot engine. Set in it is the Boyce Motometer water temperature gauge. A spirit thermometer, it was always in the driver's view.

The 1929 team of low chassis 2 Litres lined up outside Fox & Nicholl at Tolworth in May. These cycle-type wings are fixed and do not turn with the steering as Lagonda's own ones did.

PK 9203 at Tolworth, showing the shortened bodywork.

these arrangements and seems initially to have been rather the hired help. But later he became a full member of the team and paid his share of the expenses. As Le Mans was only a fortnight before the Six Hours it was felt wise to send one car to each. Only if the Le Mans car survived would it be entered in the Six Hours.

Meanwhile, Arthur Fox had secured rather better terms for himself, having got Lagonda to provide spares, repairs and overheads for his similar car. Fox & Nicholl had had two years experience racing Bob Nicholl's own 2 Litre, so it was sensible for that company to take over the running of the team and the preparation of the cars. All three were painted in the same colours, black over white, and

had consecutive registration numbers, so any onlooker would conclude they were all part of the same outfit. There was also a fourth car, plain green this time, owned by Robin Jackson. Although nothing to do with either PERR or Fox, this fourth car tended to go to the same events and was clearly similarly prepared for racing.

The three cars arrived at Fox & Nicholl's Tolworth premises towards the end of April, which was rather late for a start to be made on preparing them for the Double Twelve in mid-May. Fox registered all four cars under his name as PK 9201 to 9204, with 9201 and 9202 the PERR cars, 9203 Fox's and 9204 Jackson's.

By now the syndicate had grown more ambitious and had entered their cars in the Irish Grand Prix in Dublin (a sports car race) and the Ulster T.T. later in the summer. The cars were all prototypes of the low chassis 2 Litre with a revised front axle and the dynamo mounted on the nose of the crankshaft as on the 16/65 and 3 Litre. The lowering of the chassis was accomplished by different cross-members which allowed the floorboards to sit between the side members instead of on top of them, but principally by the more steeply dropped front axle. As a consequence, the front brake operating rods now passed through the axle instead of being attached underneath. The C-shaped lever which worked the brakes on the high chassis car vanished, no bad thing since it tended to try to straighten under heavy braking. To restore the geometry a relay lever was introduced into the front rod system. The radiator shape had to change at the bottom to accommodate the dynamo and so did the chassis cross-member beneath it. For the rear axle, the lowering was carried out by interposing spacers between the axle casing and the spring. Some merriment was caused at Fox & Nicholl when the cars arrived without these spacers, overlooked in the rush to get the cars ready, so that they were low chassis at the front and high chassis at the rear. They didn't turn up for first practice either, so the merriment was extended to the paddock inhabitants too. They got there for the race, in the end.

As you would expect at Brooklands, the Double Twelve was to be run on handicap,

based on the amount by which a given car exceeded the minimum distance calculated for it. Supercharged cars had 30 per cent added to their actual capacity when calculating this distance. Cars had to be road equipped, 2-seaters up to 1500cc, 4-seaters above, with ballast carried to represent passengers. At the start, the driver and mechanic had first to erect the hood and then run with it erect for the first 10 laps. Cars had to be catalogued models, but no one seems to have noticed that there was no mention of a low chassis 2 Litre in the 1929 catalogue, nor was there ever much of a public announcement of it. just a line of small type in the adverts. Even the instruction book didn't change.

The race was cunningly fixed for the weekend of 10/11 May, just a month before Le Mans and a good dress rehearsal for that event. It attracted an entry of 56 cars from five countries and included works teams from Bentley, Lagonda, OM, Alvis, Frazer Nash, Lea-Francis, Alfa Romeo, Aston Martin and Riley. There were five Lagondas entered, the four we have met already and a surprise entry of Mike Couper driving PK 2339, the 1928 200 mile record car, still high chassis but sporting the low chassis dynamo. It was in the programme as a private entry, but everyone recognised it.

The Double Twelve rules were quite fierce about what changes were permitted to bodywork, so the 1929 cars more nearly resembled what would become the low chassis Speed Model. A major change was the adoption of cycle-type wings, fixed on the team cars, ie not turning with the steering. Unseen inside the bonnet, the Speed Model flat cast aluminium bulkhead had given way to a more elaborate one incorporating a shelf. The new low bodies were more barrel-shaped when seen from the front and were shortened to accommodate the 25-gallon (114-litre) tank.

Many of the little touches that Kensington-Moir had thought of in 1928 were incorporated so that, for example, there were no bonnet catches, it being held down by the obligatory strap but with the lower edges fitting into aluminium channels. Last year's external oil fillers were specifically banned, although the supplementary oil tank under the scuttle was allowed. To ease the hood-erecting caper at the start, Arthur Fox hit on the idea of constructing special windscreens with a convex curve to the top which more or less followed the curvature of the top of the bonnet. He was then able to devise a special hood that could be tensioned solely by over-centre fixings at the corners of the screen and held down with just a wire loop. At the start the idea was that the car would be left in first gear; when the flag fell the crew leapt in, the driver put his wire loop over his corner of the screen and put his foot on the clutch, while the mechanic fastened his wire loop and started the engine with a button specially placed on his side of the dash. Fox made his crews practice this until they were heartily sick of it, but it paid dividends in the race and the Lagondas were first away.

The Double Twelve race, May 1929. Lined up at the start are Robin Jackson, driving No. 31, with Broomball standing behind it; Frank King (with bald head) is next to him. Howard Wolfe is driving No. 30 and Bill Edmondson No. 25. No. 32 is the high chassis PK 2339 down to be driven by Mike Couper, who has his goggles round his neck.

Nearside of the 3 Litre Special engine with twin SUs of 1930 "sloping shoulders" design. The 3 Litre is a very large heavy lump. The mechanical fuel pump is correct, but in recent years, with cars used only infrequently, many owners have fitted electric SU pumps which fill the float chambers before cranking the engine.

Black enamel finish was normal for SU carburettors in the '30s. The jets were fixed and the Ki-gass pump primed the engine with petrol for a cold start.

At the end of the 10 laps, Fox's little wrinkles came into prominence again, when more special spring-loaded clips allowed the hood to be furled and secured very quickly, while the windscreen could be opened about its horizontal axis near the top of the uprights and secured in the open, nearly horizontal, position by means of a monster thumb-wheel working on a semi-circular track fastened to the centre of the screen frame at top and bottom. Jackson's car did not have this arrangement and used merely an aero screen and the wire mesh affair used in 1928.

Although the Double Twelve rules called for normal appearance, not much was said about the mechanicals. The chassis were extensively drilled for lightness and extra dampers were added to both axles. Special camshafts gave a quicker lift and a longer dwell. Compression ratio was raised to 7.2:1 and two 35mm Zenith Triple Diffuser carburettors were fitted. The fibre gear driving the magneto was replaced by a bronze one, while the radiators held more water than standard and had the same clip-type fillers with steam valves and overflow pipes as in 1928. At Le Mans the previous year there had been trouble with rivets in the petrol tank working loose and letting the pressure down. The standard Autovac was not

Offside of the 3 Litre Special engine. Mounting the magneto the opposite way round to the 2 Litre simplified the advance/retard controls. The grey colour for the cylinder block and head is correct for Lagonda-built engines but not necessarily right for those built elsewhere.

much use for racing, where the engine was at full throttle most of the time, so the racing cars reverted to sealed tanks with a pressure pump on the dashboard. To meet this problem the 1929 cars had little copper domes sweated over every rivet, so that if it pulled loose pressure would still be held. Underneath the car a full length undertray had various bulges to fit round the moving parts and the brake linkage. The Z gearbox from the new 3 Litre Special was used, with an even closer set of ratios. The rear axle ratio was 4.1:1 and a special straight-cut bevel gear proved to be astoundingly long lived, still on the cars 30 years later. Full lighting equipment was compulsory, even though no night racing was going to happen at Brooklands. As so often with racing machines, the extra bits offset all the lightening operations, so that the finished cars weighed 31.75cwt (1613kg) ready to race.

Once Fox got hold of the cars, he was by no means satisfied with some aspects of the works' preparation and did quite a bit of re-making, despite the time constraint. The ballast had to be made up and fitted, a spare magneto fixed, and it was found the cars ran too cool in the early morning sessions, so a set of little kapok-filled yellow quilts were fitted between the radiator and the stone-

Complicated plumbing. The two large copper pipes supply petrol, main and reserve lines, to the changeover tap. Fuel then passes to the glass-bowled filter and thence to the fuel pump. The smaller copper pipe feeds the Ki-gass pump. Note the larger identity plate with three lines and no prefixes.

The brass handle of the Autoklean oil filter is prominent. Owners were supposed to turn it regularly to clear trapped grit. Later this was made automatic by linking it to the throttle pedal or the clutch. The number 397 RS3 stamped behind the lubrication instructions indicates the 397th 3 Litre engine and bears no relation to the "Engine Number" stamped on the car's identity plate, which refers to all models.

guard, one to be removed each time the engine reached normal temperature. The works had made Fox a £50 body allowance but later that year a rather involved three-way dispute between Lagonda, the syndicate and Fox arose over some of these extra items and who should pay for them.

By 1929 the propensity of the 2 Litre frame to develop cracks at the S-bend was becoming known and these special cars were fitted with a small truss underneath the side members at the curved part. This was later to become standard, but is thought to be a Fox modification as PK 9204 didn't have them in 1929.

For the Double Twelve the drivers and cars were:

Race No 24	PK9201 (OH9411) Tim Rose Richards & Cecil Randall	
Race No 25	PK9292 (OH9412) Bill Edmondson & George Roberts	
Race No 30	PK9203 (OH9413) Frank King & Howard Wolfe	
Race No 31	PK9204 (OH9414) Robin Jackson & C A Broomhall	
Race No 32	PK2339 (OH9138) Mike Couper	

When the race began it soon proved, as expected, to be a contest between the blown Alfa Romeos and the Bentleys, with the Alfas having a slight edge. But Couper's high chassis car soon established a class lead and

began to run away from the Fox cars, much to the annoyance of the syndicate. It is always possible that the older car, with 40,000 miles under its tyres, was much freer running than the new ones. Of course Couper was very familiar with both car and track compared with the other drivers, or possibly - perish the thought - the high chassis car handled better than the low ones. Not that handling, at Brooklands, counted for much.

By the end of the first day 16 cars had retired but all five Lagondas were still running, with Couper leading the class from Edmondson and Roberts. The following morning's starting endeavours with cold engines was regarded as a highlight of the event by the more cruel spectators, and great pantomime with hot oil and so on was expected. The eventual winners and other high-placed contestants didn't bother with all that, a quick check over and press the button seemed sufficient, and among the Lagondas, Couper was on his way within 10 minutes of the starting maroon. The others were not so fortunate and the Jackson/Broomhall car lost nearly an hour in getting away. So far all the Lagondas had been reliable and Couper's car continued to be, but the Fox cars were now beset with troubles, with several stops to fix broken exhaust pipes and silencers. At about 11.30am the Rose Richards/Randall car stopped for good with a broken crankshaft. It rained for quite a time on the second day, which enlivened the Bentley/Alfa duel but had no effect on the Lagonda placings. All carried on to the finish, with Ramponi (Alfa Romeo) the winner. Mike Couper won the 2 litre class and was ninth overall, having driven the 1595.5 miles unaided at an average speed of 66.48mph. Edmondson and Roberts were second in the class, 13th overall, at 64.87mph. Despite the lost hour, Jackson and Broomhall were third in class and 14th overall at 63.52mph, and King and Wolfe were sixth in class and 18th overall at 61.84mph. Turning to the team prize, Lagondas came first, second and third in their class but didn't win it since Couper was not a member of the nominated team. OM took these honours, but the Lagondas did take the Sir Charles Wakefield class prize, which ignored nominated teams.

After the race there was a lot of backbiting from the syndicate about the unexpected appearance and unmatched speed of number 32, and the upshot was that Fox was sent to beard the General at Staines and lodge a complaint. There followed a long and stormy interview that went on from noon to 5 o'clock, and although the General agreed to replace the broken crankshaft little else was achieved. Afterwards, the General wrote an extremely strong letter to the syndicate disclaiming any ulterior motives and explaining that the object of the factory entry was to show that one man could average over 60mph for 24 hours in a standard Speed Model, which had been done if one accepts PK 2339 to be standard. He went on to say that he (the General) had spent much of Saturday afternoon trying to slow Couper down as in his enthusiasm Couper had at one point been 17 laps ahead of the next Lagonda. By the end of the week passions had cooled, the syndicate accepted the general's assurances and he in his turn congratulated them on their performances, which had been very good considering that nearly all were novices and that this was a first-class international event and a gruelling one at that. He then went further, offering them PK 2339 for the Six Hours, provided Couper drove it, and the possibility of a 3 Litre Special racer if King drove that. He added, prophetically, "With a stable like this at your disposal, there should be a very fair chance of your winning the Six Hours outright and you certainly ought to win the 3 litre and 2 litre classes, and probably the Team prize as well".

The 3 Litre "Special" the General referred to was Lagonda's latest model, announced towards the end of March 1929 but not yet actually in production. It was to all intents and purposes a Speed Model 3 Litre, as described earlier in this chapter. But the indifferent performance with one updraft carburettor must have led to some searching for more horsepower at Staines, for the car that appeared for the Six Hours, although still high chassis, had a different inlet arrangement and two SU carburettors bolted directly to the head. It weighed 1.25cwt (63kg) more than the 2 Litres but the extra power meant it was at least no slower than them.

The syndicate now had an embarrassing amount of opportunity for their racing and

they had to decide a plan of campaign. The cars had gone back to Staines for overhaul, and after a meeting it was decided to give Le Mans a miss and concentrate on the Six Hours with the newly augmented team, and then go to Ireland for the Dublin GP and the Ulster T.T. It was suggested that Randall should drive for most of the time in the Six Hours to gain experience. There were to be artificial double corners on the circuit for this race and Rose Richards wanted Fox's ingenious opening windscreen removed as he felt it was a hazard to visibility. In its place he wanted a wire folding affair as used in 1928 and still used on Jackson's car.

Meanwhile, Couper was having a busy May, entering a 2 Litre, possibly the faithful PK 2339, in the London-Edinburgh Trial only a week after the Double Twelve and gaining a Gold Medal. Two other Lagondas were entered, J S Hathaway (2 Litre) gaining a Gold and Frank King (3 Litre Special) a Silver after hitting a wall on West Stonesdale. Hathaway was a keen private owner, entering everything in sight, so that we find him turning up at Shelsley Walsh hillclimb the same month.

There is a gap in the archives of the syndicate in the summer of 1929. Although we know that a sole 2 Litre entered Le Mans and that it was one of the black and white ones, it took a lot of detective work, hindered by well-meaning owners talking to former mechanics 50 years after the event and getting

Mike Couper in No. 32, the high chassis car that out-performed the lower cars in the Double Twelve.

Fitting unsprung front wings displaced the sidelamps to stalks growing out of the scuttle, another Lagonda speciality. The mirror-backed spotlamp on the windscreen frame was on the car for the 1931 road test and, remarkably, is still there.

conflicting answers, to work out that it was actually Fox's own car, PK 9203, that went. References in contemporary motoring magazines to it being a syndicate car followed from the belief that they owned all three, since they were painted alike and had consecutive registration numbers. The late Ivan Forshaw, who eventually owned all four cars, discovered in the paperwork evidence that the 1929 cars were actually rebuilds of the 1928 ones (remember, Lagonda never threw anything away). The chassis frames were different, of course, to make them the low model. This fits

Adopting cycle wings led to problems with shaping the running boards. Lagonda's solution was elegant and enabled the owner to stand very close to the engine when servicing.

in with the author's research in Surrey CC archives which show that the 1928 cars were only ever licensed for one year and vanished after that. So the syndicate and Fox and Jackson were actually paying for second-hand racers and their big discount looks less of a bargain now

For the 1929 race on 15/16 June the Le Mans course was shortened by cutting out the Pontlieue hairpin, which should have increased the lap speeds and enabled higher first gears to be used. Fox allowed for this, perhaps too much, for a lot of time was lost in practice lowering the gears again to improve acceleration. The Lagonda was noisy enough for it to be remarked on in the motoring press, just as the year before. There were 25 entries, with Bentley the favourite to win.

Fox's little dodges still worked and the Lagonda was the first car away, leading the race as far as the footbridge before the first Bentley caught it. By the end of the lap the Lagonda was 11th and was very slowly overtaken by cars initially behind it, being passed by the Alvis on the fourth lap. After two hours the Lagonda was three laps behind the leading Bentley. Three laps in 1929 was 30.46 miles, so the Lagonda must have been lapping at about 65mph if the leader was doing 80mph. Quite respectable, but no better than in 1928. However, after 283 miles the Lagonda came into its pit with the floorboards smouldering. To begin with it was thought that an exhaust pipe joint had failed, as had happened in the Double Twelve, but further examination showed the head gasket had gone. A spare was available but the race rules would not permit water to be added until the 40th lap and the car had only covered 28 laps, so it had to be retired. Bentleys went on to score the famous 1-2-3-4 walkover, finishing at a stately speed, with Barnato and Birkin's Speed Six coming first.

During the year which had passed since the last Six Hours race the Essex MC had disbanded, so the Brooklands Automobile Racing Club (BARC) took over the duty of organising it. The same 2.6-mile circuit was used, incorporating two artificial bends, one in the Finishing Straight and another where that rejoined the Outer Circuit. Once again a Le Mans start was used and hoods had to be erected and used for the first 10 laps. Cars

External electric windscreen wiper motors by Klaxon were fitted to all Lagonda models until 1935. They replaced the top of windscreen models which threatened the front passenger's head in an emergency stop. Living out in the open did nothing for longevity and they are very rare now. The wiper arms, adjustable for length, are in period too.

had to be in road trim, with lamps, wings, etc. There was an impressive array of prizes and no less than eight Lagondas came to the starting line, easily the strongest entry in the make's history so far. The arrangement reached between the syndicate and General Metcalfe resulted in the syndicate having the use of one of the 3 Litres, with Frank King to drive it. Costs were to be split 50:50 between them and the works. The second 3 Litre was probably there under a similar deal between Fox and the factory.

So the Lagonda entries in the programme looked like this:

CLASS D 2000-3000cc

Race No.	Entrant	Driver(s)
10	A W Fox	F King
11	A W Fox	J S Hindmarsh

CLASS E 1500-2000cc

12		R S S Hebeler & I Hepburn
14		W M Couper
15	A W Fox	T E Rose Richards & C S Randall
16	A W Fox	G Roberts & A A Pollard
17	A W Fox	H F Wolfe
18	A W Fox	R R Jackson & C A Broomhall

In the race, King and Hindmarsh swapped cars and Wolfe didn't appear, being replaced by Brian Lewis and B E Jervis.

The high chassis 3 Litres had the same skimpy fixed cycle wings, the extra dampers, the diagonal headlamp bracing bars and cast alloy footsteps of their smaller cousins, but there was no undershield and the windscreen was a standard two-piece affair with the

Low chassis cars, if fitted with cycle wings, normally had these louvres in the metal trim panel covering the chassis side rails. They are purely decorative.

Detail of the radiator cap and Motometer. Running temperature should not go above the black line horizontally across the middle.

upper half capable of being hinged up to the horizontal for racing. The bonnet was secured by two straps and had normal catches, not Fox's channels. What was unusual about the bodywork was that instead of being the same width as the chassis along its lower edge it widened out aft of the bonnet rear edge and also deepened so that the body sides completely obscured the chassis frame from the windscreen to the rear axle. In a year or so this was to become the standard T2 tourer body, but at the time it was unique and rather an odd choice for a competition car. Hindmarsh's car was registered PK 9160 (Z 9403), but the number of King's car is not known. It was possibly Car Number Z 9543, which survives but so altered as to prevent accurate identification.

In the customary rush of pre-race preparation it had been forgotten that the Hindmarsh car had for some reason been entered as white. When it turned up in green for the scrutineer it was not passed by that stickler for accuracy. The problem was sorted in Staines fashion by despatching the most junior mechanic into Weybridge for a tin of whitewash and a brush, and a compromise was reached with the scrutineer whereby the chassis and wheels were white - well,would be until it rained - leaving the coachwork, whose fabric finish would not take kindly to whitewash, green.

Turning to the 2 Litres, nothing is known about Hebeler's car, which may have been high or low chassis and was possibly Bob Nicholl's car since Hebeler was a pal of his.

Couper's car is an old friend. The first of the team cars, No. 15, was PK 9201 and the last, No. 18, was 9204, so it is reasonable to expect the other two to be 9202 and 9203. These cars were unchanged from their Double Twelve form and Rose Richards had not won on the windscreen issue, since the cars raced with the curved-top type. Early on in the race the windscreen of number 17 was smashed by a stone but held together for the rest of the race, a fact that Fox acknowledged in a testimonial letter to the Acetex company and which they used in adverts. One change there may have been from May was the adoption of a different joint design where the exhaust pipe met the exhaust manifold, since the recurring troubles of the Double Twelve with this area never recurred and in the later production cars a completely different joint design replaced the triangular plates found on high chassis cars.

The Six Hours race was run on 29 June and Lewis in number 17 was first away again, so Fox's tricks still worked. He was caught by the Bentleys and the big Mercedes on the first lap, as expected. The nominal race distance for the scratch cars was 175 laps and credit laps formed the handicap for all other classes. At the end of the first hour an Austin Seven and a Triumph Seven were leading at 47mph and Hindmarsh's 3 Litre was averaging 51.45 mph. This includes the time lost stopping to furl the hood and of course the time putting it up in the first place. By the end of the second hour Hindmarsh's average had crept up to 58.97mph, meaning that he was now lapping at 66.49 mph, which was more like it but scarcely faster than the 2 Litres.

At the half-way mark the Speed Six Bentley was averaging 74mph and King had passed Hindmarsh to lead the 3-litre class at 60.09mph. This was slower than the scheduled average and in fact only the largest cars and the 1500cc ones were above the schedule. Soon after half way Roberts felt the steering of his car become peculiar and it was discovered that one of the ball joints had lost its nut. Hunting around the paddock for another 2 Litre, borrowing its ball-joint nut and fitting it cost him 16 minutes. At the fourth hour Hindmarsh had regained the lead in the 3-litre class at 59.94mph since King's car had run its bearings, possibly because of

The silver knob is the Ki-gass pump and above it is a pull-out dash lamp which lights when it is withdrawn.

oil pump failure. Couper had had rocker trouble and had changed one, and Roland Hebeler had retired with what was said to be a broken magneto drive shaft, having already had one stop to change magnetos. If his car was a fairly standard one, it is more likely that this was the fibre wheel giving up, as it is wont to in times of stress, rather than the shaft failing. Fox's cars had noisy bronze wheels in place of this known weak link.

As the race entered its last hour, Hindmarsh's average speed had crept up to 61mph, compared with 70mph for the 2-litre class leader and 67mph for the best 1500cc car. Not long after, Lewis hit the sandbank at the junction with the Outer Circuit and the car

Three-brush dynamos could easily overcharge the battery on long daylight runs, hence the summer/winter charging switch. Switching on the lamps automatically brought in the higher charging rate. The key earths the magneto. This car has a dashboard water temperature gauge as well as the one in the radiator cap.

John Hindmarsh in the 3 Litre "Special" lent to Fox & Nicholl for the 1929 Six Hour race at Brooklands.

The same car in later years as rebuilt for road use and then owned by Josh Sieger, who was Hon. Secretary of the Lagonda Car Club at that time.

buried itself in sand. Lewis and his mechanic dug for a quarter of an hour to get it out and were able to continue, but they were there long enough for scores of pictures to be taken, which still reappear from time to time with humorous captions. By this time the Bentley had worn away the handicap lead of the tiddlers and the race ran out with Barnato and Dunfee the winners at 75.88mph, beating the scheduled average of 73.25mph. Out of 38 starters 23 cars finished. Rose Richards and Randall were placed ninth overall at 63.98mph, but outside their scheduled average of 67.14mph. They were fourth in the 2-litre class and the Fox team of Rose Richards/Randall, Roberts/Pollard and

Lewis/Jervis won the team prize. Hindmarsh won the 3-litre class but slower than the 2-litre and 1500cc winners. Only Rose Richards & Randall of the Lagondas completed the full 175 laps, if one adds the handicap allowance. Nevertheless the team were awarded the Mobiloil Cup, which was eventually passed by Arthur Fox to the Lagonda Club in 1957 and now is awarded as the Fox Trophy to the club member with the best performance in competition in any year.

Following the Double Twelve, Lagonda had been able to advertise, as was the way then (and now, for that matter), "Lagondas 1st, 2nd and 3rd", followed in minuscule printing by "Class E". But this kind of point-stretching was not needed for the Six Hours since the team prize was open to everyone. There was some point-stretching, though, in the statement that the 3 Litre was "a standard model driven throughout by its private and amateur owner". It wasn't standard by a long chalk and while Hindmarsh as a serving RAF officer was certainly an amateur, he didn't own the car. As the publicity department was pushing the 3 Litre at the time, I suppose it is inevitable that Hindmarsh's class win, against negligible opposition and rather slow, should be heavily boosted, while the team prize was not. After all, the 2 Litre was selling rather well now and the new low chassis cars were emerging, still with Speed Model wings, the lower-sided body and an entirely new bulkhead casting and dashboard. This last was timber as before but the central metal panel was much enlarged and elliptical in shape, containing all the instruments except the rev counter, which was directly in front of the driver. For the first time the water temperature gauge was on the dash, although some diehard owners still preferred the Boyce Motometer mounted on the radiator top, since there it was directly in the driver's eye-line and he didn't have to look down or sideways at it. The general lowering of both floor and seats brought the steering wheel, now a celluloid-covered four-spoker, much lower and nearer to the vertical. The rake was still adjustable, of course. Lucas P100 DB headlamps were standardised, frequently black as that was cheaper, and the dipping mechanism was now a switch on the steering column instead of the Barker lever. The windscreen height was reduced, for some taller drivers by far too much, so that their heads stuck up into the slipstream. As we will frequently find in Lagonda affairs, all these changes were first introduced on the 3 Litre, even on the later high chassis Specials, and then found their way on to the 2 Litre after a discreet interval.

There was an interesting change to the low chassis 2 Litre engine in 1929. As the dynamo was now fastened directly to the nose of the crank, there was no longer any need for the crankshaft-speed sprocket on the lower timing chain which had hitherto driven it. So on the first batch of engines, I believe about 50, although there is a possibility there may have been as many as 70, this sprocket was omitted and the timing chain, slightly shorter, was led above rather than below the half-time wheel between the camshafts. This had the result of reversing the direction of rotation of the camshafts. Formerly they had rotated anti-clockwise as seen from the front; now they went round the same way as the crankshaft. As the camshafts were the same items as before, the firing order had to change from 1-2-4-3 to 1-3-4-2. The magneto was also unchanged, so its skew driving gear, the fibre one, and its worm gear, had to be replaced by one cut the opposite way. On the back of the timing housing, the bulge that had accommodated the sprocket bearing now vanished, replaced by a flat plate. This modification didn't last. In only a few months 2 Litre engines reverted to the original layout. One can see the economies of deleting the sprocket, its bearing and a shorter chain, but over the years various theories have been advanced for the change back again to "widdershins" camshaft rotation. The most plausible is that on the original design you can adjust the lower timing chain without affecting the upper one. With the second version, should you adjust the lower chain, you find that doing so upsets the upper one and you have to reset that. Even at 1929 labour rates this was seen as an unnecessary expense. As the engines looked very alike, it became vital for the first time to stamp some identification on them. High chassis engines had always had extremely complicated numbers on them, which probably reflect batch order numbers, the meaning now lost. From the middle of 1929 the timing cases were stamped with a

number prefixed by an S for a high chassis engine (both types were being made simultaneously) and SL for the reversed low chassis engines. There was also the complication of stocking two different skew gear sets and identifying which was which; another possible cause of the switch back. Certainly many 2 Litre owners in later years were to telegraph the works from remote breakdown spots for a fibre wheel only to find on its arrival it was for the wrong hand.

At about the same time, the single Zenith carburettor was replaced with two and the strangler, with its multi-start thread control, gave way to the Ki-Gass pump as a starting aid. This had been a novelty at the 1927 Motor Show but could not be fitted to the car until the late-1928 addition of a fuel filter, as the reservoir which the filter bowl provided was needed as a source of petrol for the injector. There were various other trivial changes to low chassis engines. For example the camshaft cover plates ceased to be aluminium and became steel.

The earliest low chassis cars, apart from the Fox & Nicholl ones, date from July 1929. It seems reasonable to accept that this was the

1929 Six Hour race. A famous picture of Brian Lewis and his mechanic extricating themselves from the sandbank at the end of the Finishing Straight. The windscreen was held half-open, as shown, by a semi-circular rail in its centre, adjusted and fixed by a giant thumbscrew.

For the first production run of low chassis 2 Litres the sprocket that drove the high chassis dynamo was omitted, as shown, which shortened the lower chain and had the effect of reversing the direction of rotation of the camshafts. Only about 50-60 cars were built like this before reverting to the original layout.

true introduction and that the May announcement was merely to satisfy the Le Mans authorities that the car entered was a standard catalogue model. Appearing in a catalogue is no guarantee that any cars actually exist. Mind you, the only reference to the low chassis car in mid-1929 catalogues was a stuck-in slip extolling the car, with no pictures and a slightly higher price range of £555 for the chassis and £720 for the tourer. Saloons were still high chassis at this time.

Private owners as well as works-backed ones had an active season in rallies and trials. There were three Lagondas in the Brighton Rally in early July, F M Cook winning the "concours" prize for his class (£801 to £1500) in his rather *outré* 3 Litre sports saloon by Wylders of Kew (PG 1290). Gaffikin Wilkinson (3 Litre CCS) and Primrose Bancroft (14/60) also competed. J S Hathaway entered the four-day Land's End to John O'Groats Trial but was unplaced. Mike Couper's 2 Litre didn't start.

On the identity plate for the early low chassis cars an "L" was added, so that Speed

Model tourers became SML instead of plain SM. The saloons continued as SMW for Speed Model Weymann. The firm didn't bother to produce a revised instruction book since the cars were identical in every respect likely to concern maintenance. The revised brake design had no impact on how an owner looked after his car. The Speed Model was by now becoming well known and *The Autocar* published an excellent series of articles as fortnightly instalments in June and July 1929 covering its care and maintenance, illustrated with clear line drawings which were in some ways more explicit than the photographs in the official instruction book.

We left the Fox team justifiably pleased with their team prize in the Six Hours and with only a fortnight to prepare for the Irish GP in Phoenix Park, Dublin. This was a new event on a new course and inspired, one would guess, by the successful revival of the T. T. the previous year. The 4.25-mile circuit consisted of the main road through the park, dead straight, very wide and making up half the lap, which was completed by a narrower and tortuous back road linking the ends of the straight. At both ends of the straight were tricky hairpins. The Dublin authorities had gone to enormous lengths to facilitate the race, seen as a tourist attraction, even going so far as to move the Phoenix monument, hitherto placed in the centre of the main road. A two-mile straight, even if slightly uphill, was prime 2 Litre territory; the back road much less so. The start and finish point, with the pits, was about two-thirds of the way along the straight. The race was to be divided into two sections, with up to 1.5-litre cars on the Friday and larger cars on the Saturday, but with a common handicapping system, so that an overall winner could be declared. This was well thought out. Not only did the public get two starts and two finishes, but if a car got into a commanding lead on the first day, its driver could not dare ease up in case someone did much better on handicap on the second day. Each section of the race was 70 laps, giving 300 miles of racing on each day.

Fox installed the cars at McGauran's Garage on the North Circular Road and the personnel at the Four Corners Hotel on North Quay. The syndicate was by now running into trouble filling the drivers' seats for the away fixtures.

A day or two at Brooklands was one thing, a week in Dublin quite another. Fox had entered four cars: a 3 Litre for Hindmarsh and three 2 Litres. Two of these were the syndicate cars but even up to practice only Wolfe and Jackson, neither members of the syndicate, had confirmed that they would drive. Eventually, one of the syndicate cars was withdrawn and they even managed to get their entry fee back. In the end the line-up was:

Race No.	Driver	Model	Reg No.	Car No.
17	Hindmarsh	3L	PK 9160	Z 9403
23	Wolfe	2L	PK 9203	OH 9413
24	Jackson	2L	PK 9204	OH 9414

The 3 Litre was still sporting its white chassis and wheels, a souvenir of the Double Twelve. One can only conclude it hadn't been out in the rain since then. You will note that none of the syndicate drivers or their cars turned up in the end, the cars being Fox's, Jackson's and the works 3 Litre.

Once the race got under way the Lagonda performance wasn't anything to get excited about. The brakes on the 3 Litre gave out early on and Hindmarsh wasted a lot of time careering up escape roads until he adjusted his driving to suit. One piece of entertainment occurred at Montjoy corner when Wolfe's bonnet strap came loose on the second lap and his mechanic climbed out at some 60mph over the windscreen on to the bonnet to fasten it. Robin Jackson finished ninth overall at 67.81mph in 4 hours 8min 50sec. Ninth overall was getting depressingly familiar. The other two cars were still running at the finish, both with 68 laps completed. As it happened and against probability, both days were scorchingly hot, giving rise to melted tar skids for everyone, and both races were won by Ivanowsky, on Friday in a 1500cc Alfa Romeo and on Saturday in a 1750cc one.

There was now a month's respite before the Ulster T.T. on the narrow and trying Ards circuit. The syndicate, although they had entered both cars, were still in driver shortage troubles and sent only PK 9202 for Rose Richards to drive, while Fox took his PK 9203 for Hindmarsh. Jackson drove his own car. Bert Hammond from the factory went with them, some evidence of the firm's continuing interest in the Fox team. They were probably glad to have him in the primitive conditions of the garage where they were staying.

Final starting details then were:

Entrant: A W Fox, two credit laps,
                264lb ballast (120kg)
Race No. 44   T E Rose Richards, PK 9202
Race No. 45   R R Jackson, PK 9204
Race No. 46   J S Hindmarsh, PK 9203
Race No. 47   Blank in programme

In the same class were three blown Alfas, two OMs and two SARAs.

The cars were much as before, except that Rose Richards had won on the windscreen issue and his car and 9203 were fitted with the folding wire-mesh variety that fitted the curve of the scuttle when folded, leaving just aeroscreens to look through. Anticipating trouble on the bumpy course, Fox had fitted a second bonnet strap right forward, just behind the radiator. The unpopular business

Low chassis 2 Litre tourer, T body, photographed in 1968. The first low chassis cars, all tourers, retained the Speed Model long wings.

But soon the cycle-type wing became an option, still with the T body. Sidelamps on the unsprung wings would have lasted no time at all, so they were moved to stalks attached to the scuttle.

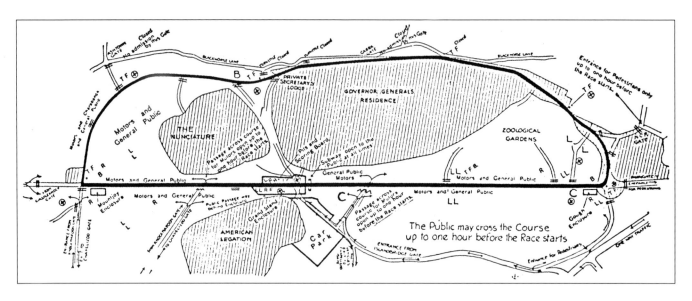

Circuit map of the 1929 Irish GP in Phoenix Park, Dublin.

Start of the over-1500cc race, Irish GP, July 1929. Hindmarsh is in No. 17, his car from the Six Hour race.

of running with hoods erected had been abandoned; in its place cars had to face the starter with hoods up and the crew's first duty was to furl them. Once again Fox's quick fastenings paid off and *The Northern Whig* published a photograph showing Rose Richards in number 44 rushing off into the distance whilst practically every other car is stationary under billows of canvas.

The sun was shining at the start, but not for long, and the race was most notable for Caracciola's inspired driving in the Mercedes under appalling conditions on roads little wider than lanes and alternating between wet and dry several times per lap. Caracciola aver-

aged 72.82mph to win from scratch and Campari's Alfa was second.

Rose Richards and Hindmarsh had fairly uneventful races but the cars were just too slow to be competitive and, inexplicably, slower than the 1928 ones. Rose Richards's fastest lap, number 18, was 13min 1sec (62.96mph) and Hindmarsh's lap 14 took 12min. 45sec (64.28mph). In 1928 Hall had lapped at 65.05mph. This rather reinforces the Double Twelve experience, but no-one has ever satisfactorily explained why low chassis car, presumed to have better roadholding and brakes, should be slower on the same circuit. Mind you, the 1929 T. T. was run in the wet while 1928 was dry, but this doesn't explain the Double Twelve.

Jackson's race is something of a mystery. The official results said he retired at 15 laps, but the author has seen the BRDC's lap times and they show Jackson to have done only two laps, counted as four with the handicap allowance, before a halt of 2 hours 58min 46sec, followed by one more lap. It is certain Jackson retired in the fourth hour and either the one final lap was intended to prove the car was raceable or it proved it wasn't.

The T. T. had an odd arrangement at its conclusion. The race did not finish when the leader crossed the line at the end of his last lap. Instead, all the remaining runners were allowed a further 30 minutes to see if they could beat their handicap. If they could not they were "flagged off". So we find at the end Hindmarsh was 21st of the 22 finishers, having taken 6 hours 11min 17sec to cover the 30 laps, a running average of 61.81mph. Rose Richards was still running but was flagged off and Jackson had retired. Hindmarsh was third in his class behind two Alfas.

There was only one more outing in 1929 for the Fox 2 Litre, which was driven by Howard Wolfe in the Brooklands closing meeting in September, scoring a second and a third place. This ended the Fox & Nicholl team's adventures for the year, and by the end of it the 2 Litre had become reliable enough to enter any long-distance race where the circuit didn't have too many corners, but no amount of tuning could make it fast enough to be really competitive. The basic problems were excessive weight and the strangled breathing that resulted from the tortuous inlet passages. The factory was aware of this and was experimenting with superchargers, but the weight problem was always going to be there. The syndicate was less than satisfied with the year's work and put up the cars for sale. Bill Edmondson bought 9201 and Tim Rose Richards placed 9202 with Malcolm Campbell's sales showroom in London. But this was the autumn of 1929, the time of the Hatry crash in New York, and the American Depression was beginning to spread ripples across the Atlantic. It was December before 9202 was sold and the syndicate had got some of its money back. Just to round off the story, in 1930 Bill Edmondson made an attempt to get from London to John O'Groats in daylight on midsummer's day in 9201. Knowing his engine's talent at bending rockers he took a boxful of spares, did London to Edinburgh in eight hours, but ran out of rockers and light at Dornoch, 70 miles short of his objective. For the 1930 season the syndicate turned their attention to MGs, which seemed to win on handicap inordinately often. They were to return to the Lagonda world in 1933 as the trigger which led to the M45 4½-litre model, but that is outside the scope of this book.

The same issue of *The Autocar* as carried the lengthy report of the T. T. also had an article about how Lagonda Distributors (London) Ltd, one of the main dealers, had imported a 6.9-litre Duesenberg chassis, converted it to righthand drive (with some difficulty) and sent it to Barker's for a sporting body for their customer. This looked as if it

Robin Jackson in his 2 Litre at the Irish GP.

The start of the 1929 T.T. Fox's little dodges allowed Rose Richards to get away well before everyone else had folded their hoods.

was going to be a money-spinner for the company but in fact only this one car was so treated and the concession passed to Malcolm Campbell Ltd.

After the rather uncertain start, the 3 Litre Special was now ready for proper production, and a tourer was made available for *The Motor* to road test in September 1929. There had been some changes since June, notably two SU carburettors bolted directly to the cylinder head, the inlet manifold being

The Fox & Nicholl team on board Ulster Monarch *on the way to the 1929 T.T. Left to right: Bert Hammond, Lloyd (a mechanic), Robin Jackson, Arthur Fox, Donald Wilcockson (Fox & Nicholl's chief mechanic), C A Broomhall, Tim Rose Richards, Dobson.*

internal to the casting. It had also discarded the six-branch rake-type exhaust manifold in favour of two three-branch ones, leading to two vertical downpipes by numbers 1 and 4 cylinders. Both pipes were wrapped in asbestos string to avoid too much heat reaching the driver's feet. The fan had grown another two blades and a revcounter drive contrived off the half-time shaft which already drove the magneto, water pump and camshaft. The obvious place for this drive, off the back of the camshaft, was buried behind the flywheel housing. The fuel supply to the carburettors was still by Autovac, but the hydrostatic head from it to the float chambers looked dangerously small. The bodywork stayed a longer version of the 2 Litre, but although this car was still high chassis, it had acquired the new low chassis dashboard, with its elliptical central panel for the instruments. Speed Model wings remained, but in keeping with the dignity of a £1000 car the little tweaks at the back of the rear ones vanished and a much more sober shape continued down below the axle line.

The Motor explained that to convert the original 3 Litre to the Special the engine had been mounted nine inches further back in the chassis. It is assumed that the side-members of the chassis were also altered in the same way as happened in 1927 to convert the original 14/60 frames to Speed Model ones.

The Speed Model, now low chassis for the tourers but still high for saloons and coupés, was almost unchanged for the 1930 model

year, but there was another revision to the exhaust manifold "as a result of racing experience". Prices were slightly increased, but to offset this Triplex safety glass was standardised. Triplex glass proved totally reliable, unlike the first make Lagonda tried, which all de-laminated and cost the company a fortune in warranty claims. Lagonda were now offering 18 separate models on five distinct chassis, with prices varying from £650 for a 14/60 tourer to £1100 for a saloon on the 3 Litre Special chassis. As the nation entered into a period of Depression, this was a formidable list for a small manufacturer and one suspects some sense of desperation as they sought to have a model for every gap in their chosen market. There wasn't room on the Olympia stand for more than four cars but they took advantage of the proximity of Bill Oates's premises in Hammersmith Road, only yards away from Olympia, to show the rest. One of the cars on the stand, a blue six-light Weymann 3 litre saloon, was sold immediately to Raymond Mays, then just coming into prominence, and a large sign on the car confirmed this, though it didn't mention the discount he had obtained.

During the year a number of extra dealers had been appointed, some of which would prove to be short lived, like Henly's, while others, such as Central Garage in Bradford, would sell scores of cars over the years. Central Garage, under "Mac" McCalman, had a special gift for selling cars to rich Yorkshire wool merchants, frequently a new car each year. The dozens of surviving Lagondas with KW or KY registrations all originated from Central Garage.

Lagondas turned out in force for the 1929/30 season of trials. In the MCC Sporting Trial of October G W Gemmell in YV 6652 gained a First Class award, J S Hathaway in UE 7826 gained a Silver Medal and R S Latham-Boote in UV 4850 didn't finish. Then, in the London-Gloucester Trial in early December, Mike Couper drove PG 3033, a low chassis tourer, to a Premier Award and Gemmell got three awards, one for the best performance in a car (motorcycles took part too), one for the best performance by an MCC member, and the third for the best performance by a member of the promoting club, the NW London MC. Hathaway also entered and gained a third class award.

The big event of the Christmas period, the London to Exeter Trial, had eight Lagondas in it, one of them being driven by Lord de Clifford, soon to become one of the make's more high-profile drivers. Results were as follows:

255 R S Latham-Boote 2 Litre Speed model
UV4850
Gold Medal
256 S C H Davis 3 Litre Special
Silver Medal
257 J A C Patterson 2 Litre Speed model
PH3928
Silver Medal
258 Lord de Clifford 3 Litre Special PG3024
Gold Medal
262 H R Attwood 2 Litre
did not finish
263 J S Hathaway 2 Litre UE7826
Silver Medal
264 W M Couper 2 Litre
Silver Medal
269 P W White 2 Litre
Silver Medal

Of these cars, Patterson's and Lord de Clifford's were definitely works cars and Couper's and Davis's probably were. The de Clifford car was entered in the Trial as 2985cc, which was either a mistake or indicated scrupulous attention to accuracy over a car which had been rebored slightly oversize (about 15 thou).

So 1929 came to an end; one of Lagonda's best years. The racing teams had had favourable comment from most quarters and even if the depressing succession of ninths overall hadn't secured much silverware, Dunlop were now prepared to release tyres to them without demanding cash. They had arrived on the racing scene and the company had actually made a bit of money. The 3 Litre had emerged from its ugly duckling era, well, the tourer had anyway, while the low chassis 2 Litre was up to the minute in appearance and there were periods when the factory could not keep up with demand for it. In fact, someone who should know, Donald Bastow, responsible for the chassis of the 1947 LB6 2.6 litre, reckoned that in 1929 Lagonda could have sold far more cars than they did but the factory was simply unable to turn out any more with its limited facilities. Quite rightly, the management was not going to compro-

mise on quality by cutting corners to get production numbers up, not with the ten-year warranty period they had introduced in March. This was divided into five two-year periods; at the end of each the owner had to agree to whatever work the factory deemed necessary, and when this was completed the warranty was extended for a further two years. So the management looked forward to 1930 with confidence, so much so that they abruptly cancelled the arrangement with Fox & Nicholl at very short notice, forcing Fox to turn to Talbots. They were sure that the 3 Litre, although no faster than a good 2 Litre, would reel off a string of class wins as the opposition was thought to be negligible. It is interesting to note that under Fox's guidance

The 1929 team re-assembled for the Lagonda Centenary celebrations at Brooklands in 1999. All four cars belonged to the late Ivan Forshaw but only PK 9201 has so far been repainted in Syndicate colours.

A second carburettor became an option on low chassis cars.

Although low chassis 2 Litres and 3 Litres carry similar bodies, the extra bonnet length needed for the six cylinder engine is noticeable in this profile view.

there had been 19 starts and 19 finishes, so reliability was excellent, but the unanswered question is how much of this was down to Fox's meticulous preparation.

At some time in the autumn of 1929, probably around the October Olympia Show, the abbreviations used on the cars' identity plates was altered. Until then 14/60s and 16/65s had carried T, S or SS, representing tourer, saloon or Semi-sports. Speed Models had added SM and SMW to this. Then the 3 Litre had come along, coded Z3, followed by the 3 Litre Special (Z3S). The low chassis 2 Litre tourers gained an L to become SML. The new system was more detailed. Under "Type" the entry now read in two parts, separated by a dot. So a low chassis 2 Litre Speed Model tourer became OHL.T and its companion on the 3 Litre Special chassis would be Z3S.T. Turning to the saloons, the Weymann bodies had continued to be called plain type W even after the 1928 changes to the appearance, but with the advent of the 3 Litre Special a completely different body was called the W2, and since this was available in both 4-light and 6-light versions, these became W24 and W26 respectively. At this time an external luggage boot became available for the first time (if you exclude the CCS body, which always had one). To fit it without lengthening

the car, the interior was shortened, so clearly the owner, if specifying a boot, had to do so at order stage. A further confusion was the short production runs of low chassis 2 litres with the opposite-hand engines. These came into the earlier "SML" categories but for some odd reason these engines continued to be fitted to saloons after being dropped in tourers. Such saloons were designated "LOH" on their identity plates to distinguish them from other saloons and were generally plain W2 bodies, not W24. When the car was supplied as a bare chassis for another coachbuilder to perform on, the notation after the dot read "CH". At about the same time the prefix OH or Z transferred from the engine number to the Car Number. But this only occurred after an interim period when the prefix either appeared on both panels or on neither. By early 1930 this more precise system had settled down and was to persist until the 1935 bankruptcy.

The 1930 catalogues showed a new development, the introduction of cycle-type wings for all the more sporting models. They were an extra, at extra cost. Lagonda's choice of design was unusual in that they were fixed to the backplates of the front brakes and hence turned with the steering. In this unsprung position they had to be fairly massively

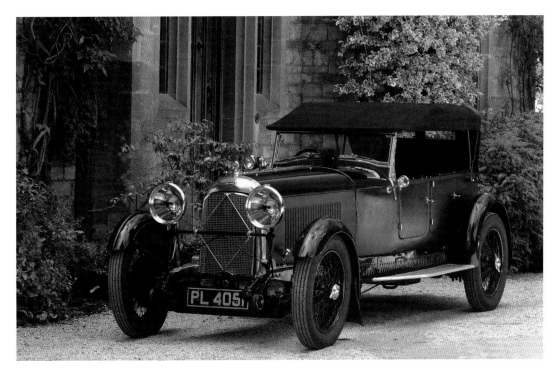

The mirror on the spotlamp became vital once the hood was erected, as the view from the tiny rear windows was severely restricted. But when this car was new not many vehicles were going to overtake it.

Lord de Clifford (in beret) at the finish of the 1930 Monte Carlo Rally. Bert Hammond is next to him and the other members of the crew are Edwin Mills and E H Paul. Few rally drivers today wear a waistcoat, watch chain and tie.

constructed to survive, and they appear to be a retrograde development brought about by fashion. Such wings had become very much the vogue; they undoubtedly assist in placing the wheels in tight cornering and the Lagonda variety had the benefit of not shooting mud in the driver's eyes on right-hand bends. But there was a hidden reason. The steeply-dropped low chassis front axle had brought with it a problem, in some cars at least, with axle tramp under braking, especially on rough roads. Increasing the unsprung weight had the tendency to put the natural frequency of resonance into a different range, hopefully away from those normally encountered. To catch sideways splashes, leathercloth valances were attached to the wings, reaching down to the backplates. An incidental advantage of these wings was that they allowed far better access to the engine by permitting the owner to stand close to it, but they also posed the aesthetic problem of what to do with the front portions of the running boards. This was solved by tapering them to a point alongside the chassis, or, for the very sporting, abandoning them altogether and substituting little oval footsteps under each door, plus one for the driver, who still had no door on the T body. To tidy up the vast length of chassis now exposed, most Speed Models with cycle

wings were fitted with louvred aluminium covers running the whole length of the exposed chassis frame. The louvres were purely decorative, of course. It was not going to be a good idea to mount the sidelamps on these unsprung wings, so they were repositioned on streamlined stalks growing out of the scuttle, which were to become a Lagonda trademark for a few years. If the owner speci-

fied the Speed Model long wings, the side-lamps remained on them as before.

Following the decision to take the racing team in-house, it is no surprise to find Fox's own car for sale in White & Mears showroom in Piccadilly, "guaranteed to do 100 mph", right at the end of 1929 and priced at 480 guineas (£504).

Lord de Clifford started off the competition year for Lagonda as he was frequently to do in the future, driving a 3 Litre Special tourer, PG 3024, in the Monte Carlo Rally. Starting from John O'Groats with Bert Hammond as mechanic and Edwin Mills and E H Paul as co-drivers/navigators they were 46th on the road at the finish, suffering from the system that awarded higher marks to starters from the more far-flung places like Tallinn or Athens. But in practising for the Mont des Mules hillclimb, "Ted", as the noble lord was known, skidded off the road and plunged over a cliff, severely damaging the car. This car was a high chassis tourer. PG 3024 had Speed Model wings and the enormous side-lamps found on early 3 Litres, complete with tripod bulb supports matching the P100s and somewhat larger in diameter than the small foglamp which seems to have been the only extra added for the rally, apart from the spare petrol can on the running board. It won first prize in the open car class of the *concours de confort*, presumably before going over the cliff.

Quietly, in the late winter, the high chassis

2 Litre Speed Model saloon and coupé were dropped, and were replaced by low chassis equivalents at slightly increased prices (£820 each), with the cycle wing option extended to them. In March the firm produced a new catalogue, and not before time since the 1928 one was beginning to be laughable. The new catalogue featured a model which seems never to have gone into production, the 2 Litre Special. It was intended to be a competition version of the low chassis Speed Model, and although it was almost identical outwardly some of the less vital parts had been dropped to save weight. There were no running boards, for example, and the chassis side rails were bare, with no decorative louvres. The major difference was under the bonnet, where the tortuous inlet passages had given way to a pair of downdraft carburettors by Zenith mounted between the camboxes. The photograph in the catalogue was a dead side view and it isn't clear where the sparking plugs were. None of these cars survive, nor any downdraft heads. The author concludes that the photograph of the engine is a mock-up and that the factory was actually concentrating on adding a supercharger, which could be done relatively cheaply in comparison with the cost of new cores and a different head casting. In recent years, keen Lagonda Club members have explored this downdraft head idea with considerable success, but there is no evidence that the factory pursued it in 1930. Surprisingly, the Special was to have been offered at the same price as the normal Speed Model tourer.

The 3 Litre came in for some changes too. On the Special the low hydrostatic head available for the Autovac had given trouble after all and a new AC mechanical pump replaced it, driven off the camshaft and drawing its fuel from the 20-gallon (91-litre) tank. Ordinary 3 Litres persisted with a 14 gallon (64 litre) tank. The two three-branch exhaust manifolds were re-designed to be symmetrical, so that the outlet pipes were by numbers 2 and 5 cylinders instead of numbers 1 and 4. Probably the biggest change was to fit the Special engine, with its two SU carburettors, to all 3 Litres. Prices were revised, too, so that the Standard chassis was now £775, the longer one £845, a five-seat tourer on the standard chassis was to be £945 and both the

Speed Model Weymanns got the low chassis only in 1930. Lucas had introduced the P100 headlamps and this car has dispensed with running boards in favour of steps for the occupants. The louvres along the chassis cover plates are purely decorative.

Weymann saloons £1050 each. A coachbuilt saloon on the 10 t 9in (3.28m) standard chassis was £1065 and a Weymann limousine on the long chassis £1150. Prices for the Special versions were unchanged at £835 for the bare chassis, £1000 for the tourer and £1100 for a Weymann saloon. All these cars were now on the low chassis but nothing was mentioned in any literature about this change, which must have simplified the stores position in the works by giving all models the same front axles and braking systems.

The Special chassis had originally appeared with a 4.1:1 rear axle and the ZE set of intermediate gears, giving 5.15, 8.05 and 12.88:1. The same set of ratios within the OH gearbox of the Speed Model were retained but for the low chassis car the rear axle ratio was changed to 4.4:1 (9 x 40) and this gave intermediates of 5.53, 8.64 and 13.83. The more pedestrian models had shorter ratios than this and the wider ratio ZC and intermediate ZD sets were still available, together with their equivalent OH sets in the earlier gearbox.

There had been rumblings from the racing authorities over the very abbreviated rear wings on the team cars (and on other people's models too) which tended to throw stones into the face of following cars. So for 1930 the rear wings were extended down to hub level, deleting the horizontal tweak on which owners were wont to rest their beer mugs at social gatherings. At the front, both 2 and 3 Litres gained a streamlined dumbiron fairing which extended from the number plate to the base of the radiator, held in place by

quick-release clips to allow the starting handle to be inserted. The little truss under the chassis side members, first found on the 1929 team cars, had become standard and was stressed up at the works so that the chassis member had a positive camber before the body was added. The joints in the truss were then sealed and the owner told not to meddle with them on pain of loss of warranty. As the search for sales grew tougher with the world-wide recession, Lagonda virtually abandoned any strict model policy and you could have any body on any chassis and in any colour, although there was an extra charge for a non-standard colour to reflect the cost of cleaning the equipment before and afterwards.

The search for power, exemplified by the 2 Litre Special's downdraught head, led the factory to seek more power for the 3 Litre,

F M Cook was a frequent competitor in concours d'elegance with this high chassis 3 Litre. The coachwork was by Wylders of Kew. The wings look more like a bird's than most and the huge Lalique glass mascot stands on a special bracket attached to the radiator cap. Cadmium-plated brake drums were a current fad. Clearly expecting trouble, the car can carry three spare wheels.

The high chassis 3 Litre Special, photographed in November 1929. The more sober rear wing line, extended down to hub level, indicates that the car was a 1930 model, already in production.

whose 50% larger capacity didn't really produce a great deal more performance. Top speed of the Special tourer, as established by *The Autocar* in November 1929, was 80 mph with 70 in third, compared with exactly the same speeds "guaranteed" by the company (although rarely achieved without special tuning) for the 2 Litre Speed Model. So the expertise of Ricardo & Co. was sought. Ricardo had developed their "High Power Head", an inlet-over- exhaust layout, for the 4 Litre Bentley with good results, so a 3 Litre engine was sent to them early in 1930 to undergo the same treatment. This was very successful and the ioe Ricardo head increased the 3 Litre Special engine's output from 79bhp at 3800rpm to 100bhp at 3600rpm. This would have transformed the 3 Litre and achieved the desired performance distance between the two models, but unfortunately Lagonda decided they couldn't afford it. It meant, of course, a completely different head casting, different valve gear and no doubt other changes, perhaps to the brakes, as any extra performance from this weighty car might have overloaded them. Plus, of course, stores full of obsolete parts from the existing model. The one engine built survives, or did in the 1970s, although not in a car.

Another route to more power was offered by supercharging. This was regarded as very exotic at the time, not without reason, for some machines could be temperamental and the management of their lubrication was seen as a black art; too little lubrication seized the blower, too much fouled the plugs, and only tiny changes went from one extreme to the other. On the other hand, a supercharger could be added to the 2 Litre engine with very little trouble by devising a bevel drive between the nose of the crankshaft and the dynamo, moving the latter forward to accommodate a bevel box. There need be no stores full of obsolete parts. In the event it wasn't quite as simple as that, and we will return to the superchargers in the next chapter.

At Easter 1930 five Lagondas entered the London-Land's End Trial and all got Gold Medals. To the familiar gallery of Gemmell, Hathaway, Latham-Boote and Couper (back in PK 2339) we must add W H G Tom. His car, TR 3270 (OH 8630), was fourth hand but new to him. Out of 400 entries, only 112 were "clean", showing the event to have been tougher than some earlier ones.

Lord de Clifford entered a 3 Litre in the Paris-Nice Rally in March, navigated by Mike Couper, but the results have not come the author's way. Although no longer driving works cars, Bill Oates was still a familiar face in Lagonda affairs, with his London dealership. Already a radio ham he was, in 1930, building an experimental television set. The photograph illustrating him in the "Familiar Faces" series was taken, inevitably, in his 11.9 racer at Brooklands and showed the incredible number of rivets needed to hold the rear springs to the body over the notorious bumps.

The JCC Double Twelve was to be held on 9 and 10 May and after the success of the 1929 race was a keenly anticipated event, with speculation for weeks beforehand. Having severed the Fox & Nicholl connection, the factory was going to enter four cars under Alfie Cranmer's name. In addition, Gaffikin Wilkinson entered a 2 Litre for D E Sharman and T E Stone. The works cars were three 3 Litres numbered 11, 12 and 14 in accordance with time-honoured superstition. Drivers were to be Eddie Hall/Frank King; Tim Rose Richards/O Saunders Davies and Eddie Hayes/Louis Real respectively. Real was one of the factory testers, following the Bert Hammond tradition. The fourth car was a 2 Litre for Mike Couper, driving alone and numbered 35, and the "Gaff Wilks" car was number 40. As before, the race was to be run on handicap, and although the fastest cars were bound to be Malcolm Campbell's Mercedes and its rival troupe of Bentleys, blown and unblown, the chances were that one of the shoal of tiddlers would survive the pounding and take the race. The 3 Litre class, which also contained Arthur Fox's new and untried Talbots, was set a minimum average speed of 57mph, to the 2 litre class's 54mph.

There is every reason to believe that the whole Lagonda team consisted of new cars. All last year's 2 Litres had been sold and all the cars were low chassis. One of the 1929 3 Litres survives and is still high chassis, so the 1930 cars must have been new ones. Gaff Wilks's car looked exactly the same as the works 2 Litre and in fact proved the better car in the race. This was PG 8804 (OH 9657). Just how much factory involvement there was in this car, the Sharman/Stone vehicle, became clear in 1990 when the author was able to examine it closely as it was being restored. Fortuitously for the historian, the car had had very few owners and none of them had altered it much. For a start it had a magnesium gearbox casing and a magnesium timing case, which contained an extra access hole for timing the inlet camshaft. The bodywork of the scuttle had no aluminium panelling, consisting solely of criss-crossed upholsterer's webbing, red one way, black the other. This was covered with Zapon fabric and painted to look solid. A "streamlined" tail was made of very thin plywood and hinged up to reveal the 24-gallon(109-litre) copper fuel tank and the spare wheel. Clutch, flywheel and gearbox internals were riddled with holes for lightness. The gearbox had normal ZE ratios except for second, which was 1.82 instead of 1.96. The engine was a cross between a normal 2 Litre and the as yet unannounced supercharged version, having the later crankshaft with its wider connecting rods (polished all over) and a mechanical fuel pump driven off the inlet camshaft. Compression ratio was about 7:1 and a bronze gear, rather than a fabric one, drove the magneto. The camshafts were non-standard, surprisingly giving less lift but opening earlier and for longer. The rockers, long a weak point, were the latest stiffer type, soon to be standard on the blown engine. The mechanic, relieved of having to pump up fuel pressure by the provision of the mechanical pump, now had the reserve oil supply to contend with, this being a tank under the scuttle and a pump to transfer the oil to the sump when needed. The dashboard was dominated by a huge rev counter and an oversize oil pressure gauge. Lamps and magneto switches were porcelain and bakelite household items very neatly engraved with their function.

The bodywork was even shorter than the 1929 cars, ending at the rear axle line, where a vertical plywood bulkhead took the weight of the petrol tank, the spare wheel and the beetle-like tail. The driver's cutaway in the body side was enlarged to a squarer shape, so that it was half the depth of the body side, giving less chance of bruised elbows on the notorious Brooklands bumps. On the near side one huge door gave quick access for Le Mans starts. The radiator was a new design, deeper than hitherto and supported by trunnions attached to the chassis at each side. This overcame the 1928 Le Mans problem where the bottom-mounted earlier design had begun to leak around its fixings after prolonged bashing from the rough roads. The huge P100s disappeared, replaced by tiny 6-inch (152mm) lamps on minimal supports and sporting domed covers to minimise wind resistance in the race. There was to be no malarky about running with the hood up this year, so Fox's quick-fix hoods were abandoned and all the cars ran with a curved wire mesh windscreen folded flat and two aero screens erect. The wings were fractionally longer than last year's and no longer had the sidelamps mounted on them, the normal scuttle stalk type being used. Under the car a

PG 8804 in the 1930 Double Twelve race, driven by Sharman and Stone. Technically entered by Gaffikin Wilkinson, it was clearly "works" prepared.

bulbous undertray extended from the clutch to the rear chassis cross-member and at the front the dumbirons were faired in with an aluminium tray.

The other 2 Litre entered, PG 5920, has not survived, but it looked exactly the same as the Sharman/Stone car so one suspects it was prepared in exactly the same way. The Lagonda strategy of entering two identical cars, one admittedly a factory product, the other "private" was quite a cunning ploy. If the factory car did well, then the resultant publicity would sell cars. If the "private" one did well, then this showed what good cars Lagonda made, allowing a private owner to compete with or beat the factory product.

None of the 3 Litre cars seem to have survived, but outwardly they were very similar to the 2 Litre ones and it is a safe assumption that they were tuned in much the same way.

In practice, the Talbots astounded everyone with their speed and in the Lagonda pit faces grew longer as the confidently expected 3 litre class win faded alarmingly. 85mph lap speeds were beyond the Lagonda 3 Litre, but 24 hours is a lot of racing and the Talbots were new and untried.

At the start, Tim Rose Richards was first away and led the race as far as the banking, when he was engulfed in Speed Sixes, but at the end of the first lap he was ninth, having been passed by all the Bentleys and two of the Talbots. Two more Lagondas were 11th and 12th and in all 59 starters flashed past the spectators. The Talbots, only 2.3 litres and in the hands of a none-too-experienced team, proved to be reliable as well as fast and began to run away with the 3 litre class with embarrassing ease. The first inkling of trouble for the Lagondas came at 12.30 when Rose Richards coasted into the pits with a broken timing chain, a habit of the 3 Litre when flustered. He and his mechanic set about replacing it, a hot job since the radiator had to come off to get at it. Half an hour later Hayes spun off at the junction of the Finishing Straight and the banking, but he was able to continue. During the afternoon the blown Bentleys began to disintegrate but the works Speed Sixes thundered on, leading both on the road and on handicap. It was then Mike Couper's turn to break his timing chain, but he was much

further from the pits and had to push the car the best part of a lap, so he was very ready for the pint of beer the General had ready for him before setting about another removal of a radiator. The next Lagonda disaster struck the Hayes car, which broke a connecting rod, knocking a hole in the crankcase. The driver heard the bang, but because of the odd nature of the break the oil pressure did not drop, so he carried on in an ever thickening smokescreen until the pit finally convinced him he should stop to investigate. Having stopped, the engine would not restart, so that car withdrew.

At three minutes to seven, as recorded by the stoppage of the electric clocks, two of the Talbots crashed into each other at the end of the Finishing Straight and catapulted into the crowd, just at the place where the party from the Lagonda factory were watching. One of the Talbot mechanics, Ted Albery, was killed, as was a spectator, Mr Hurworth. Nine spectators were injured and Colonel Rabagliati severely so, although he eventually recovered. The whole affair caused a sensation, the worst ever crash at Brooklands. Arthur Fox withdrew the remaining Talbot at the end of the first day and the crowd went home in suitably oppressive drizzle.

They came back the following morning, more than ever being attracted by the drama of the previous day, to watch the pantomime of a cold start after 12 hours of racing and 12 hours of parc fermé. Fifty-nine cars had started the first day and 42 were still running. Couper had not finished his timing chain job the previous evening, so the spanners came out at 8am, as they did in the next door pit where Rose Richards was installing a new battery and Frank King was under his 3 litre renewing a run big-end. Only the Sharman/Stone 2 Litre seemed to be trouble-free. The Rose Richards/Saunders Davies 3 Litre started once the new battery was in but was three hours down after Friday's adventures. King changed the connecting rod but the bearing metal had got everywhere and very shortly another bearing went and the car was withdrawn.

The race ran out in deteriorating weather, with the Bentleys slowing to a canter and winning by a 200 mile margin. Sharman and Stone were ninth overall at 69.61mph and second in their class to the Ivanovsky/Eyston Alfa Romeo. A good result for a "private" entrant but rather spoilt by realising that the Riley that won the 1100cc class was faster. The Rose Richards/Saunders Davies 3 Litre came second (out of two) finishers in its class, 26th overall of 27 finishers. They averaged 57.84mph. The team prize was won by our old friends the PERR syndicate in their MGs.

The 1930 Double Twelve was rather a watershed in many ways, not least in Lagonda affairs, for it saw the last full-scale team effort by the factory in first-class racing for nine years. The 3 Litre was plainly not up to racing over long distances and even if it could be made more reliable, was just not fast enough, while the forecast series of class wins against negligible opposition had been knocked on the head by the appearance of Fox's Talbots. Some kind of poetic justice for having so summarily sacked him at the beginning of the year. The 2 Litre was by now more reliable but still tended to be outclassed on speed. Both models were, and still are, charming road tourers with useful performance but it needs working up to and their excessive weight and strength, which may well be the reason why we can still admire and preserve them, prevented them from being truly competitive with the Alfas and Bugattis of their day, half the weight and able to reach peak revs along comparatively short straights. Sensibly, the works teams only contested events like Le Mans and other long-distance

classics where durability was of some account and fizzing acceleration less so, but with the Depression biting the world there was not enough money coming in to risk racing unless wins were likely to be forthcoming.

The Double Twelve was to be run once more in 1931, when an attempt was made to make it safer by running clockwise round the track, so that the braking point for the only corner wouldn't coincide with the spectator enclosure. There were also more stringent requirements for driver experience. With hindsight and a knowledge of Sod's Law, it was very unwise for Talbot to head their advertisement in the 1930 programme "Britain's Safest Car".

The saucy tweak to the rear wing line found on high chassis cars vanished when cycle wings came in.

2 LITRE LOW CHASSIS SPEED MODEL
As High Chassis except

Engine

LOH models	Camshafts revolve clockwise. Firing Order 1–3–4–2
Oil capacity	2 gallons (9 litres)
Coil ignition by 1932	

Chassis / Gearbox / Rear Axle

Kerb weight	Chassis	23.25cwt (1181kg)
	Tourer	27.75cwt (1410kg)
	Saloon	30cwt (1524 kg)
Rear axle ratio	4.4:1 (1930)	
Overall gear ratios	4.4:1, 5.53:1, 8.64:1, 13.83:1	
Mph/1000rpm in top	20.96	
Tyres	5.00 x 21 from 1932	

Prices	1929	1930	1932
Chassis	£430	£555	£430
Tourer	£595	£730	£595
Weymann Saloon	£695	£820	£695

Chapter Seven

Superchargers

T he financial crash of late 1929 carried across the Atlantic and 1930 was not a good sales year for Lagonda or any maker of expensive cars. So the factory was instructed to forget about racing, pursue more sales and concentrate on the 2 Litre. The weakness of its design had always been the

John Walker has owned PL 7016 for well over 30 years and it is one of the rare Lagondas whose complete history is known. The combination of the stoneguard frame and the headlamp support stays almost replicates the double diamond door trim.

strangled breathing and we have seen before that a version with freer-flowing inlet tracts had been advertised, but not sold, in the spring of 1930. An alternative approach was supercharging, which met all the problems, and the Experimental department had been charging about since March in such a car. From the sales angle, the blown car won hands down since it was possible to charge a much higher price for a supercharger while the cost to the factory was much the same as a revised cylinder head casting would have been. The customer would see that the super-charger itself must bring about a price rise, not to mention the performance gain, whereas a new head would look much like the old one and he would resist paying more for it. However, the development ran into a lot of trouble and outside consultants such as Harry Weslake and Charles Fisher became familiar faces at Staines during 1930.

It is rarely possible to put new wine into old bottles without blowing a few corks and the extra heat and torque generated by the supercharged engine proved extremely troublesome to accommodate. The actual drive to the supercharger caused little bother, the dynamo drive from the front of the crankshaft being moved forward and a bevel gear interposed, driving a vertical tubular shaft at crankshaft speed. This drove the blower, which thus came to live vertically in front of the timing case. A single 1⅜in SU carburettor

on the side fed the mixture and a long inlet pipe curved round the engine to the original inlet manifold. Obviously, with no manifold depression, the Autovac had to go, and a mechanical AC petrol pump was mounted at the rear of the inlet camshaft, displacing the rev counter drive to the other camshaft. The carburettor varied in position according to which design of blower was used. The cams themselves were the Speed Model design, but re-timed to open the inlet valve at 9 degrees BTDC and close the exhaust at 6 degrees ATDC, so that the 9 degrees overlap on the unblown car was increased to 15 degrees. The 0.004in rocker clearances were doubled to 0.008in, probably in the justified expectation of increased valve stem temperatures. The ignition was advanced and a freer-flowing exhaust manifold probably produced better breathing.

The increased length of the engine meant that the radiator had to be repositioned further forward and the opportunity was taken to rethink the chassis at this point. The 1928 racing cars broke their radiators because of the hammering these got from sitting directly on top of the pressed-steel chassis cross-member. This member was now in the way of the supercharger drive, so it was scrapped and replaced by a tube, sufficiently far forward to clear the dynamo on the unblown car; for the blown one an inverted U-shaped bend was introduced to provide clearance. The radiator was then mounted on brackets projecting from the side of its shell and supported on trunnions bolted to the chassis side members. No only did this solve the cracking problem, but it led to the possibility of extra depth to the radiator without any other changes. Further, the ends of the front dampers could be attached directly at this strong point. The extra strength here led to the designer deleting the tube which joined the front dumbirons. The resulting "raw" look

John Walker's supercharged 2 Litre shows the T2 body with a third door and revised cutout for the driver's elbow. The bulge in the bonnet behind the offside headlamp is visible evidence of the blower.

PL 1240 (chassis OH 9711), the first supercharged 2 Litre, in the yard at Staines, outside the paint shop. This was the debut of the T2 body, which featured an additional door in the rear and a deeper cutout for the driver's right elbow. This car had a standard top-hinged windscreen but production ones folded flat. For the first time the bonnet top and scuttle top were painted, not fabric covered. Possibly the extra heat brought on problems here.

From this angle only one detail distinguishes this car from PL 4051 and that is the over-centre clip fitting on the fuel tank filler.

to the chassis was hidden by a streamlined shield. There seems to have been no coherent policy about this front cross-member and from 1930 on the OH chassis seems to come with or without it to customer's choice. If present, it carried a metal ring which acted as a steady for the starting handle and the dumb-iron shield had a bump in it. If absent, a shorter starting handle was supplied and the shield was smooth.

Most of the development work was done on Car Number OH 9711 (PL 1240) and the first supercharger tried was the Powerplus, a single-rotor type made by George Eyston's company. It was very reliable but blew at about 15psi (1.03 bar), which was rather higher than really needed. It was also rather expensive. Lubrication of the rotor was by means of a small oil pump on the top of the casing, drawing its oil from a tank on the bulkhead. In addition, oil was added to the petrol. The engine's compression ratio was reduced to 5.4:1 and endless experiments with plugs, timing and mixtures ensued. It had been expected to announce the car at the traditional spring launch of new models but it was July before the management was sufficiently confident to do so. At the Lagonda fete at Brooklands PL 1240 was on hand as a demonstrator and was made available to *The Motor* for road test the next month.

It was the firm's habit to let the press have and describe a development car. This car often had a greater performance than later production ones and differed in detail from them. Most Lagonda models were variable anyway at the whim of the customer. The supercharged 2 Litre, however, is almost bewildering in its varieties and the old remark that Lagonda "never built two cars alike" particularly applies to it, albeit many of the variations are small.

PL 1240 was also pioneering a revised body style for the 2 Litre, later to be called the T2 body. The most noticeable feature was the extra five inches depth of the body sides, which now covered the chassis side members

The T2 body swept out and down to conceal the chassis side rails. A leather strap across the bonnet was a requirement of the Brooklands authorities.

Triangular leathercloth shields were fitted to the front wings to prevent stones and mud gritblasting the bodywork when on lock.

aft of the scuttle, the lower edge of the body curving down from the bulkhead to a point under the front door hinge. The new body was no wider, although it looked as if it was. The nearside doors remained the same but an additional door was arranged for the offside of the rear compartment, but set back further than the nearside one, necessitating a cut-out in its rear edge to clear the wing. The driver was still not allowed a door but the cut-out for his elbow grew much deeper and was shaped more elegantly than before, the new line being approximately that of the driver's forearm when holding the wheel. The rear seat gained a centre armrest. A new wind-screen was designed for the T2 body although, as is the way of these things, it wasn't fitted to PL 1240. Instead of the hori-zontal division between the opening upper rectangular screen and the lower fixed trian-gular parts, the new screen was all one piece, with a curved lower edge to match the curve of the scuttle and opening about its hinged upper edge.

The new design of radiator brought with it a new filler, an over-centre clip replacing the screw down cap with its Motometer attached. A similar quick-release cap also appeared on the fuel tank. This first design of cap had its operating arm crossways. The radiator support trunnions were concealed behind polished aluminium covers fixed to the chassis top.

The bonnet of the blown car was, of

Close up of the supercharger. Cuthbert raced with an outsize Powerplus but this is a Zoller, possibly made by Lagonda under licence.

Nearside of the supercharged engine with festoons of extra oil pipes. A blow-off valve in the centre of the inlet manifold is a vital safety device. An SU electric fuel pump has replaced the original mechanical one.

Low chassis 2 Litre engines took advantage of the repositioning of the dynamo to fit much beefier exhaust manifolds.

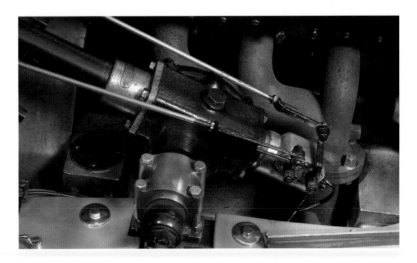

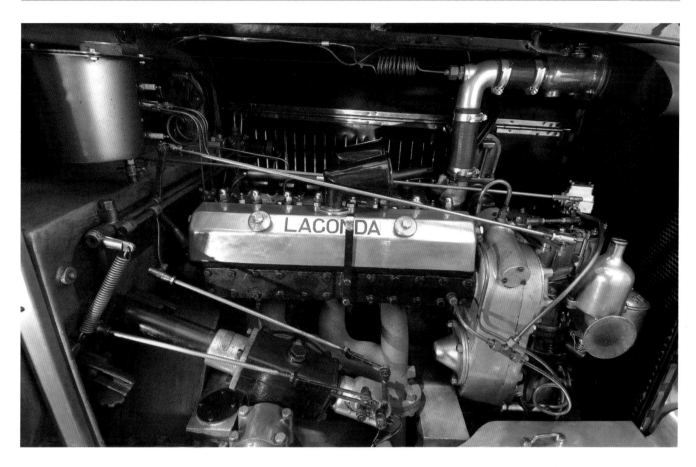

Offside of the supercharged engine. Adding the
blower in front of the timing case has called for a
bundle of extra oil pipes and re-routed control rods.

Detail of the inlet side of the supercharger.

PL 7016's first owner was W A Cuthbert, a garage proprietor from
Guildford, who regularly competed at Brooklands. Here he is in the 1932
Whitsun race meeting on the Mountain Circuit. Note that he has even
removed the sidelamps and their stalks. He didn't finish this race, breaking
an oil pipe, but in an earlier one he lapped the Outer Circuit at 83.94mph
from a standing start. The overflow pipe to the radiator is clearly visible.

for the T2 tourer and £875 for the Weymann saloon, all these being about £50 above the corresponding unblown cars.

The Brooklands fetes were now so well patronised that the company was able to secure a summer Saturday date, 19 July, in 1930. There were 11 events, plus two demonstrations of the supercharged 2 Litre. Many of the events had progressed to two laps from the earlier one. Event 1 was won by D R Sharman of Fox & Nicholl, who should by then have known his way round Brooklands, in contrast to E Grimaldi, a dealer from St Albans, who took a wrong turning at the Fork but made up for it by winning Event 2, a Mountain race. Some of the events were so popular that they had to have heats and a final, and one would love to know exactly what happened in the Obstacle Race (Event 10), where there was a tie between D H Searle and L McCardle. A playoff was ordered in which both were disqualified and Lord de Clifford declared the winner. Both *The Autocar* and *The Motor* sent photographers as well as journalists, and the Lagonda Club archives now have copies of the pictures. In one shot there is a quaint Lagonda service van, built on a 16/65 chassis with artillery wheels. The cab has no side windows, just D-

Nobody at the 1930 Lagonda Fete at Brooklands could have known that this would be the last one. It has never been explained why the Brooklands authorities stopped them.

course, longer than the earlier car's and had a small bulge low down on the offside to accommodate the carburettor. At the front the trimmings of the 3 Litre Special were added, the high-set P100s (their tops level with the top of the radiator), the stoneguard with distinctive diamond-shaped bracing, the ready-wired fog lamp bracket and so on. Prices were to be £610 for the chassis, £775

Over 70 years of opening and shutting the bonnet have taken their toll of this cutout that accommodates the steering box and drop arm, so a reinforcing piece has been added. The rod bolted to the underside of the chassis frame is part of the truss which strengthens this part of the low chassis frame.

The offside set of grease nipples show signs of over 70 years of wear.

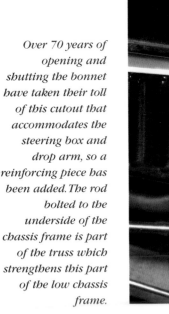

In this head-on view you can see how the deeper supercharged radiator extends below the stoneguard, designed for the normally aspirated car.

Magneto detail. Supercharged cars were originally fitted with a special one to aid starting, with a changeover switch to normal running.

Cuthbert sold PL 7016 to Leslie Hawthorn (Mike's father), who passed it on to Major J A Rycroft, shown here on the left at the July 1937 JCC Members Day at Brooklands. P100s produce formidable wind drag, hence the business of turning them up.

Weather equipment included six sidescreens, stored behind the back seat squab in dry weather. The originals were glazed with celluloid which eventually went yellow but modern plastics are better behaved.

The London to Edinburgh Trial, June 1930, with R S Latham-Boote in his high chassis Speed Model UV 4850 on the way to a Gold Medal. This is not the most direct route to Edinburgh.

shaped openings above the tiny doors. Also prominent is the outrageous 3 Litre coupé by Wylder (PG 1290) with its sketchy wings and giant Lalique glass mascot. A then famous comedian, Gillie Potter, did the public address commentary.

The fetes had been extremely popular and various other companies held similar festivities but suddenly at the end of 1930 the Brooklands authorities stopped them all without giving any reason. At this distance in

time it all looks rather dog-in-the-manger and it generated considerable ill-feeling then. C G Vokes, the filter manufacturer and lifelong Lagonda enthusiast, was so incensed that it led him to set up the original, factory-backed, Lagonda Car Club in 1933. Returning to 1930, the star of the day was W T Barnes, who won three events. Class A of the Appearance Contest was won by H (Mac) McCalman, then of Central Garage, Bradford, but later to be Lagonda's Sales Manager in the Bentley era. One of the novices making his first stab at racing was T A S O Mathieson.

On the same day, the Irish GP was held at Phoenix Park, and although a 3 Litre was entered by C E A Flewitt there is no record of him starting. The ending of the works team after the Double Twelve seems to have meant that the classic trials were temporarily shunned too, for the four Lagonda entries in the 1930 London-Edinburgh were all private owners. R S Latham-Boote, W H G Tom and W G Leslie all secured golds, while L E Goldsworthy failed Park Rash and had to be content with a silver. On the distaff side, Margaret Allan took her 2 Litre on WASA's London to the Lake District trial in July and finished, although outside the medals.

The Motor published their road test of the supercharged 2 Litre at the end of July and

As originally supplied the windscreen wiper motor would have been on the windscreen frame top edge, driving the left blade directly. To avoid endangering the passenger's head many cars have had it moved to a safer place.

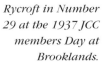

It is difficult to spot this on the car but it is the maker's name for the windscreen.

Rycroft in Number 29 at the 1937 JCC members Day at Brooklands.

The windscreen opens about hinges along the top edge. These stays hold it in the desired position against the wind pressure. Many blown tourers have a fold-flat screen.

A fold-down centre armrest for the rear seat was one of the improvements which came with the T2 body.

found the car quite transformed. I think they were expecting a rorty beast that had to be revved hard, but Cranmer and his team were conscious of the limitations of the crankshaft and had gone for torque and tractability, so that the standing start figures were all vastly improved. At this stage PL 1240 retained the Speed Model 4.4:1 axle, which helped the acceleration, but she was still able to reach 90mph in top without bursting anything. The actual figures were 0-50mph in 12.5 seconds, 0-70 in 22.6 seconds and 0-90 in 50 seconds. That last 20mph took a long time arriving, but it was there and these were exceptional

The "double diamond" only featured on the front door. The rear one contained useful storage.

The oval panel dashboard from the unblown car was carried over, with a boost gauge added.

figures for 1930 and for a car taxed as a "thirteen". The car was fitted with the close-ratio ZE set of gears and could manage 80mph in third, while at the opposite end of the scale some juggling with the ignition control permitted a snatch-free 5mph in top. The all-up weight was 28.75cwt (1460kg), not greatly

in excess of the Speed Model, which had been putting on middle-aged spread itself, and the 20mpg fuel consumption was excellent considering the hard driving associated with a road test. Somewhere between the fete and the road test the supercharger blow-off valve had been moved away from the casing

Vintage and near-Vintage hoods fold flat since they are not lined. Later lined hoods look messier when furled and can obstruct the all-round vision expected from an open car.

Lagonda were proud of their bodywork and fitted this plate to the doorsills.

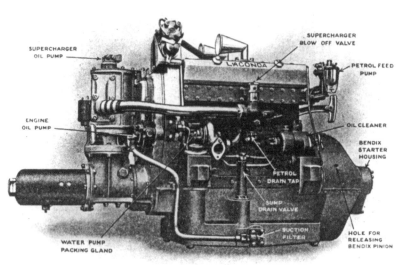

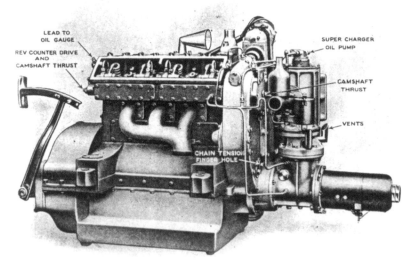

All low chassis cars have their dynamo dogged to the nose of the crankshaft. On supercharged ones it is even more prominent and the tubular chassis cross member was bent upwards to clear it.

Instruction Book photographs of the supercharged engine.

to a new position at the rear end of the inlet manifold, a bit further away from the sparks.

Undoubtedly orders were generated as a result of the eulogistic road test but there seem to have been no deliveries before September, and a number of changes took place in the interim. PL was then tested by *The Autocar* and was found to be faster still, largely as a result of fitting a 4.2:1 rear axle from the 3 Litre, which increased the track by 2 inches (51mm) and gave a flying half-mile speed of better than 88mph. Production cars began to appear, some with the Powerplus blower and others with a Cozette No. 9. These were made under licence by Gallays and blew at a lesser pressure, around 4-8psi. (0.27-0.55 bar). Recent experience suggests

the Cozette produced a better bottom end boost. The separate oil tank had disappeared and oil was now fed from the main supply to the blower's oil pump — a mixed blessing since 2 Litres are great sludge producers and it gets everywhere. Some trouble seems to have been experienced with crankcase ventilation and the perforated nuts on the rocker boxes were replaced with rather comic "ship's ventilators" pointing forwards. The exhaust valves grew thick sodium-cooled thick and, unseen inside the engine, bolt-on balance weights and wider big end journals had appeared on the crankshaft. The blown car's ability to hold 4500rpm in the intermediate gears was beginning to blow the corks that I mentioned earlier. A new oil pump increased the recommended pressure to 30psi (2.07 bar), and a special magneto was fitted which incorporated an induction coil for easy starting, with a change-over switch on the dashboard. This too was to prove a mixed blessing, since owners were inclined to forget to switch back to the "run" position and burn it out.

Once the public got their hands on the blown cars all sorts of atrocities were committed. The extra power output proved the OH gearbox to be marginal and the stronger Z gearbox from the 3 Litre was substituted. Owners' new-found delight in jackrabbit starts brought on the stronger heavy rear axle, already noted. Valve seats cracked, heads cracked, pistons seized; there were all sorts of troubles and the legend grew that the excess cost of the blown car was to cover a couple of replacement blowers in the first warranty period. Pistons with much heavier crowns were introduced, with wide ring gaps, and stronger connecting rods appeared. Basically the problems led back to hurried development, so that the early customers finished it off for the factory. Allied to this was the type of customer attracted to the "supercharged" label, who tended to be in the "boy racer" mould, rich enough not to be put off by high insurance costs. The car's handbook recommended a pint of oil (0.6 litres) to every 8-10 gallons (36-45 litres) of petrol, but modern experience suggests this is insufficient and may lead to seized blowers. Much of the trouble was just over-enthusiastic driving, perhaps coupled with the difficult changes in the Z gearbox, so that the less skilled went everywhere in third.

On the other hand, the balanced crankshaft was a great success, removing for the first time the tendency of 2 Litre cranks to wear the centre main journal eccentrically due to a "skipping rope" action developing, this effect being worse on the low chassis crank, which had thinner webs.

The factory at this point were faced with an identity problem. There were now five versions of the 2 Litre engine: the original 14/60, still available; the high chassis Speed Model; the low chassis standard; the low

chassis "cackhanded" and now the super-charged version. Although there were differences between them, a number of these were internal and not visible once the engine was assembled, so it was at last deemed to be a good idea to stamp on the engine some clue as to which version it was. 14/60 engines had always been stamped with complicated numbers that no-one can now decipher, and high chassis engines continued with an equally obscure system, but prefixed with an S. To illustrate how obscure this was, engine number 986 was stamped S2259/2/853 and engine number 1141 was marked S2259/5/853. In fact the problem had begun to appear earlier with the short-lived early low chassis engines, whose camshafts revolved in the same direction as the crank-shaft (as distinct from the normal

Recent photograph of a supercharged engine. An owner has fitted an SU fuel pump instead of the AC mechanical one originally fitted.

A different version of the supercharged 2 Litre engine with the carburettor on the other side, leading to a very much longer inlet tract snaking across from the offside.

2B is the code for the supercharged engine and this is the 1052nd 2 Litre engine.

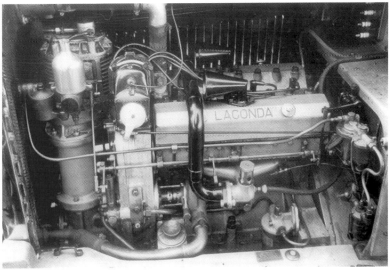

Cuthbert fitted this elaborate steam valve and it has been on the car ever since. For racing, a rubber tube connected it to a catch tank.

"widdershins" version). On these engines the prefix SL instead of S was followed by a simple number and all the other complicated strokes and other numbers vanished, so that the earliest "clockwise" engine that we have record of was SL900, indicating the 900th 2 litre engine since the first 14/60 and the clockwise camshafts. At this time the company was making and selling both high chassis and low chassis engines simultaneously, so engines with S and SL prefixes are all mixed up in production sequence. The blown engines were coded 2B (B for blown?) and although considerably different internally, would look much the same until the blower was attached. But the SL series had ended, so from the middle of 1930 we find 2B blown engines sharing the production line with normally aspirated low chassis engines coded OHL2. Initially the 2B engines were made in batches of 10 or 12 but as 2 Litre production tailed off they dwindled away to the odd one or two.

Lord de Clifford was keen to exploit the supercharged car's extra performance, and the car he drove, PL 2089, probably belonging to the factory, was soon figuring in the popular trials, usually accompanied by the regular gang of private owners: Hathaway, Gemmell, Latham-Boote and sometimes a new member, F H P Gardner. Nor must we ignore Margaret Allan, who competed in the big open trials as well as the WASA ones, which were confined to women. In the MCC High Speed Trial of October 1930 "Ted" de Clifford lapped Brooklands for an hour at an average of 82.04mph. His car was road tested by *Motor Sport*, who got a top speed of 92mph and a 0-60mph time of 18 seconds, very quick for the period. Unusually for a supercharged 2 Litre, PL had the long Speed Model wings and the monster sidelamps found on the 3 Litre Special. The car also scrubbed up well, for Lord de Clifford won his class in the Eastbourne "Concours" of September 1930. The new-found power also

Proof that racing improves the breed. The Le Mans cars broke their radiators through sitting directly on a cross member. The longer radiators for the supercharged cars were mounted on trunnions on each side, covered by these aluminium housings.

encouraged him to enter the Shelsley Walsh hillclimb in September, which for reasons of weight no 2 Litres had ever attempted, and PL 2089 appears again when he won a bronze in the MCC Sporting Trial at the end of October, as did Hathaway and Gemmell.

By the time of the Motor Show at Olympia the blown car was no longer news and the visible changes were concentrated on the 3 Litre and particularly its bodywork. Three 3 Litres were displayed on Stand 119, two Specials in black over white and a standard coachbuilt saloon in black. The 3 Litre chassis had acquired a similar tubular front cross-member to the 2 Litre one and this had allowed a deeper design of radiator, which now extended downwards, splitting to avoid the dynamo. As a result there were two bottom tanks with a drain tap in each. Having done this, the dumbiron shield got in the way of the cooling, so it was removed and the stoneguard extended also. There were no important changes to the engine but it did grow a trumpet-shaped ventilator on the front of the rocker cover. Changes to the bodywork only affected the Weymann saloon; they were subtle but unmistakable if one compares a 1930 and 1931 car side by side. One obvious difference was the adoption of a semi-panelled construction. There had been numerous complaints about the lower panels of fabric-covered Weymann saloons rotting, and to meet this the lower panels, up to the waistline, were now panelled in aluminium and cellulosed. Most other makers of Weymann bodies did the same at this time. It did mean, of course, that Monsieur Weymann's principles of flexibility began to be compromised, but one has to remember that only the major roads in rural areas were hard surfaced at this time and the amount of mud and stones kicked up by the wheels would mean the rot set in very quickly, certainly within the warranty period. The compromise became even worse the following year when Lagonda hit one of its

This overcentre clip fuel tank filler cap was introduced for the blown car to encourage owners to think of their car as "race ready". A similar one went on the radiator (although not on this car). Versions of this survived until 1940 on all subsequent models.

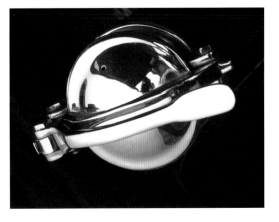

Black with red trim was an extremely popular colour combination in the 1930s.

The clip type radiator cap displaced the water temperature gauge and it reverted to the dashboard.

Lagonda at this period did not put red lines on their rev counters.

A speedometer reading to 100mph was less of an affectation on a 90-plus supercharged car.

The boost gauge on the extreme right of the dashboard was an additional instrument for the blown 2 Litre.

Supercharged 2 Litre saloon. Still a fabric Weymann body, but the boot was, at this time, unique to the blown car. The 1930 bodies had a more "one-piece" look compared to 1929. A side-mounted spare wheel was normal with this body style, fitted either to the left or right, to the owner's choice.

periodic cash shortages and in desperation substituted steel for the aluminium, steel being a great deal cheaper. The author has examined a semi-panelled Weymann saloon 3 Litre of undoubted authenticity on which only the bonnet sides, boot and bootlid were aluminium, the rest being steel. On the cars' identity plates a P was added to denote the semi-panelled version, the commonest being W24P, representing the four-light version of the second Weymann saloon, semi-panelled.

On these bodies the waistline became much more prominent now that it defined a change of material, and a 1½-inch wide waist moulding was introduced from the wind-screen to the rear edge of the rear doors, narrowing to half an inch around the rear of the car and along the bonnet. This strong horizontal line had a very noticeable effect on the profile of the car and the whole of the saloon part of the body was lowered so that this moulding could be horizontal from the shoulder of the radiator to the top of the boot. In addition, the doors were lengthened so that the valance between them and the running board disappeared once again. (It had re-appeared in 1930 with the low chassis saloons; high chassis saloons not having a valance.) Deeper side windows had the glass louvres over them surrounded by a plated frame. The bonnet boards, hitherto aluminium-faced timber, now became plain, thick, aluminium sheets and hence were less noticeable when cycle wings were fitted. The boot shape changed to have a roof-like top with a ridge on the centre line of the car, and the rear window above it changed from a single rectangle to two parallelograms, matching the boot section. The drop-down bootlid was strong enough to carry several cases and the extremely comprehensive toolkit was carried in a fitment inside the lid with sorbo rubber in place to stop rattles. Two scuttle ventilators met the complaints about hot feet, and the high-pressure area just

in front of the windscreen was exploited by fitting air intakes here in the underside of the roof peak, feeding cool air to the crew's faces. Most of these changes affected 2 Litre saloons, too, except that only the blown version had a boot.

Although the Show car was fitted with the Cozette blower, the Experimental department were testing the Zoller unit. Designed by a Swiss, Arnold Zoller, who lived in Berlin, it was manufactured in Britain by McEvoy in Derbyshire. The attraction of the Zoller was that it was made of simpler parts, whose lack of inertia gave a snappier response if the throttle was opened suddenly. Even more tellingly, McEvoy was prepared to let Lagonda

Late 1931 2 Litre and 3 Litre Weymann saloons adopted metal panelling to the lower half of the body, prone to rotting the fabric of earlier cars. The material change was concealed by a more prominent chromed waist rail. This is the rare 6-light version.

One of C G Vokes's earlier 3 Litres, a 1929 car, shown on a fishing expedition to Scotland. As it is sporting a Lagonda Car Club badge this picture must be 1933 or later. Note the enormous fishing rod strapped to the offside. With no doors on this side it isn't an obstacle.

make it themselves, paying him a royalty. As everyone at Staines had a healthy suspicion of everyone else's workmanship, this was a clincher. The Zoller blew at about 7psi boost (0.48 bar), a lot more than the Cozette, so was likely to bring on the overheating problems again. To go with it, a new Y-shaped inlet manifold was evolved with yet another blow-off valve arrangement, vertically upwards this time and thus allowing for the first time the fitting of a drain tap, for a reluctant-to-start blown 2 Litre was quite capable of filling its manifold with petrol. But the Zoller No 5 did not totally replace the Cozette and both types were available until the end of production.

There is no doubt that rapid wear could be a problem with these early superchargers. It is recorded that the blown MGs in the 1934 BRDC 500 Mile race started with a boost of 25psi (1.72 bar) and by the end of it were down to 10psi (0.7 bar), solely due to rapid wear. More oil or opening up the clearances just led to oiled plugs.

Lagonda had been spreading their wings a little further in the quest for sales and for the first time exhibited at the Scottish Motor Show in November 1930, on the stands of the Scottish Automobile Co. and Andrew Downie Ltd. Further south, Gaffikin Wilkinson was now the "Special London Agent" in contrast to Kensington-Moir and Straker, who were "Specially Appointed Lagonda Agents", different but equally obscure.

In contrast to its predecessor, 1930 had not

been a good year at Staines, but then it hadn't been a good year for anybody, with the Depression tightening its grip. The blown car was the only novelty but it was really only a minority interest. In the summer some publicity had been gained when it was agreed to transfer the warranty to a second owner, provided the car was newer than 1 September 1927 and was sent to the factory for assessment and rectification.

There were five Lagondas in the London-Gloucester Trial in early December, driven by Lord de Clifford, Margaret Allan, Mike Couper (in PL 1240), G W Gemmell and J H Baker. Miss Allan won the Ladies Cup in YW 6895 (OH 9126) and Lord de Clifford gained a silver to Couper's and Baker's bronzes.

The start of the London-Exeter Trial had been moved to Virginia Water, where there was more room than at the traditional Staines start point, and the event attracted six Lagondas. Of these Couper, Baker and de Clifford got golds, W Tom a silver and L Goldsworthy and G Randall bronzes. The blown cars of Couper and de Clifford were noted for their noisy exhausts and blower whine, and on the timed ascent of Black Hill only Aldington's Frazer Nash could out-accelerate Couper, still driving PL 1240.

A month later Lord de Clifford had another go at the Monte Carlo Rally in PL 2089, starting from Stavanger, surviving a big crash in Norway on ice and coming fourth in the general classification. This was his and Lagonda's best performance in this event. In his book on the rally Humphry Symons was full of admiration for his lordship's ability to average speeds of 40mph over roads so slippery that it was nigh impossible to stand up on them when out of the car. After a good wash, the car then went on to win the "Open cars over 1100cc"class in the *Confort* competition. Also competing was Conrad Mann in another blown 2 Litre, GK 3466 (OH 9741). He started from Glasgow, which carried lower marks, and came 34th overall but second to de Clifford in the *Confort* part. However, he excelled in the Mont des Mules hillclimb, winning his class and also winning the Condamine Cup for the best performance in the braking and acceleration tests on the promenade. This was the year Donald Healey won outright in an Invicta.

A stainless steel exhaust system is a sensible modern replacement.

2 LITRE SUPERCHARGED SUMMARY STATISTICS
As Low Chassis Speed Model except

Compression ratio	5.4:1	Water capacity	4 gallons/18.2 litres (short radiator)
Crankshaft	Counterbalanced and has wider journals		5 gallons/22.7 litres (long radiator)
Valve timing	io 9° BTDC, ic 47° ABDC,	Rear track	4ft 8in (1422mm)
	inlet open 236°	Fuel capacity	20 gallons (91 litres)
	eo 50° BBDC, ec 6°	Kerb weight	Chassis 24cwt (1219kg)
	ATDC, exhaust open 236°		Tourer 28.5cwt (1448kg)
	1938 version io ½° ATDC,		Saloon 30.75cwt (1562kg)
	ic 52° ABDC, inlet open 231°	Gear ratios	4.1:1, 5.154:1, 8.052:1, 12.886:1 (ZE set)
	eo 55° BBDC, ec 18° ATDC,		
	exhaust open 253°		
Brake horsepower	110 at 5000rpm	**Prices (1931)**	
Ignition	Impulse starter magneto ML ER4	Chassis £610	
Ignition timing	44° BTDC fully advanced	Tourer £775	
Sparking plugs	Champion L10S	Saloon £875	

Chapter Eight

The Selector

By mid-1931 low chassis 2 Litre saloons were designated W2, standing for the second design of Weymann. This car has one of the "cack-handed" engines although it is doubtful if it did originally.

The Lands End Trial of 1931 attracted eight Lagondas out of 271 cars. For the first time, Porlock was omitted but three new hills were added and one of these, Hustyn, failed no less than 98 contestants. Of the Lagondas only G W Gemmell got a gold. Hathaway and Baker gained silvers and Tom and E J Boyd bronzes, but Boyd appealed and was eventually upgraded to gold. T C Mann, C H Mann and D M Reid retired.

Unexpected publicity came from the Sunbeam MCC's second "Pioneer Run" from Tattenham Corner, when George Burtenshaw entered his Lagonda tricar LN 3252. This was alleged to be a 1904 machine but the wheel steering, water cooling and other details suggest it was actually built in 1907. In 1931 "old crocks" were regarded as hysterically funny and very few took them seriously. But Burtenshaw's machine was authentic enough to carry the vast acetylene headlamp beloved of the Edwardian tricarist, even though it also had gimmicky attachments aimed at publicising his business.

Preparations were now in hand for the Double Twelve, which, as related above, was a rather muted affair after the 1930 disaster and was run the other way round the track. There was to be a system of qualifying for inexperienced drivers, which was run off during the previous week, and since all the drivers knew they were on trial they drove like vicars and lap speeds were very Edwardian. Mike Couper had entered a blown 2 Litre but had by March 1931 left Lagondas and joined Tim Birkin in Welwyn Garden City running Birkin & Couper Ltd, who tuned sports cars and made the Blower Bentley, much to W O's annoyance. Couper's Lagonda, carrying race number 14, was the only entrant in its class in a race dominated by the "tiddlers", there being 24 entrants in the 750cc class and 28 other entrants in all the other classes put together.

The identity of Couper's car has been lost, although it might have been OH 9891, whose ID plate says "2B.COMP". It looked almost exactly the same as the 1930 cars except for

Early 3 Litre Selector Special. The body is a semi-panelled Weymann with a boot and helmet front wings that do not turn with the steering, enabling the sidelamps to be mounted on them.

the longer bonnet needed to accept the supercharger. The race started at 8am in mist and rain, a typical May morning, and Couper, distinctive in a green crash helmet, was lying sixth at the beginning, the Lagonda making a lot of noise but not running properly. But it gradually improved and wasn't doing too badly at the end of Friday's racing. Saturday was fine and warm and Couper was away within 40 seconds of the starting maroon. A lot of the opposition were starting on fairly serious rebuilds, apart from the little MGs, which were running like clockwork toys. Just after noon the Lagonda broke a valve, which chipped a lump from No. 4 piston and called for a long pit stop, during which the spare cylinder head was fitted. Couper restarted, after permission had been obtained to use the starting handle, but now the supercharger began to play up and had to be changed, causing more delay. Eventually the car expired on the track and had to be pushed a long way to the pits. When time ran out the Lagonda was technically still running but was excluded for being outside the required distance, having completed only 568 laps (1462 miles). The winning MG only did 601 laps but the race was on handicap and MGs took the first five places.

This was the last appearance of the 2 Litre in first-class long distance racing and apart from the efforts of private owners, the competition activities of Lagonda reverted to rallies

and trials until the 4½ Litre came along in 1933. Works participation had stopped in 1930 and there really wasn't enough money in the kitty to support a racing team. In fact the only part of the firm to make any money in 1930/1 was the social club, which ran a company shop selling sweets and cigarettes and the like. It also surreptitiously ran a bookmaking business that management knew nothing about. This was sufficiently profitable to finance the outing of the entire factory to Ostend, an event so beset by alcohol it is best forgotten.

The London-Edinburgh Trial of 22/23 May was as popular as ever, and of the 171 entries eight were Lagondas, all privately owned. E J

The T2 tourer body quickly found its way on to the unblown 2 Litre tourers. This car is from March 1931.

Boyd did best, gaining a gold and also the special triple award which went to anyone scoring gold in the MCC's three main trials, the Exeter, the Land's End and the Edinburgh. Of the other Lagonda drivers, C H Mann and H C Hobson both failed Park Rash to win silvers; W H G Tom, R Lester-Williams and J S Hathaway finished outside the medals and C H Fish and L E Goldsworthy retired. All these people were driving 2 Litres, Lester-Williams's one being supercharged. By contrast, the MCC's Land's End to John O'Groats trial had deteriorated into a touring holiday with minimal competitive element and the 1931 event only attracted 30 entries, three of them Lagondas, which all gained premier awards - but so did all but five entrants. The Lagonda people were T C Mann, R Latham-Boote and W H G Tom.

On 1 June 1931 the company revised its guarantee arrangements from a possible five two-year periods to three three-year ones, with the same proviso about repairs at the end of each period as before. Not many customers kept their car that long and the crippling depreciation of the 1930s meant that the possible bill at the end of each warranty period was likely to exceed the value of the car. The company made surprisingly little of these generous guarantees in advertising. In contrast "All British" and "Buy British" featured prominently, as it was continually necessary to explain that Lagondas did not originate in Venice.

Mike Couper had a busy summer in his Double Twelve car, entering it in several small club and inter-club events at Brooklands but without any noteworthy success, probably following the handicappers' perpetual suspicion of supercharged cars. In June Margaret Allan won a premier award in the Brighton-Beer rally, with T C Mann also entered. In September the Brighton and Hove MC high speed trial at Brooklands saw the reappearance of a 1929 team 2 Litre, PK 9203, in the hands of Major G D Pillitz, winning a first class award.

At most times in the development of the motor car there has been some particular aspect of design on which rival firms have been concentrating particularly, whether as a result of customer complaints, in an effort to reduce costs or just to steal a march on the opposition. In the first years of the 1930s it was easy gear-changing that brought the heavy mailbags to motoring journals and produced the droves of patent applications for systems of varying degrees of complexity or nuttiness. General Motors in America had fitted synchromesh to their Cadillac in 1929 and this system, which was cheap, effective and could be fitted to existing gearboxes with merely a redesign, was gaining ground in the USA very rapidly, but much more slowly in Europe. This is not to say that no one was working on it -- far from it.

At Lagonda there was a persistent feeling that the 3 Litre didn't sell as well as it should, and various theories were floated as to why this should be. With hindsight, all that appears to have been wrong was the price differential between it and the 2 Litre. For over £200 more than the smaller car, the 3 Litre buyer got increased running costs but precious little extra room and not a great deal more performance. Admittedly the 3 Litre was a more relaxed car to drive and those wary of changing gear could do most of a day's drive in top, for the ignition timing control was very effective if used properly. The gear change on the Z 'box was a tricky one, though, and needed learning. Thus it is no surprise that Alfie Cranmer began experimenting with alternative types of gearbox which might be easier for the non-expert driver.

The one that he fixed on was Maybach's *Doppelschnellgang* (dual overdrive), which that firm had introduced for its vast 7-litre V12 DS7 "Zeppelin" car in 1930. The engine alone of the DS7 weighed half a ton and the rest of the vehicle was in proportion, including the gearbox, which was about the size and weight of an 11.9 engine. Lagondas always tended to the weighty in their components. The Maybach 'box had two sets of four ratios, rather as in a Land-Rover, but the transfer arrangements from high to low ratio were incorporated inside the gearbox instead of being a separate unit, and it was intended that the driver should use all of the gears, or most of them, in normal driving. Thus the spread of ratios was nowhere near as wide as in an off-road vehicle, ranging in the Lagonda's case from 3.66:1 (high ratio top) to 16.5:1 (low ratio first). In keeping with the gearbox's origins in such a huge vehicle the

Lagonda's page in the instruction book for the Selector probably left the average owner little the wiser. The various types of dotted line indicated the power train in each of the gears.

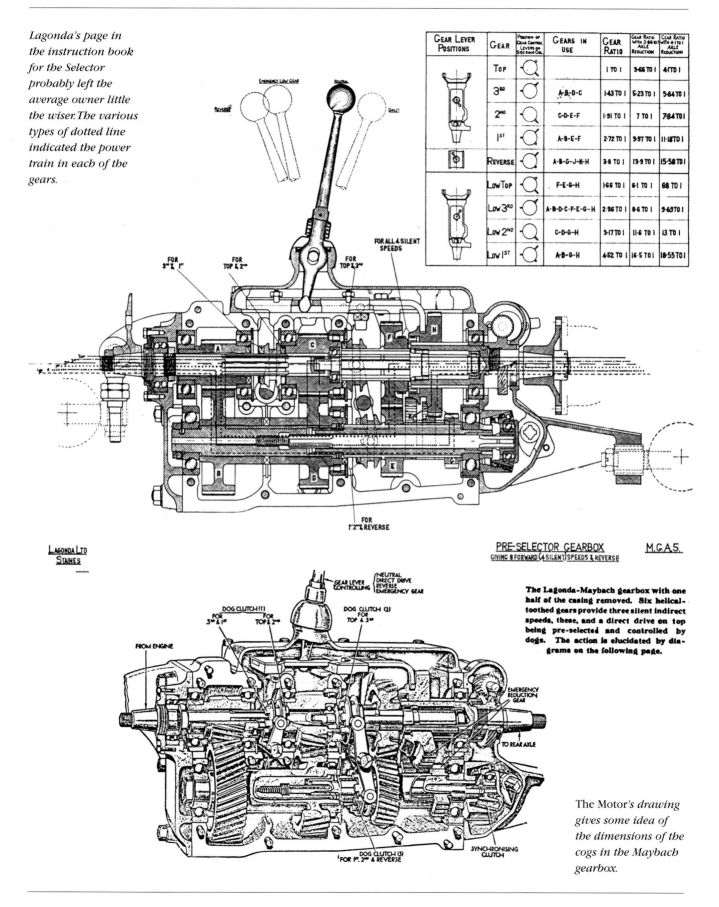

GEAR LEVER POSITIONS	GEAR	POSITION OF GEAR CONTROL LEVERS ON STEERING COL.	GEARS IN USE	GEAR RATIO	GEAR RATIO WITH 3·66 TO 1 AXLE REDUCTION	GEAR RATIO WITH 4·1 TO 1 AXLE REDUCTION
	TOP			1 TO 1	3·66 TO 1	4·1 TO 1
	3RD		A·B·D·C	1·43 TO 1	5·23 TO 1	5·84 TO 1
	2ND		C·D·E·F	1·91 TO 1	7 TO 1	7·84 TO 1
	1ST		A·B·E·F	2·72 TO 1	9·97 TO 1	11·18 TO 1
	REVERSE		A·B·G·J·K·H	3·8 TO 1	13·9 TO 1	15·58 TO 1
	LOW TOP		F·E·G·H	1·66 TO 1	6·1 TO 1	6·8 TO 1
	LOW 3RD		A·B·D·C·F·E·G·H	2·96 TO 1	8·6 TO 1	9·69 TO 1
	LOW 2ND		C·D·G·H	3·17 TO 1	11·6 TO 1	13 TO 1
	LOW 1ST		A·B·G·H	4·52 TO 1	16·5 TO 1	18·55 TO 1

EMERGENCY LOW GEAR

REVERSE

NEUTRAL

CLUTCH

FOR 3RD & 1ST

FOR TOP & 2ND

FOR TOP & 3RD

FOR ALL 4 SILENT SPEEDS

FOR 1ST, 2ND & REVERSE

LAGONDA LTD STAINES

PRE-SELECTOR GEARBOX   M.G.A.5.
GIVING 8 FORWARD (4 SILENT) SPEEDS & REVERSE

GEAR LEVER CONTROLLING

NEUTRAL DIRECT DRIVE REVERSE EMERGENCY GEAR

FROM ENGINE

DOG CLUTCH (1) FOR 3RD & 1ST

FOR TOP & 2ND

DOG CLUTCH (2) FOR TOP & 3RD

EMERGENCY REDUCTION GEAR

TO REAR AXLE

DOG CLUTCH (3) FOR 1ST, 2ND & REVERSE

SYNCHRONISING CLUTCH

The Lagonda-Maybach gearbox with one half of the casing removed. Six helical-toothed gears provide three silent indirect speeds, these, and a direct drive on top being pre-selected and controlled by dogs. The action is elucidated by diagrams on the following page.

The Motor's drawing gives some idea of the dimensions of the cogs in the Maybach gearbox.

Cockpit of a Selector Special tourer. The two levers on the right of the steering wheel boss change the gears once the driver lifts off the accelerator. Later cars had a little diagram on the dashboard as a crib to where the gears were to be found.

cogs themselves were of the proportions normally only encountered in watermills, and nearly every one had a bearing on both sides of it, there being no less than 13 ball and roller races in the whole 'box. The method of operation was complicated and ingenious. The basic layout was of a constant-mesh, three-shaft design, but the layshaft was split in the middle and the two halves could run independently or be dogged together. Each half carried two gear wheels, the front pair and one of the rear ones being constant-mesh gears. There were two gears running on the input side of the mainshaft and either could be dogged to the shaft. Similarly, the ouput half of the mainshaft could be split into two parts or both could be dogged together. The dog clutches that locked together the necessary gears and shafts to enable the gearbox to work were made with tapered teeth to give some of the effect of over-running clutches and worked in pairs, connected by a rocking lever so that one or the other would go into engagement easily. To assist this process a conical brake, rather like a big synchromesh cone, was fitted to the rear end of the layshaft and operated by a cam connected to the gear selector. The actual process of changing gear, apart from starting from rest, did not require use of the clutch. Instead the act of releasing the throttle pedal produced a surge of

vacuum (if you see what I mean) in three large vacuum cylinders and these did the actual changing.

The prospective driver of a car equipped with the Maybach gearbox was confronted with a normal clutch pedal for getting away from rest, a normal-looking gear lever in the centre of the floor which was used to select high or low ratio, plus neutral and reverse, and a pair of small concentric levers on the right of the steering wheel boss labelled, rather obscurely, 1334 in the 2 o'clock position and 4221 at about 5 o'clock. One lever was longer than the other, for ease of use. Assuming for the moment only the high ratios, one selected high ratio with the floor lever, depressed the clutch and placed the longer steering wheel boss lever in the upper position, the shorter lever in the lower position and moved off as normal. To change to second gear, the longer lever was moved to join its brother (hence the 22 marking). Nothing happened until the throttle pedal was released, when the vacuum servos were able to change the gear once the loads had come off the dog clutch teeth. There was a synchronising cone clutch mounted on the layshaft to permit the re-engagement. For third gear, both levers moved to the top position and for top the longer lever moved down, leaving the shorter one at 2 o'clock. These steering column levers worked Arens cable controls that opened and shut valves to feed manifold depression to wherever it was required. The whole setup was amazingly complicated and the monstrous gearbox, designed to cope with the Maybach car's 100bhp, was enmeshed in a maze of pipes, servo cylinders, cables and rods. To use the low ratios, the driver first changed to them with the floor lever and then the procedure was the same, with the difference that the four high ratios were constant mesh and silent, while the low ones were sliding mesh and anything but silent, the worst offender being low third which involved all five shafts and eight cogs, all revolving at different speeds. No one but a demonstrator would use all eight speeds, of course, and in effect the Selector was a five-speed car. Most owners would start in low first, change to high first with the floor lever and then operate the four high ratios. An amusing side effect of the design was that selecting reverse with the floor lever still allowed all four preselected gears. Nothing was said about this officially, but the fellows in Experimental soon discovered it and so did journalists on road test. H S Linfield of *The Autocar* got up to high-ratio third in reverse down the Finishing Straight at Brooklands, something like 60mph, but not a word of this appeared in the road test.

Once development of the car began, various troubles appeared. The principal one was that the massive weight of the new gearbox cracked the chassis frame at its weak point just behind the clutch. Additional triangulating stiffening flanges were tried but these resulted in two cracks instead of one. Also, the extra weight began to show up shortcomings with the brakes, still the 2 Litre design. Finally Alfie Cranmer grasped the nettle and designed a completely new chassis for the Selector model. At this time the word "preselector" was used widely for any design with this feature. It was only later that it came to be confined to epicyclic 'boxes such as the Wilson type.

The new frame had side members deeper in section and much straighter in plan view. They were parallel from dumbiron to clutch and then diverged at a slight angle to each other without ever returning to the parallel. The front dumbirons were not connected, but a tubular cross-member a foot or so back picked up the damper loads. The weight of the Maybach gearbox was taken by two massive curved tubular cross-members of 4-inch (100mm) diameter. The front of it was suspended by a yoke from two adjustable mountings on the first tube, and the rear by a single point, also adjustable but in a different plane, attached to the second tube. Three more cross-tubes connected the rear spring mounting points and carried the 20-gallon (91-litre) fuel tank. The rearmost tube came in for redesign very soon and was braced by a little triangular truss. As well as a new frame, new axles and more powerful brakes were featured. The deeply dropped low chassis front axle had caused some problems with

F Gordon Crosby's drawing for The Autocar *of the 3 Litre Selector chassis. He had to cut away part of the chassis side-member to show the complicated pipework. What looks like a central gearlever only selects high or low ratio, plus neutral and reverse. Small levers on the steering column did the gear changing.*

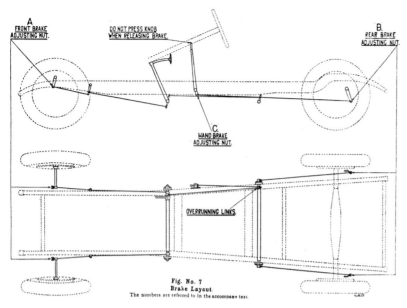

A
FRONT BRAKE
ADJUSTING NUT.

DO NOT PRESS KNOB
WHEN RELEASING BRAKE.

B
REAR BRAKE
ADJUSTING NUT.

C.
HAND BRAKE
ADJUSTING NUT.

OVERRUNNING LINKS.

Fig. No. 7
Brake Layout.
The numbers are referred to in the accompany text.

Having established that in practice compensation between brake shoes was unnecessary, provided the setting-up was done properly, the ZM chassis design had none.

tramp if the brake drums wore eccentrically and the new design passed over the spring instead of underneath, achieving clearance under the dynamo by inserting three short straights at obtuse angles. A new rear axle looked like the earlier Z axle but had the conical tapered arms of the banjo extended right out to the spring anchorages. Ball races rather than rollers carried the inner ends of the half-shafts and the whole thing was, if anything, even sturdier than its predecessor. More attention was paid to keeping the brake backplates square to the axle and stiffening ribs appeared for this purpose. The extra gear ratios in the new gearbox permitted a new higher axle ratio of 3.66:1 (12 x 44).

The new braking system was a complete reversal of the 1925 design, which had had compensation in every conceivable direction. Subsequent modifications had reduced this as people grew less afraid of four-wheel braking. The new layout had no compensation anywhere and was as simple as possible. There were two cross-shafts mounted on self-aligning bearings, carried on substantial trunnions. The front cross-shaft worked the front brakes via rods and had the pedal mounted on it. Similarly, the rear cross-shaft worked the rear brakes via rods and a further rod connected both cross-shafts, with a second parallel one working the handbrake, fitted with a slot that allowed, in theory, only the rear brakes to be actuated by the handbrake lever while the footbrake applied all

four without moving the lever.

The brake drum size was increased to 16 inches (406mm) and chromidium cast iron was used instead of pressed steel. Four circumferential ribs were cast on the outside to aid cooling. At the rear, only a single pair of shoes was now used in each drum and a novel means of transmitting the braking effort from the lever to the shoes was employed at both axles. Instead of a cam bearing directly on the ends of the brake shoes and thus sliding on their faces, a pair of "diabolo-shaped" toggles were interposed, working in circular housings in both cam and shoe; thus the motion involved was circular, producing less friction and wear. At the front, the Rubery system was replaced by the Perrot pattern, with the Perrot shafts above the axle, their inner ends being mounted on the top of the chassis frame just in front of the radiator mountings. The front backplates were aluminium castings, as indeed were the rears, and were extended beyond the brake drum over nearly half their circumference to provide a firm anchorage for the cycle wings. At the outset, not much attention was paid to water exclusion and the first few chassis proved nearly unstoppable in the wet, so a labyrinth was added which cured the problem.

The new chassis had no little rows of grease nipples, because Lagonda had adopted Silent-bloc rubber bushes with relish and applied them to all suspension joints as well as supporting the engine, radiator and gearbox. At the rear, the compliance inherent in Silent-blocs was vital, since the rear springs diverged at the same angle as the chassis frame side members; if the mountings for the shackles had been totally rigid, in theory no movement at all is possible, although the constraint is very small. There must have been problems with the rubber bushes too, for the firm went back to lubricated joints after a couple of years. The sheer size of the Maybach gearbox and its associated impedimenta allowed only just enough room for the starter motor and none for the battery, so this was banished to either side of the propeller shaft under the back seats and one twelve-volt gave way to two sixes.

The new chassis was called the "M" chassis, presumably for Maybach, and the code on the identity plate became ZM. Development continued through 1931 prior to the October announcement. It was soon found that although downward changes were very quick, upward ones could be very leisurely as all those huge cogs took their time about engaging. It was even worse when the gearbox was cold. So the normal Lagonda clutch stop was re-introduced, reducing the time taken for an upward change by 8 seconds. This was a huge improvement, as you can judge with a stopwatch by timing 8 seconds, but of course it rather made a nonsense of the clutchless idea. But at least there were no more of those grarking noises.

Lagonda normally revealed their new programme in September, but for 1931 the announcement was delayed until October, just before the Motor Show. The Selector took all the attention, of course, being referred to as a "12-speed Lagonda" in various places, which may have confused the public even more than they might otherwise have been. PJ 463 was the press car and featured a special new tourer body, the T3, which had an extended tail incorporating a boot with a drop-down lid. The tools now lived in a wooden tray built into the bootlid, with a sorbo rubber layer to quell rattles. The rest of the body was unchanged from the T2 and the extension looked rather ungainly. With the hood up it looked gormless and Lagonda were careful never to erect the hood when photographers were about. This body was also offered on the supercharged 2 Litre, but not on the normal Speed Model. The advent of the boot displaced the spare wheel to a sidemount, normally on the nearside, but a second offside one was an option. At the other end of the car a new radiator design with a new badge distinguished the Selector from the other models. For the first time the radiator had a separate shell, chromium plated(another first), and was deeper in section front to rear and generally more rounded, except for parallel vertical sides. It also marked a change of core, the original honeycomb design being replaced by the newly available film type, which increased the throughput of water as well as being easier to make. A slightly revised design of clip-type filler was now turned through 90° so that its operating bar was longitudinal. The

new badge, which was to last until 1940, featured a stylised headless eagle in copper around a blue enamel panel with "Lagonda" set in it. The stoneguard, as on the earlier cars, moved up close to the radiator core, but after a short time disappeared altogether as thermostatically operated vertical shutters came to be fitted. These overcame any tendency to overcooling during the warm-up stage, which could be lengthy with all those gallons of water. Actually, chromium-plated radiators had crept in unannounced in the middle of 1931 on the earlier pattern, but while dealers would emphasise the benefits of chromium plate, the factory never remarked on it.

A host of small changes came in with the M chassis, but true to tradition PJ 463 didn't have half of them. Headlamp dipping regulations had been announced in 1931, to come into effect in October 1932, so Lagonda's system changed and now on pressing the dipswitch button the offside headlamp went out and the nearside one dipped, having a moveable reflector built into it. The charging system changed to constant voltage, using a two-brush dynamo which meant the end of the summer/winter charge switch. An Autoklean oil filter was added to the lubrication system. This filtered the oil through the edges of a multitude of parallel discs mounted on a common axis and was cleaned by the rotation, controlled by the throttle pedal, of a further set of discs between the fixed ones. The Autoklean was fixed just in front of the clutch and it displaced the suction filter further forward.

A revised oil breather took the form of a long ½in diameter pipe from the crankcase right down to the back of the car, where it puzzled small boys by appearing to be a second, smaller, exhaust pipe. The vacuum offtake needed by the Maybach gearbox was taken from the rear of the cylinder head, where the 3 Litre's integral manifold lurked. Access to the camshaft was improved by reverting to three large cover plates and coil ignition replaced magneto, although the vast majority of surviving 3 Litres of this era have been converted back to magneto.

Although the steering gear looked much the same as before, it was in fact by Cam Gears of Luton, using the Bishop design. As the gear-

C G Vokes was an important link between the Lagonda factory and the owners. He amassed quite a fleet of Lagondas and used them as mobile test beds for his filter business. This is the engine of one of his 3 Litres, fitted with the world's largest oil filter and a non-standard rocker cover breather. It also had air filters, removed in the photograph.

changing levers were on the steering wheel boss of the Selector, this was enlarged so that it could also accommodate the advance/retard lever and the dipswitch. There was no room for the hand throttle as well, so this migrated to the dashboard. The windscreen wiper motor also got moved from its position at the top of the windscreen, where it imperilled the passenger's head in an emergency stop, to outside on the bonnet top, where its messy appearance with no proper housing spoilt the appearance of that part of the car. On the saloon version of the Selector a new front wing design, the "helmet" type, made its debut. This was a more civilised version of the cycle wing, much deeper and more rounded in section and not turning with the steering, so not contributing to unsprung weight. On top of the helmet wings Lucas's new type 1130 "snail" sidelamps replaced the traditional Lagonda stalks growing out of the scuttle. To go with the helmet wings, the running boards were extended forwards and fitted with turned-up ends, like monster skis. The helmet wings were made from two halves, welded together on a joint not quite at the peak, so that flatting prior to painting didn't weaken the weld. They went a long way towards remedying the narrow-chested look of a saloon with cycle wings, which latter were still available as a £10 optional extra over Speed Model wings. It is ironic that the M-type front axle was the first one designed from the outset to accommodate

cycle wings properly, and was introduced just as cycle wings began to go out of fashion.

Lagonda occupied Stand 152 at Olympia and coupled the introduction of the new Selector and Selector Special models with reduced prices for many of the older models. It needs a table to explain: 1932 prices first, with 1931 equivalents in parentheses.

2 Litre Speed Model

chassis	£430 (£555)
tourer (T2)	£595 (£720)
Weymann saloon	£695 (£820 + £25 for semi-panelled)

2 Litre Supercharged

chassis	£610 (£610)
tourer (T3)	£775 (£775
Weymann saloon	£875 (£875 + £25 for semi-panelled)

3 Litre Special

chassis	£752 (£835)
tourer (T3)	£900 (£1000)
Weymann saloon	£990 £1100)

3 Litre Selector

chassis	£827
Weymann	£1065 (panelled)
tourer (T3)	£975
11ft 6in chassis	£827
limousine	£1120

3 Litre Selector Special

chassis	£827
tourer (T3)	£975
Weymann saloon	£1065 (panelled)

There was a further economy measure in that for the 2 Litres, only black, maroon or green bodies were available at the quoted price. Other colours were £10 extra. There was now no extra charge for safety glass, as this was to be mandatory from 1st January 1932.

The difference between the Selector and the Selector Special has now become lost and cannot have been much for them to sell at the same price. The author suspects that it was basically the position of the engine, with the Special using the more rearward position. It certainly had smaller section tyres, 5.25 to the other version's 6.00.

The Motor managed to borrow PJ 463 for a brief road test on the day the Selector was announced and reported on the new gearbox

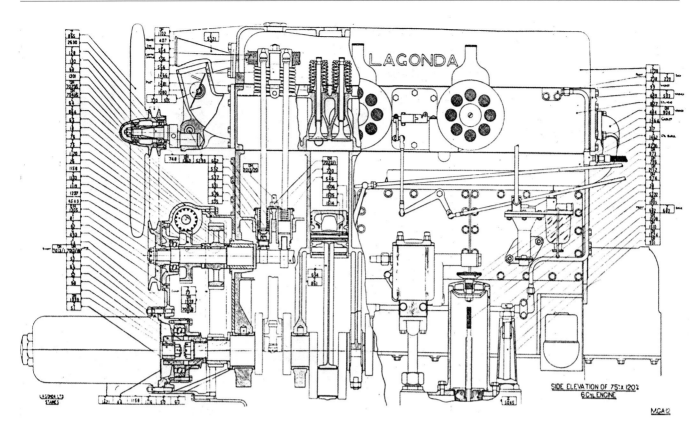

with enthusiasm. One of its major attractions was that if a novice made a complete hash of it no harm would result; the gears would refuse to engage and the car would gently come to rest without damage. The published performance figures were extremely good, so much so that one wonders if PJ had something non-standard in the engine department. Standstill to 60mph in high ratio took 20.8 seconds, slightly more if a fifth gear was employed. Top speed was 82mph. The acceleration figures are equal to or better than the same magazine's results for the blown 2 Litre tourer. Lagonda undoubtedly did tune their demonstrators and apparently never suffered from irate owners complaining that their car wouldn't match published figures.

A more direct comparison became possible in December when *The Autocar* published a road test of PJ 729 (Z9991). This was a panelled Weymann saloon with the helmet wings. In April 1930 they had tested PG 5999, a fabric 3 Litre Weymann of the then current pattern, and comparing the two tests is illuminating. Almost all the acceleration times are, within a second, the same. The exception was a result of the Z gearbox's high third, which

gave a 10-30mph time of 11 seconds, whereas the Maybach's more evenly spaced ratios allowed the Selector to do this increment in 9.2 seconds. Top speed of the 1930 car was 75.3mph to the 1931 car's 73.2mph, and fuel consumption of both was 20mpg. The Selector was 3½cwt (190kg) heavier and also higher geared in top, so that these two factors tended to balance each other. The braking distance had improved and the turning circle, still stately at 43ft (13.1m), was better than the previous 47ft (14.3m). The change to helmet wings probably explained this, since they didn't hamper the full lock position so much as cycle wings. *The Autocar* liked the Maybach gearbox too, but didn't remark on the two features that modern experience reveals. One, that the speed of change varies with the temperature of the oil in the gearbox (and this large piece of engineering takes a very long time to warm up). Two, and more important, there is an unwanted and sometimes disconcerting upward change if the driver has to lift off after he has preselected a higher gear.

The fact that the new, more expensive model was no quicker than its predecessor

Longitudinal section of the 75mm 3 Litre engine, introduced in the search for more power to counteract the Selector's weight. A mechanical fuel pump is shown but many owners have changed to electric ones for easier starting with a car that stands idle for substantial periods.

Lord de Clifford's car in the 1932 Monte Carlo Rally. It was a Selector Special with the T3 body. With the hood up the T3 would win no prizes for beauty, but it did win its class in the confort competition.

a supercharged 2 Litre saloon, PJ 378, and found it very nearly as fast as the open version while actually using slightly less fuel. Reading between the lines, the writer of the test was clearly upset by the rather ludicrous acceleration times he was asked to measure, which gave no true idea of the sparkling performance of the car. The magazine's standard procedure was to measure times for accelerating from 10 to 30mph in each gear. So for the blown 2 Litre saloon we find times of 5.2 seconds for first gear, followed by 7.0, 12.8 and 17.2 seconds respectively for the other gears, measured over the same increment of speed. One feels that the procedure had been laid down in horseless carriage days when gear changing was avoided like the plague. It certainly gave no indication of the performance a reasonable use of the gearbox would achieve. One new feature of the saloon was a boost gauge on the dashboard, not found on the earlier tourer road test and useful to check how well the blower was working.

Only one Lagonda, that of J F Falconer, was entered in the 1931 London-Exeter Trial, which was run on a shortened course and ended at Shaftesbury. Falconer had fitted a close-ratio gearbox, whose high first gear defeated his efforts on four hills, and he only

led to the next development, which was to bore out the engine to 75mm, increasing the capacity to 3181cc. This slight boost in power was enough to balance the extra weight and keep the 1932 model at least the equal of the earlier cars. This change came in January 1932. The 75mm engine is actually slightly taller than the 72mm version and uses longer pushrods, so there must have been other changes.

In November 1931 *The Autocar* road tested

The same car in the 1932 RAC Rally and showing evidence of contact with a hard object on the offside front wing. Lord de Clifford is on the right with his crew watching. This early version of the Selector radiator has not yet acquired the vertical slats that aid warming up.

gained a bronze medal. Lord de Clifford had contested the London-Gloucester Trial on 12 December (the result has been lost) but had then set sail for Umeå in Sweden, his chosen start point for the Monte Carlo Rally. Donald Healey, the 1931 winner, had started from there and this start attracted very good marks. De Clifford took a 3 Litre tourer, PJ 1867, fitted with the T3 body and Speed Model wings. In the interests of acceleration it was also fitted with a 4.7:1 rear axle, the 75mm engine and a manual gearbox. His navigator was H B Browning. After the traditional adventurous journey he came 20th overall and won a prize for best open car over 1500 cc in the *Confort* competition. The other Lagonda entrant was T C Mann in his blown 2 Litre, GK 3466, starting from London and finishing 37th overall. Mann's forté was the Mont des Mules hillclimb, where he won the 2 litre class in 3min 33.6sec, a new class record. It has to be admitted that the absence of any handicap on supercharged cars was of considerable assistance. In the same hillclimb Lord de Clifford came fifth in the 5 litre class with a time of 3min 46.4sec. It was won by Donald Healey in 3min 14.8sec.

As a piece of light relief, in January 1932 Sir Dennistoun Burney, in the process of trying to launch his rather weird Burney Streamline, announced that he had "practically completed negotiations to take over the Lagonda company, whose supercharged 2 Litre engine was giving 110bhp at 5000rpm on the test bench and was well suited to the rear-engined Burney". The only trouble with that was that no-one at Staines was aware of any impending takeover.

The RAC Rally was held at the beginning of March and no less than 18 Lagondas entered. The event was a trifle more onerous than some of its British rival rallies but still had little competitive element on the road section. All the various starting points converged on Torquay, where the eliminating tests were held. For the 1932 event a car that would proceed very slowly in top gear was essential. The only Lagonda to feature in the prizes was the 3 Litre tourer of Lady de Clifford, PG6711 (Z 9630). Between completing the road section and the tests Lady de Clifford was taken ill and her navigator, Charlotte Naish, could not or was not allowed to drive, so a substitute driver, Paddy Naismith, took over for the tests. In the main event, the best placed Lagonda was the 3 Litre saloon of E A Morris, who came 20th, just pipping Lord de Clifford, who was 21st.

3 LITRE (75mm bore) SUMMARY STATISTICS

Engine

As 73mm except

Capacity	3181cc
Bore & stroke	75 x 120mm
RAC rating	20.94hp
Compression ratio	6.43:1
Brake horsepower	79 at 3800rpm

Chassis

As 72mm except

Track	Front 4ft ¼in (1429mm), rear 4ft 9¼in (1454mm)
Weight	Chassis 25½cwt (1346kg) Tourer 32cwt (1626kg) Saloon 35cwt (1778kg)

Prices	1932	1933	1934
Chassis	£827	£827	£827

Gearbox

Type	Z type sliding-mesh by Lagonda as earlier or Maybach "Selector" (to 1933)
Overall ratios	
Maybach	High 3.66, 5.27, 6.95,10.61:1 Low 6.09, 8.65, 11.62, 16.54:1 Reverse 13.9:1
ENV 110 preselector (available from 1933)	3.66, 4.55, 7.14, 11.49:1

Rear Axle

Type	Spiral bevel by Lagonda
Ratios	3.67:1 or 4.1:1 or 4.7:1
Wheels & tyres	5.25 x 31 (1932) 600 x 19 (1933)
Tyre pressures	35psi/2.41 bar (tourer) 38psi/2.62 bar (saloon)

Chapter Nine

The 16/80

T here were five Lagondas, all 2 Litres, in the Lands End Trial at Easter 1932. None gained a gold but T C Mann, R Lester-Williams, W H G Tom and J F Falconer all got silvers and G V F Lacon retired. Mike Couper was guilty of desertion to drive a Triumph, although he was to return to the fold later in the year.

At the end of April a new model was announced. This was the Continental and represented the last fling of the 2 Litre. Most of the chassis was unchanged but wheel size was reduced to 18 inches, with a compensating increase in tyre section, up to 5.50 from 5.25. The rear axle ratio was unchanged so the overall gearing was reduced by approxi-

A 2 Litre Continental tourer of 1932. This is the T4 body, distinguished from earlier ones by the sloping, shuttered radiator, smaller wheels and steel bodywork.

mately 8%. The cast iron brake drums of the Selector 3 Litre had proved to be excellent, so a similar pattern, with the cooling/stiffening ribs, was introduced for this 2 Litre. Lagonda had been phasing out the Zenith carburettor, both 3 Litres and blown 2 Litres using SU instruments, and the Continental followed this trend by having a single SU.

The bodywork was given a facelift. The previous autumn, when Speed Model prices had been cut, the management had decided there was room for a rock-bottom cheap model, akin to the K model 11.9 of ten years before. To cut costs, steel replaced aluminium in the bodywork and smaller 18-inch wheels were used, while cheaper lamps, one wiper blade and less kit in the interior were all specified. The works were unhappy at building such a car, labelled it the "C" (for cheap) model, and stamped the ID plate thus. When the new cars got to the sales people they were horrified and sent them back as unsaleable, quite outside Lagonda's quality image. Everyone else was cutting prices but not quality. So the cars went back to the works to be transformed into Speed Models. Then another problem arose. The fabric covering was applied over a kapok filling which was stuck to the body panels with a rye-based glue. In use, a fungus was known to grow in this kapok, and whereas on aluminium there was no problem, on steel panels it started severe corrosion which

Brian Savill's 1933 16/80 saloon is coded W24P, standing for Weymann body, second type, four light, semi-panelled.

would go right through the panel if left. The solution was to go for a lead-coated steel panel, but this was just as expensive as aluminium and made the weight problem worse. Then, as the spring selling season approached, management admitted defeat and went into reverse, stripped off the fabric covering and loaded the car with all the luxury bits and pieces, putting the price up rather than down. The result was the Continental, which had a very short production life, only four months. So far as is known, it was never road tested by any magazine. Thus no contemporary weight figures are known. More recent measurements suggest the Continental is about 3cwt (152kg) heavier than a low chassis Speed Model, but the lower gearing compensates to some extent and in fact in hilly conditions the car may even be faster, at the expense of fussier cruising. Although few in numbers, the survival rate of the Continental has been phenomenal, perhaps because the steel body panels stiffened the structure so much. The identity plate for them carried the code CB, which may have stood for Continental Body or the B version of the C model.

As well as the steel tourer a saloon version was produced which was steel panelled up to the waistline. A new radiator design was a cross between the Speed Model design and the more deeply domed Selector design. It was mounted in a raked position with the

bottom about 3 inches (76mm) further forward. The stoneguard vanished and chromed vertical shutters covered the radiator core. These were thermostatically operated to open as the engine reached working temperature. The clip cap from the supercharged car was mounted longitudinally. The actual distance from radiator cap to windscreen was unchanged but the opening part of the bonnet was made longer, so that its rear edge was now only about 9 inches (229mm) in front of the screen, and the side panels ceased to be plain rectangles. Instead the lower and rear edges were one long curve, with fewer, wider louvres varying in length to match. A new windscreen folded flat, as on

Saloon version of the Continental. The side-mounted spare wheel obscures the curved rear bonnet edge and, curiously, the bonnet louvres are vertical whereas on the tourer they slope to match the radiator. This is a semi-panelled Weymann but one assumes the panelling was steel, not aluminium.

The essence of a sporting saloon in its day; comfortable and fast.

the blown car, and at the tail of the tourer body the sides were cut down so that the folded hood could lie flush. The petrol tank was reshaped so that it didn't protrude above the rear dumbirons and the space was faired in. Cycle wings were standard and for the first time were painted body colour instead of always being black. Although in profile this new tourer body, the T4, is extremely similar to the T2, it always looks more slab-sided and it is possibly wider at the scuttle.

The saloon Continental body looked very similar to the semi-panelled Weymann but was in fact coachbuilt and not a Weymann at all. It acquired the twin rear windows of the 3 Litre and supercharged saloons, but not their external boot. Both models had Lucas P100

headlamps along with a PL40 spotlamp mounted centrally and a CAV spotlight on the windscreen pillar.

The Continental did not replace the Speed Model but was offered as an addition at £30 extra over its equivalent, although the chassis prices was identical. By April 1932, then, Lagonda was offering 20 catalogued models if you count bare chassis as separate types. Even though lots of parts were shared, parts control must have been a headache. The associated problem of supplying instruction books for this mass of products was solved by introducing a loose-leaf system with individual sections for each permutation of engine, gearbox, axle and so on. As the section lengths varied, the resulting page numbering was rather haphazard and owners were constantly ringing up to locate what they thought were missing pages. Just to confuse the historian, from time to time revisions were introduced and only the dated printer's coding gives any clue as to the dates of issue of these revisions.

Lagonda car numbers had got into five figures in November 1931 when OH 9999 had been built, and the first Continental had been OH 10101 at the end of April 1932. True to Staines tradition, it wasn't typical, having a standard vertical radiator and not the sloping, shuttered one.

These angled glasses were called louvres and permitted a window cracked open in wet weather without the occupants getting wet or steaming up. On later Silent Travel bodies the plated frame was omitted and the glasses were built into the doors.

The competition world, as far as Lagondas were concerned, was strictly a private owners' one. The days of Wilbur Gunn proudly recording successes every week had long gone. In March, W A Cuthbert in a blown 2 Litre, PL 7016 (OH 9869), came second in a Mountain Speed Handicap at the Brooklands Easter meeting and in April W A L Cook scored two third places at the JCC Members Day, where T C Mann won his class in the driving-skill test. In June C Morgan won the 2 litre sports car class at Shelsley Walsh. Margaret Allan had traded her first 2 Litre in for a blown one, PL 4158 (OH 9787), and with it won the Ladies Prize in the Scottish Rally. Mike Couper returned to the Lagonda family by having the firm build him a special car for the gruelling Alpine Rally, which ran from Munich to San Remo over seven days. It was a fabric-bodied T2 tourer with twin SUs and Speed Model wings, but featured the Continental radiator, mounted upright. Although penalised, he won a Glacier Cup in JH 2463 (OH 10145) but was rather cross when Lagonda failed to publicise this class win. In the Lagonda Club's records is a note that Alfred Grosch entered a 3 Litre tourer in the same event but there is no trace of this in the official papers; he may have finished outside the awards or not finished at all. Unfortunately the Alpine Rally story is very confused, with sometimes up to three rallies calling themselves this in any one year. In the London-Edinburgh Trial Falconer didn't start but E Boyd got a silver medal.

A study of car numbers shows that Lagonda sold about 100 cars between November 1931 and April 1932, and a further 60-odd between April and July 1932, the main selling season. The 2 Litre took the brunt of this drop; 3 Litre sales held up reasonably well, but they were always the minority. Clearly something had to be done about the 2 Litre. The problem was the industry's headlong rush to six-cylinder engines, then in full cry. Any car above one litre was expected to have six cylinders by the buying public, and in the depressed 1932 market the buyer's wishes were paramount. A new six-cylinder engine was out of the question for two reasons. First, the cost, but just as important, the time it would take to design and test it before production could start. So a large part of 1932 was spent casting about for

a suitable six-cylinder 2 litre engine to replace Lagonda's own four. Ideally, it should produce more power than the OH engine, have more low-end torque and of course be of sufficient quality to carry the 10-year warranty. Eventually the Crossley Shelsley model was fixed upon. This had been introduced in outline in late 1927 and launched properly in the spring of 1928. It was perceptibly more sporting than the usual run of Crossley products and had been brought out at the time when every manufacturer thought he should have a Speed Model, complete with fabric-covered body and a radiator in the Cricklewood Gothic style. The engine was a

Most 16/80s came with P80 headlamps, but upgrading was simple. P100s were probably available at extra cost.

These later pattern P100 headlamps had only one bulb and the dipswitch put both out and brought in a central "passlamp". The radiator now had a separate chromium plated shell and thermostatically operated shutters.

The semi-panelled body is metal skinned up to the waistline and fabric above. Only the front passenger door has an external keyhole. On leaving the car, all the other doors are locked internally and the driver leaves by the front passenger door and locks it.

conventional in-line six with vertical overhead valves operated by pushrods. Both block and head were in cast iron and both crankshaft and camshaft had four bearings. Bore and stroke were 65 x 100mm, giving 1991cc, and the engine was thus more of a 2 litre than the 2 Litre at 1954cc. Crossley had done some development work on it for use in a new

As the shape of the scuttle differed between saloons and tourers, the sidelamp stalks take up different angles on the two types. The spare wheel sits in a little well in the running board but most of its weight is taken by a dummy hub attached to the bulkhead.

model called the 2 Litre Sports, raising the power output to 60bhp at 4000rpm from the original 45bhp and using a 6.5:1 compression ratio, quite high for 1928. Lagonda needed more than this if the new model was to outperform its predecessor and set about experiments before confirming their order. At the time, no figures were published, but *The Autocar*, in a retrospective article published in 1945, quoted 61bhp at 4500rpm, very nearly the same but at a higher crankshaft speed. This meant that, provided the gearing allowed it, the car should be that little bit faster than the Speed Model and could boast the desired six-cylinder engine. The name chosen for the new model was the 16/80 Special Six, representing the RAC rating (15.7hp) and the top speed rather than the brake horsepower.

The Experimental team at Staines were confronted with two sets of problems: firstly the physical changes necessary to the engine to get it into the 2 Litre chassis, which hadn't been expected to take it, and secondly, extracting more power without sacrificing reliability. The Crossley engine was in unit with its gearbox so a new clutch bellhousing was needed, and this was designed to have the starter motor bolted rigidly to it on the engine side, since it would foul a chassis cross-member if left where it was. The engine itself was longer than the 2 Litre, but no longer than the blown version. A new radiator was very like the Selector's, mounted vertically. It was shorter than the Selector radiator and had no extensions below the chassis rails. It carried the winged badge, in contrast to the Continental, which had continued with the rectangular one. The deeper (fore and aft) radiator called for a kink to be introduced in the cross bar of the head-lamp support framework, although the first car didn't have this. The rest of the chassis was the same as the Continental 2 Litre's, with the exception that the Z gearbox and Bishop Cam steering were fitted. Both these changes smack of long overdue standardisation of components, since one doubts that the OH gearbox would have given any trouble. One suspects there were problems adapting Lagonda's home-made clutch to the Crossley engine and their Borg & Beck proprietary item was used.

As stated before, the engine was a conventional pushrod overhead-valve unit with one chain driven camshaft fairly high up on the nearside of the block prodding the valves with steel pushrods. The timing chain also drove the dynamo and magneto in tandem with a vernier coupling. Both of these were carried in a hefty aluminium cradle fixed to the timing case and the whole cradle and its contents could be moved to adjust the chain. The rather bulbous aluminium timing case concealed a torsional damper fixed to the nose of the crankshaft, which was located by its rear main bearing and cross-drilled for oil supply. Connecting rods were Duralumin forgings with die-cast big end bearings. Aluminium alloy pistons had three rings above the floating gudgeon pins and split skirts. The valve gear was lubricated via the hollow rocker shaft from the rear pedestal, which incorporated a bypass valve. The oil was cleaned by an Autoklean filter attached to the bellhousing and operated by a link from the clutch pedal, it being thought that this was more positive than the 3 Litre's throttle-operated version. Cooling was by water pump and a four-bladed fan, the design anticipating modern practice by making the water pump the centre of the fan and driving both by belt from a pulley attached to the half-time wheel.

Both inlet and exhaust ports were on the nearside of the cylinder head, their being three inlets and four exhausts. Crossley had only ever used one carburettor. Lagonda never tried anything but twin SUs, but they tried these in every conceivable arrangement. To begin with, semi-downdraught instruments were used and photographs exist showing them at varying distances from the head, ranging up to about a foot away on the end of precarious-looking Y-shaped manifolds. The press car, PJ 7395 (S 10168), had a shorter version of this design when demonstrated in August but production started with a long rake-type manifold with a horizontal SU at either end, one pointing forwards and the other backwards. In this arrangement, the inlet gases passed above the exhaust manifolds so that an element of "hotspotting" was present - and apparently much needed according to early road tests. Rather comically, the photographs of the engine which

accompanied *The Motor*'s road test in September showed the semi downdraught layout in the picture of the nearside and the back-to-back arrangement in the picture of the offside. The final layout of the inlet manifold, and the one most commonly seen today, had a pair of horizontal SUs side by side in the middle of a rake-type manifold.

The 16/80 used the Continental 2 Litre chassis, which included finned cast iron brake drums to replace the earlier pressed steel ones. These are modern replacements to the same design.

Hydraulic dampers were in their infancy in 1933 and Lagonda stayed with friction Hartfords until 1934. What appears to be a sidelamp is in fact a flashing indicator, added for safety reasons.

Offside of the 16/80 engine, supplied by Crossley and then rebuilt by Lagonda.

16/80 engine seen from above. This oil filler design, here in the centre of the rocker cover, was a carry over from earlier Lagonda-built engines and re-appeared on the 1934 M45 Rapide.

Throughout, the exhaust manifolding was a pair of Y-shaped cast iron castings. The fuel feed was by the newly introduced SU Petro-lift, an electrically operated plunger type pump, mounted in the centre of the scuttle shelf, next to the jack.

Some of Lagonda's alterations to the Crossley engine had a knock-on effect. For example, the new starter position fouled the oil-pressure relief valve, which had to be relo-cated further forward with different plumbing. A larger sump was provided, holding 2½ gallons (10.2 litres). It was still a two-piece aluminium affair but shallower at the front and with Crossley's rather vulnerable vertical drain plug moved up to the side. No quick-drain facility was provided, probably because there wasn't time to design one. A giant oil breather was added to the crankcase but only after production had got under way. Inside the engine a more sporting camshaft super-seded the Crossley one (see the statistics section at the end of this chapter) and most surviving engines are found to have all the water transfer ports blocked off except the rearmost one, leading one to suppose that the intention was to increase water velocity round the block and head. This may have been connected with the decision to use Crossley's water pump, which used the opposite method of cooling to Lagonda's norm. Instead of pumping cool water into the block, the Crossley pump sucked hot water out of the cylinder head and sent it straight to the radi-ator. In later years the combination of a radiator full of scale and enthusiastic revving of the engine in the intermediate gears has given many a 16/80 driver an unlooked for

Nearside of the 16/80 engine. After numerous experiments, production inlet arrangements were as shown, with side by side SU carburettors. The metal shield keeps petrol drips off the exhaust manifold.

shower bath of hot brown water when the choked passages couldn't accept all that output. The new radiator and cooling system had a capacity of 5 gallons (22.7 litres) against the 2 Litre's 4 gallons (18.2 litres), although the recently introduced long radiator for the blown 2 Litre also boasted a 5 gallon capacity. After a year's production, the 16/80 cooling system was redesigned, which we will come to later.

The next headache was who was actually going to assemble the engines. Crossley were prepared to put "Lagonda" on the rocker cover but wanted to assemble the engines at Gorton. Lagonda, on the other hand, had been making their own engines since 1913 and were suspicious of other people's standards. Added to that, Lagonda, not Crossley, were going to carry the warranty. The eventual solution was for Crossley to assemble and no doubt test each engine, then send it fully built up to Staines, where it was taken to pieces, checked, built up again and tested. In the process of re-assembly Lagonda introduced its favourite ANF threaded cylinder head studs with special nuts using BSF sizes to avoid spanner problems. Nine years is a lot of guarantee.

The shape of SU dashpots changed in the 1930s. The bronze body hints at its age.

The low chassis 2 Litre dashboard was carried over for the 16/80 unchanged. The saloon version, as here, had a flat top in contrast to the curved one on open cars. The original exterior Klaxon windscreen wiper motor has expired and been replaced with an indoor one.

Driver's door. The long plated lever shoots the window down with spring assistance for instant hand signals. Closing it again is slower and requires quite an effort. Intermediate positions are possible. Electric indicators were not yet available.

Rear passenger's door. This has a conventional window winder. The small catch at lower right is the internal lock.

Handbrake on and gearlever in neutral. Both scientifically placed for maximum interference with trouser legs, but it is easy to slide across and use the other door. Originally both levers would have had leather gaiters to keep out draughts.

The 16/80 chassis retained the grouped lubrication nipples of the 2 Litre but the advent of pressure lubrication at garages brought on one change. Over-enthusiastic pressure greasing of hubs had been known to fill the brake drums with grease, so now a special screwed plug replaced hub grease nipples and a special adapter was added to the already generous toolkit so that a hand greaser could be used

The tourer and saloon bodywork chosen for the 16/80 were developments of their predecessors. The tourer was based on the Continental but some subtle shaping had taken away the slab-sided look. The fold-flat windscreen disappeared as it had proved a little unstable at speed, and the earlier top-hinged variety re-appeared but with stiffer supports. The neater hood stowage, by a cut-down tail, was retained, and so was the

dashboard location of the hand throttle, an innovation on the Selector. The first tourer, chassis S10168, called this body the T2P, which is what it really was, but by the time production started it was decided to call it the T5. Fabric-covered finishes had now gone out of fashion and all T5 bodies were bright metal panelled, whether steel or aluminium. The saloon body was a panelled Weymann, just like the Continental one in appearance, but with the supercharged car's boot added. The bonnet side panels returned to the normal rectangular shape. But an unexpected additional model was also announced. This was a

The change to Bishop Cam steering boxes displaced the hand throttle on to the dashboard. At the same time the Ki-gass pump was relocated to a more convenient position for the driver.

Some instruments and the pushbutton switches have grown plated bezels. The ignition switch has been separated from the lighting one.

An owner has fitted a contemporary electric cigar lighter, shown working with the element glowing red.

Photographic proof that Lagonda dismantled all the Crossley engines for the 16/80 and rebuilt them. This is a 1932 shot of the engine shop at Staines.

sporting 2-seater with a body designed by Vanden Plas. The bodies were started by that firm and driven to Staines for Lagonda to finish them. The 2-seater was Lagonda's first such design since the 12/24 and was clearly a sports car in appearance, with a long curved sloping tail which rather clashed with the very vertical front end. Mechanically the car was standard and, as it was very little lighter, performance was indistinguishable. Most examples had a folding dickey seat occupying the long tail, sometimes with a step on each side of the rear body to assist entry. The doors were rather extraordinary in that the hinge line was raked to match the angle of the shutting edge and the windscreen. Thus, when they were opened wide they dropped nearly to ground level, being restrained only by check-straps. The hood, which only covered the front seats, had external and rather untidy stowage for its irons when folded, between the door hinges and the rear wings. The wings, which one might have expected to be cycle type, were a new design, flowing in a smooth reverse curve from above the front axle to meet the start of the rear ones, which in turn were extended to the rear to match the body profile. Following the new regulations, the 16/80 had a flat-top beam centre lamp, which came on when the main lighting, a pair of Lucas P80s, was extin-

The Vanden Plas 2-seater was an unexpected new model in 1932. This is the first one, delivered fully finished and photographed at the Lagonda factory (Car No. S 10155). Most of the other 15 were started by VdP but delivered untrimmed to be finished at Staines. The hood, when erect, only covers the front pair of seats. On later cars the rear edge of the bonnet was raked to match the windscreen and bonnet louvres.

guished by the dipswitch. The middle lamp also doubled as a fog lamp.

The actual introduction of the new model was rather muted as Lagonda was not advertising very extensively in 1932. The prototype, PJ 7395 (Car Number S 10168), was around from early August but advertising only really got under way when colour front cover pictures appeared in September. A new catalogue was required and to save money the 16/80 had its own one, pending a complete new one for the whole range. It is obvious that the catalogue was being produced before any cars were ready, for the picture of the tourer is actually a Selector 3 Litre (you can see the dynamo) and the saloon picture is also a 3 Litre. The 2-seater is illustrated by a drawing that does the car no favours and has a number of features altered before production began. One of them, the fold-flat screen depicted, was denied by a sticker added at a later date. The prices fixed were £450 for a bare chassis, £595 for the tourer, £695 for the saloon and £635 for the Vanden Plas, spelled wrongly as three words in the catalogue but subsequently corrected. Extras quoted were £27 for long wings, £3 for a spare wheel bracket and £1 for a fuel tank fairing.

It was decided to call the car the "Special Six", a thoroughly confusing name for a firm already selling a Special that was also a six

and a Selector Special that was also a six. To add to this, the T5 tourer was called the "Speed 4-seater", thus coming dangerously close to being a Speed Six, a name someone else had used... It was stated that the ordinary 2 Litre would continue, which would have meant 21 models in the reange, but in practice very few owners ordered a 2 litre after the 16/80 appeared, and although the blown car was still advertised the unblown one wasn't. The distinguishing code on the cars' identity plates was an S. The Crossley engines also bore an S number stamped on the timing case and later, after the major revisions that

Early 16/80 tourer with the T5 steel body. Only the later radiator and lack of fabric distinguishes it from a 2 Litre. The British motor industry's rush to six cylinders was universal. In 1928 64% of UK cars had four-cylinder engines; by 1932 it was down to 22%.

A cosy period interior. The dangling handles are known as "dowager pulls" in the trade. The blind above the back window is controlled by a cord terminating by the driver's right ear. The upholstery would have been pneumatic originally but may have punctured and been replaced.

came after the first year's production, an engine number in the form Sxxx/S2 to denote the later version.

The Autocar and *The Motor* road tested PJ 7395 in successive weeks in September and commented on the increased low-speed torque and flexibility and the appreciably lighter clutch action. As a prototype, this car had a number of features which differ from the eventual production, such as a straight bar joining the headlamps. To compare performance with the 2 Litre we have to go back to 1928 road tests, since the low chassis unblown car was never tested. In the interim, testing methods and what was actually measured had changed. However, the 16/80 was

perceptibly more accelerative, probably as much to do with lower overall gearing as anything else and its maximum speed of 80mph was exactly the same as that of the high chassis car. From rest to 60mph occupied 19.2 seconds, which compares well with the 20.8 recorded for the Selector 3 Litre and 22.6 seconds to 70mph for the blown car. *The Motor* published acceleration graphs in the gears, which are instructive: 0-40mph in second took 8 seconds in the 16/80 against 14 seconds for the Speed Model. Acceleration from 10 to 60mph solely in top gear took 35 seconds against 50. So the 16/80 was quicker than the high chassis car, as one would hope it would be four years later in a period of rapid change. In fact the performance figures were quite comparable with the supercharged car over the lower speeds, but lost out at higher ones, when the blown car "got up on to the cam" and really began to fly. There are some odd discrepancies between the two reports. *The Autocar* quoted a 4.4:1 rear axle and the ZD set of gear ratios whereas *The Motor* said the car had a 4.6:1 axle and the ZE sporting intermediate ratios. They couldn't agree on the overall length of the car either. Both testers commented that the Lagonda gearbox was not easy to master and were

Early 16/80s used 2 Litre running boards, pointed at the front. But the 3 Litre had gone in for helmet front wings and running boards turned up at the front, like giant skis. By 1933 these had found their way on to the 16/80 as well.

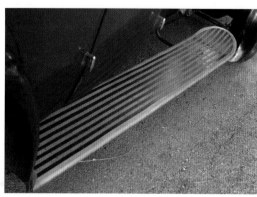

pleased that the increased flexibility overcame this to some extent.

The new loose-leaf instruction book system came into its own with this new model. All that was needed was to write a new engine section, lifted largely from the Crossley book anyway, and drop it into the existing book. This was done so quickly that even the spelling mistakes got perpetuated, like leaving the second "s" off Ki-gass.

In the period just before the Motor Show the Eastbourne Concours d'Elegance was attracting increasing attention and a certain "showbiz" element began to creep in, attracted by the column-inches that got spent on it. There were 32 classes in all, so practically everyone won something, even if it was for "The Most Distinctive Car" sort of prize. Mike Couper, by now a motor trader in St Albans, came second in the open car class £501 to £700. Class 13, which was confined to Sussex residents, was won by a faithful Lagonda fancier, Major Maurice Cohn, military

Heat from the engine gets into a saloon quite easily, given the rather basic insulation provided by the bulkhead, so ventilators for the crew's feet were provided. The mesh keeps insects out.

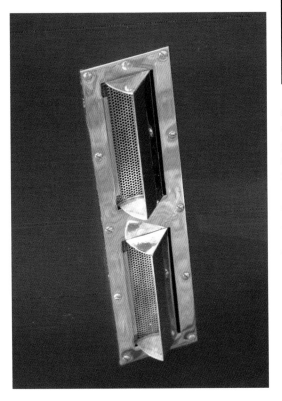

attaché at the US Embassy. At that time he drove a supercharged 2 Litre but he later graduated to an M45, whose radiator virtually disappeared under the number of badges he fastened to it.

Lagonda had Stand 23 at Olympia in October and displayed on it two 16/80s, a standard T5 tourer and a Vanden Plas 2-seater, and two 3 Litres, a semi-panelled Weymann saloon on the Selector Special chassis and a long-wheelbase Selector carrying the latest saloon body. The latter was a Silent Travel design, built under licence. Silent Travel Ltd were neighbours of Lagonda Distributors (London) Ltd in Albemarle Street and had been set up to exploit the Daste patent form of body construction. This was another attempt to accommodate the flexible

The winged badge was introduced in 1931 for the 3 Litre Selector, as was the more deeply domed radiator top tank. The filler cap was a revised version of the blown 2 Litre but mounted with the arm longitudinal.

Detail of the front of the car with the apron removed and starting handle in place. The top photo shows the apron and number plate in place.

Even by 1935 use of the starting handle was not ruled out, so the front apron was made easily detachable, held by a pair of these spring clips.

chassis of the period. While the Weymann idea was to make the body as flexible as the chassis, so that it would not squeak or fidget as the chassis flexed, the Daste view was that the body should be rigid, but mounted flexibly on the chassis. To this end, each Silent Travel body consisted of, basically, three stiffly built units: the floor, the scuttle/windscreen unit and the roof/rear quarters assembly. Each of these was attached to its neighbour with joints involving large-diameter pins and Silentbloc rubber bushes. The idea had been taken up by Delage and Vanden Plas and later developed into a pillarless saloon design, where the B post vanished and the door locks operated vertical bolts into bushed sockets in the roof cant rail and body lower valance, leaving the centre of the side of the car completely clear and unrestricted. A small advantage was that all door edges were perfectly plain and bereft of locks to catch clothes on. In Lagonda's case they were covered in plated trim. The 1932 Motor Show had pillarless Silent Travel saloons on the MG, Delage, Charlesworth and William Arnold stands, these last two being coachbuilders, of course. The Lagonda one was a large six-light limousine, not typical of later production. The Silent Travel body on the 10ft 9in (3277mm) wheelbase 3 Litre was coded ST24, (since it looked rather like the W24P) but was easily distinguished by the rear-hinged rear doors. It always had a boot and had a revised method of ventilation for the occupants. A flap was fixed to the inside of the front wings (assuming these were not cycle type) and from here a tube led cold air to the occupants' feet, closed off within the car when not required. It was claimed that this system would eventually be developed to pipe warm air in the winter, but it never was. Later cars, notably the M45, provided plenty of heat for the driver's feet without any extra plumbing. Weymann attempted to counter this new rival system with a more complicated version which involved hollowed-out sections, but labour costs, even in 1932, made it uncompetitive and Weymann turned his attention to bus and railway work.

There were several other coachbuilders exhibiting their wares on Lagonda chassis at Olympia, notably a smart drophead coupé by Carlton on the 16/80 and an exotic close-

A 3 Litre saloon with Silent Travel body (ST24) and helmet wings illustrated in the catalogue. Pillarless construction meant that the rear doors had to be rear-hinged.

coupled fixed-head coupé by J Gurney Nutting on the Selector. This had no running boards and elaborate teardrop-shaped wings front and rear with wide chromed bands running down the sides. It was finished in black and was probably the first Lagonda to have built-in direction indicators. T H Gill showed a drophead coupé on the Selector chassis with a spring-compensated hood for ease of erection. Not for the first time it was noted that the rounded top of the Lagonda radiator - and the Selector radiator was even more rounded than its predecessors - made life difficult for the body designer as there was no pronounced shoulder at the top which the waistline could meet, so any horizontal trim was inclined to have a rather arbitrary look to it.

There were several novelties at the 1932 Show that were later to feature in the Lagonda programme. ENV Ltd announced that they had taken up the manufacture of epicyclic gearboxes to the Wilson patents; Smiths were preparing to offer their built-in jacking system, the "Jackall", and André were publicising their Telecontrol system for remotely controlled dampers.

The switch to an all six-cylinder line-up was undoubtedly right at the time and sales picked up immediately, with well over 100 sold by the end of the year. Some Lagonda stalwarts disagreed, Mike Couper for one, and for these people exceptions could be made and a 2 Litre built for them, usually employing the 16/80 radiator and metal bodywork. The six-cylinder car was undeniably faster than the

The frame of a body built under Silent Travel patents : this view shows where the special shock-absorbing bushes are fitted.

normally aspirated four but had to rev higher in the process, so the dispute came down to "fizzers" versus "thumpers".

In November 1932 the firm arranged for a photographer to tour the works and a set of 33 pictures emerged which were sold to the staff. Sets have survived and make an interesting contrast to the 1921 set. The forests of flapping belts driven by overhead line shafting have not disappeared, but they are now driven by electricity, not a gas engine, so stoppages brought on by the latter's temperamental behaviour had ceased, but belts still broke on occasion and in the wood mill usually contrived to dislodge the sawdust of centuries and fill the place with fog. In the chassis frame assembly shop they were drilling Selector frames when the photographer came round and Mr Feeley Senior is

From late 1932 Silent Travel saloons began to replace Weymanns, only on the 3 Litre to begin with but later on the 16/80. This drawing illustrates the principles of the Daste patents, with Silentbloc rubber bushes giving flexibility between stiff sub-assemblies. Lagonda bodies were pillarless and dispensed with the B pillar in the centre of each side.

The Silent Travel principle was even applied to the large "Family Saloon" that Lagonda produced almost unchanged from 1926 to 1935. This retained the forward engine position of the original 3 Litre to maximise passenger space.

operating one end of a two-man power drill. Suspended from the roof, which has been reinforced with extra trusses of dubious structural value, is the large jig with which all body mounting bolts were positioned. When the ZM chassis appeared the management baulked at the cost of a new jig, so the same one was used, with the helpful result that all pre-1935 Lagonda bodies will fit on any chassis, give or take a bracket or two.

The various bodyshop pictures show a rich variety of styles being built, mostly steel coachbuilt tourers and Weymann saloons on the 16/80, but with the occasional Silent Travel Selector and limousine. The method of construction varied: tourers were built up, trimmed and painted on a dummy chassis called a "buck", and only fixed to the chassis at a very late stage, whereas saloons were built on their intended chassis from the outset. Hiram Harris, the bodyshop foreman

at the time, was responsible for all timber purchase, travelling to the London docks to do so and secretly marking every piece to ensure he got what he had selected and not anything inferior. Naturally, certain specialisms developed. One man made all the petrol tanks, for example, and another all the bonnets. But the place was versatile and Frank Feeley recalled them making filing cabinets for the office in slack times.

The engine shop provides photographic evidence that Lagonda did indeed tear all the Crossley engines apart and rebuild them. In the trim shop, which was across one end of the body shop, a trimmer can be seen applying the fabric to the roof of a Weymann saloon using the Buckingham method described earlier. In another part of it, dozens of women are seated at a vast table machining the seats and other soft furnishings. One of these ladies later became Mrs Frank Feeley. In the stores the roof purlins came in very handy for the storage of bulky items like Speed Model wings.

In the winter of 1932 C G Vokes, the founder of the filter company and a keen Lagonda owner, put the idea of a Lagonda Car Club to General Metcalfe, seeking factory backing. The General was enthusiastic and Vokes wrote to *Motor Sport* to advertise the idea of an inaugural meeting and also wrote to 100 known owners whose names he had got from the service department. About a dozen responded and a meeting was held at Vokes's factory. This set up the club, with

Lagonda's sidelamps were always more substantial than the law demanded, although nowadays they wouldn't be legally permitted so far from the front of the car.

General Metcalfe as President and Vokes taking on the jobs of both Secretary and Treasurer. Mike Couper was to be Trials Secretary and Bill Oates took the chair of the Committee. The annual subscription was set at one guinea (£1.05) and for a further guinea a member could buy an attractive badge designed by F Gordon Crosby which took the form of a miniature Selector radiator with a full-sized winged radiator badge fixed across it and "Car Club" engraved in the tail feathers of the stylised bird. As well as the officers the club elected four committee members, one of whom was a director of Lagonda Distributors (London) Ltd, so the trade got a voice. In these early days the club bore some resemblance to an offshoot of the public relations department. The first event was held at Hanworth Air Park on 28 March 1933 and was a cross between a rally, a gymkhana and an air display, concluding with a dance in the evening.

Lagonda Distributors (London) Ltd were very active and it is believed they were responsible for the Vanden Plas two-seater becoming a listed model. In December 1932 they went further and arranged for Vanden Plas to build drophead and fixed head coupés on the 16/80 chassis and also a less extravagant Gurney Nutting saloon. Not to be outdone, the works then offered a Vanden Plas drophead, but with four seats instead of the two in the rival car. They followed this with a very similar body on the 3 Litre, distinguishable only by the bonnet length.

The works having stolen their thunder, Lagonda Distributors (London) Ltd went into liquidation following the departure of Jack Olding, who was to become an earth-moving expert with a large sales operation on the Barnet Bypass. But it immediately rose again, phoenix-like, as Carr's Ltd at the same address, and continued as a Lagonda dealer. At about the same time Dobson's, a dealer on Staines Bridge, only yards from the factory, was upgraded to be a distributor, probably in recognition of its status as the outlet for all the Lagondas taken in by the factory as trade-ins. This was a bad time to be selling expensive cars and it was quite easy to find so-called "shop soiled" new cars at knock-down prices. In one of the motoring magazines in December 1932 one could find offers of a new, unregistered 3 Litre for £580 against the list price of £900 or a supercharged 2 Litre for £200 off.

Mike Couper took his Alpine Rally 2 Litre on the London-Gloucester Trial in December and got a bronze medal, but for the first time in years there were no Lagondas in the Exeter Trial at Christmas, most of the keen drivers having transferred their aspirations to the Monte Carlo Rally in January. Tallinn was the favoured starting point, given its high marks. Lord de Clifford trundled off there in his latest toy, a Bentley saloon fitted with a Gardner diesel engine. It isn't clear how he kept the fuel liquid in the minus-35 degrees Fahrenheit recorded there, but he must have somehow. The Lagonda entrants, all private owners, were a fraction less adventurous, opting to start in Britain. D C Love (2 Litre), T C Mann (2 litre s/c) and H Welch (3 Litre) all started from John o'Groats and the Liddells (2 Litre) from Harrogate. Welch crashed in a snowstorm in France but all the others got through to Monaco, Mann finishing 33rd overall, Love 36th and the Liddells 57th out of 71 finishers. Lord de Clifford was the best of the British contingent, fourth overall. T C Mann was as ever more interested in the Mont des Mules hillclimb, where he bettered his own class record time, winning his class at 31.55mph. This was the last time this event was held. Weight being paramount in hillclimbs, it isn't that surprising to notice that Aldington's Frazer Nash won the 1½-litre class at a higher speed, 33.21mph.

All Lagonda wheels and wings were stove enamelled black, whatever final colour was required. Other colours were oversprayed.

Roads in the 1930s were just as quiet and not much wider than this one.

Two 3 Litres on tour in Germany in 1936. The car on the right is a 1932 semi-panelled Weymann, KY 2118 (Z10105). On the left is a Gurney Nutting 3 Litre Selector Special, KY 3510 (Z10238), a copy of the car on the Gurney Nutting stand at the 1932 Motor Show. Photo J P Wood

Mann also won his class in the *Confort* competition for the fourth year in succession. Lagonda, for no very clear reason, made a huge splash about this. Their advertising had become very intermittent, probably to save money, and was rarely more frequent than once a month in *The Autocar* only, but for the 1933 Monte Carlo results the 36-point black type was dragged out and "1st Prize" and "1st, 2nd and 3rd" dominated the page. The Lagonda Car Club was also mentioned, as part of a recruiting drive. There were three Lagondas in the Lands End Trial at Easter, R Lester Williams getting a silver medal after only failing Lynmouth, and G E Ferguson in KR 7200 (3 Litre, Z9725) failing four hills on his way to a bronze. D Percival (2 Litre) retired.

In April the company edged all its prices

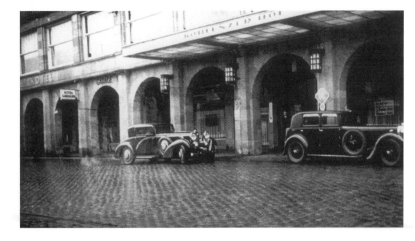

up, announcing their intention to do this a month in advance to get some "buy now while stocks last" impact. The 16/80 tourer went up from £595 to £640 and the saloon from £695 to £750, all the other models having comparable increases. At about the same time the supercharged 2 Litre went on to its third cylinder-head design, with a change to a 14mm sparking plug which allowed more water around the valves. The second design had retained the 18mm plugs but had offset them to get slightly better cooling for the exhaust side. It is believed that no production car was fitted initially with the 14mm version; they were kept by the works for trouble-shooting with very recalcitrant engines. In the same way, Invar strut pistons had been adopted, without any announcement, for the blown engines.

At this point the PERR Syndicate re-enters the story. They were prepared to underwrite the costs of two exciting developments, one of which was to result in the Rapier and the other the M45 4½ Litre. In the end the deal fell through but it would have gained the syndicate a royalty on every Rapier and M45 sold. In return the factory got the development costs of the two models for nothing, or at least very little. The 4½ Litre project was a simple one; just shoehorn a Meadows engine into the Selector chassis. The 9hp Rapier scheme was a "clean sheet of paper" project and Tim Ashcroft was hired to do it, with one

Lagonda draughtsman to help him. Neither model concerns this book's subjects, so we will leave it at that.

In March the second RAC Rally attracted 11 Lagonda entrants, three of them 3 Litres, the others 2 Litres including T C Mann's blown car. Mann had the best result, coming 20th overall, with others trailing in up to 93rd (H A Barham, 2 Litre DHC by James Young). The splendidly named Cecil Lowthorpe-Lutwidge failed to start..

The 16/80 underwent a series of minor changes in the spring of 1933. The SU company had introduced their Type L electric fuel pump, delivering 8 gallons an hour at 1psi, and although it was stated that it didn't supersede the Petrolift, Lagondas thought it did and began to fit it immediately. The 3 Litres were still using the AC mechanical pump. The Crossley water pump had several shortcomings and Lagonda designed a new one to replace it which reversed the water flow round the engine, drawing cool water from the bottom of the radiator and pumping it into the cylinder block below the dynamo via the original inlet. This new pump was fixed to the front of the dynamo and driven by it. Such cooling problems as there had been were now banished. At the same time Crossley's rather crude pressed steel four-bladed fan was replaced by an aluminium two-bladed one of much superior aerodynamic design. The next change was less noticeable. The steel 5⁄16in (7.9mm) pushrods were replaced by stouter duralumin ones 3⁄8in thick (9.5mm). One presumes this was to lighten the reciprocating valve gear but of course the clearances when cold had to be increased from 0.004in to 0.015in (0.10mm and 0.38mm), to allow for differential thermal expansion rates, and the later engines are noisier when cold. Also not noticeable externally, the oil filtration system was changed from the Crossley version, which only filtered the oil after it had been through the engine, to one which did the filtering first. These second series engines can be distinguished externally by an S2 stamped on the timing case after the S series engine number.

Bigger changes came at the end of June with the announcement of a revised design of tourer body and the availability of an epicyclic gearbox by ENV on both the 16/80

and the 3 Litre, confined, on the latter, to the Selector, an admission that the Maybach 'box had not sold well and was effectively dropped. It also meant, although this was not expressed, that supplies of 72mm chassis, the Z3S, had been used up and henceforth all 3 Litres would use the later Selector chassis, regardless of which transmission was fitted. The ENV gearbox came in 75bhp and 110bhp versions and, perhaps for simplicity, Lagonda chose to fit the 110 version to both models. The 3 Litre needed it, just, but the 16/80 could have coped with the smaller one. As ENV used a four-point mounting, a new subframe had to be devised and fitted in place of Lagonda's three-point system. A right-hand gear change lever was still used but operated fore-and-aft rather than in a gate, with reverse at the front, protected by a catch, followed by neutral and then the four forward gears in turn, with top at the back. When neutral was selected the left-hand pedal stayed halfway down. As no clutch was fitted, there was a problem with creep in neutral, particularly with cold oil, and this was never overcome by ENV or Lagonda. It was particularly annoying because the epicyclic gears tended to growl in neutral. In 1934, when the same problem arose with the Rapier, the company relented and fitted a plate clutch to save wear on the first gear band and went further by adding a catch that held the clutch out in neutral, killing the growling, but this useful modifica-

Lagonda never offered a factory-bodied drophead coupé before the Bentley/Good era but there was a growing demand for them and in early 1933 a short run of Vanden Plas-bodied 16/80s were offered. After four 16/80s and one 3 Litre (shown in the picture) Lagonda started to build their own to VdP design 886. Four of these have been traced but there may have been more. VdP-built cars are coded VP and the Lagonda-built ones DHC1.

tion seems never to have reached 16/80s or 3 Litres. On the 3 Litre the ENV 'box came without extra charge but the 16/80 customer had to pay £25 more for his. On the cars' identity plate the letters WS (for Wilson) were added, so 16/80s were stamped SWS and 3 Litres lost their Z to be noted as MWS (M chassis, Wilson 'box).

The new tourer body was a development of the T5 and was virtually identical back to the rear axle line. But the rear was different, seven inches (178 mm) longer and adding a swept tail with a substantial enclosed boot and the spare wheel carried on its lid. It was hinged at the bottom and could be used open flat to carry extra luggage, provided one could arrange some way of displaying the number plate, normally carried across the spare wheel and secured by the same monster wing nut. Quite incorrectly, *The Autocar* stated that this body was of Vanden Plas design and this "fact" has often been repeated since. Not true; it was purely a Staines product throughout. What was stolen from Vanden Plas was the wingline, that went with this new T6 body. This had first appeared on the short-lived VdP two-seater and in elevation was one long reverse curve from the front axle line to the start of the rear wings. The "snail" sidelamps from the helmet wing shape now appeared on these new wings. Cycle wings had gone right out of fashion but were still available if required. There were detail changes to door handles, bonnet catches and the fuel tank filler, which was now a copy of the Maserati one, sold as a Bonora. The dashboard didn't change, except for a move of the Ki-gass pump to the driver's side.

The Autocar published a road test of the

A Wilson-type preselector epicyclic gearbox by ENV became an option for 1933 and standard on the 16/80 later in the year. This picture shows the revised gear selector lever with a catch protecting reverse. Black instrument bezels were sometimes demanded by drivers.

preselector 16/80 with T6 body on 14 July and were at great pains to allay the fears of diehard readers that the new gearbox might have taken all the fun out of the car. The Lagonda announcement had omitted to mention that the rear axle ratio had been altered to 4.67:1, giving a 6% increase in engine revs at any given speed. This was probably to combat the extra 1.5cwt (76kg) of the new body and it is not surprising that the lower gearing and extra weight dragged the top speed down from 80mph to 77.6. You would have expected, though, that the lower gears, which had a more progressive set of ratios than the Z gearbox, would have improved the acceleration times at lower speeds. But the reverse was the case. The manual gearbox car had gone from 20 to 40mph in third in nine seconds. The ENV one took 11 seconds. Acceleration from 30 to 50mph in top now took 17.6 seconds against 14.8 seconds earlier. To compare "through the gears" times we have to compare the *Motor Sport* road test of January 1933 with the epicyclic car. Here again the manual car is quicker, despite the sustained-power upward changes that the ENV gearbox permits. The early car did 0-60mph in 22 seconds against the later one's 26.2 seconds.

The competition arena was rather bereft of Lagondas in the summer of 1933, although there were entries at Shelsley Walsh and in the London-Edinburgh Trial. E J Boyd, driving a blown 2 Litre, GG 2276 (OH9818), gained a Principal Award and G E Ferguson in KR 7200 (Z9725) won a bronze medal.

In late June General Metcalfe was taken seriously ill and the Chairman, Sir Edgar Holberton, took over the reins. This rather scuppered the PERR Syndicate's attempts to subsidise their racing. Mrs Metcalfe wouldn't let anyone near her husband and although he emerged from hospital in late July, he never fully recovered and was to die early in 1934. But the levering of a Meadows 4½-litre engine into a 3 Litre chassis continued at Staines and by the summer of 1933 a prototype was on the road, clearly a modified 3 Litre with the T6 body. To make driving a touch more civilised a "Silent Third" version of the Z

Spot the difference. This is the T7 tourer body on a 16/80 of 1934. The sole difference from the T6 is the angled bonnet rear edge and the matching rake to the bonnet louvres. Very similar bodies were fitted to 3 Litres and M45s, although the latter had a different dashboard. For 1935 the T8 body had a driver's door but was otherwise similar.

gearbox was installed and fitted to the first batch of production cars, but it proved to be not up to the job and Lagonda were forced to use Meadows's own T8 gearbox, recalling the cars with the Z 'box for a replacement.

For the exciting new model Lagonda brought in new tourer and saloon bodies. The T7 body abandoned the two small doors on the nearside in favour of one huge one, with its top cutout to match the driver's elbow-clearing one. It retained the small rear door on the offside, although this was slightly enlarged. The opening part of the bonnet was extended back nearly to the windscreen and its louvres were now raked at the same angle as the windscreen instead of being vertical. This body was also now mounted on the 3 Litre and 16/80, with the exception that the

M45 had a totally new dashboard whereas the smaller cars made do with their ordinary ones. So the T6 body had a remarkably short life, from roughly June to October 1933. One of the changes to the 16/80 in the summer had been the change-over from Weymann panelled saloons (W24P) to Silent Travel (ST24), bringing the smaller car in line with the bigger one. For the saloon M45 a new saloon body, still by Silent Travel, was the ST34, which was lower than its predecessor, had a larger boot and no peak over the windscreen. The selling point for this last change was the "eddy-free front". The 3 Litre carried on with the earlier ST24 design, but with the eddy-free front added, becoming the ST24A, also fitted to the 16/80 for 1934.

With the exciting new models - for the Rapier was also prematurely announced at the 1933 Motor Show - Lagonda overhauled its dealer network and appointed a professional PR firm to handle press matters. This was Woodwright Publicity and Press Service, operated out of Warwick Wright's premises in Bond Street by J Stanley Woodward. The press cuttings album that Woodward kept is now one of the treasured archives belonging to the Lagonda Club Heritage Trust.

Lagonda had Stand 143 at Olympia with a pair of M45s, a prototype Rapier and the latest saloon versions of the 16/80 and 3 Litre on show. Martin Walter also showed a drophead coupé on the 3 Litre chassis. Freestone & Webb showed an enormous six-light limousine on the 11ft 6in wheelbase (3.5m) 3 Litre which could seat six in the back, using three folding occasional seats. Changes to the smaller cars were slight. The ENV gearbox was now standard on the 16/80 and the silent third gearbox standard on the 3 Litre.

The prices fixed for the M45 were surprisingly low and the smaller cars had theirs cut to stay below them, the 16/80 tourer coming down to £595 from £640 and the 3 Litre tourer to £695 from £900. Comparable saloon prices were: 16/80 reduced to £695 from £750 and 3 Litre to £750 from £990. It was soon discovered that these were "too" low and the following spring they went up again, although not to the earlier figures.

Eventually the 16/80 got the Silent Travel saloon body. Recent photo by David Hine.

16/80 SUMMARY STATISTICS

Engine

Configuration	6 cylinders in line, pushrod overhead valves
Capacity	1991cc
Bore and stroke	65 x 100mm
RAC rating	15.7hp
Compression ratio	6.5:1
Firing order	1, 5, 3, 6, 2, 4
Valve timing	S1 io 0.5° ATDC, ic 52° ABDC, eo 55° BBDC, ec 18° ATDC. Inlet open 231.5°, exhaust open 253°. Overlap 17.5° S2 io TDC, ic 50° ABDC, eo 55° BBDC, ec 20° ATDC. Inlet open 230°, exhaust open 255°. Overlap 20°
Tappet clearances	0.004in/0.102mm cold (steel pushrods), 0.015in/0.381mm cold (alloy pushrods)
Brake horsepower	61 at 4500rpm
Main bearings	4
Main bearing diameter	1⅞in (47.6mm)
Big end diameter	1⅞in (47.6mm)
Oil capacity	2.5 gallons (11.4 litres)
Cooling system	Water pump, thermostat and fan. Capacity 5 gallons (22.7 litres)
Ignition	Magneto by Scintilla, PN6 at 1½ engine speed
Ignition timing	44° BTDC fully advanced
Contact breaker gap	0.012-0.016in (0.305-0.406mm)
Sparking plugs	Champion 17. Gap 0.018in (0.457mm)
Carburettors	2 x SU HV3
Fuel supply	SU Petrolift. Later SU Type L electric pump. 14-gallon tank.
Dynamo	Lucas
Starter	Lucas type M45
Clutch	Single dry plate by Borg & Beck
Batteries	2 x 6 volt 11-plate tall

Chassis

Wheelbase	10ft (3048mm) or 10ft 9in (3277mm)
Track	Front 4ft 8in (1422mm), rear 4ft 7¾in (1416mm)
Overall length	Tourer 13ft 7in (4140mm) Saloon 14ft 4in (4369mm)
Turning circle	40ft (12.2m)
Kerb weight	Chassis 22.5cwt (1143kg) Tourer 28.5cwt (1448kg) Tourer with ENV gearbox 30cwt (1524kg) Saloon 30cwt (1524kg)

Gearbox

Type — Z type sliding mesh by Lagonda

Ratios	Top	3rd	2nd	1st & reverse
with 4.4:1 axle	4.4	6.01	10.13	16.21
with 4.67:1 axle	4.67	5.8	9.10	14.6
with 5.44:1 axle	5.44	7.45	12.51	20.02

Rear Axle

Type	Spiral bevel by Lagonda. Ratios as above.
Mph/1000rpm in top	19.6 on 4.4:1 axle, 18.47 on 4.67:1 axle
Wheels & tyres	5.50 x 18 (tourer and saloon) 5.50 x 20 (4-seater saloon on long wb)
Tyre pressures	32psi (2.2 bar) all round
Steering	Bishop cam & peg
Propeller shaft	Hardy Spicer. Plain bearing until 1933, needle roller after.

Prices

	1932
Chassis	£450
Tourer	£595
Saloon	£695
VdP 2-seater	£635
LWB saloon	£695

Lubrication instructions had altered by 1933. The gearbox oil was no longer castor-based, but it was still used in the rear axle.

Chapter Ten

The 3½ Litre

Bryan Hyett's 3½ Litre tourer has the Lagonda T9 tourer body, shared with the M45 Rapide, frequently but wrongly attributed to Vanden Plas.

In February 1934 Brigadier-General Metcalfe died, having never really recovered from the previous summer's cancer. He may have been an unlikely candidate to run a motor company but he was very good at finding and dealing with customers. He ran the factory as he had his regiment, firmly but fairly, was trusted by everyone and repaid that trust. I will give one example. The company had an issued share capital of only £115,000, which isn't a lot if your products cost nearly £1000 each. So there were frequent cash-flow problems. One week,

probably in early 1933, things got so bad that there wasn't enough money to pay the wages. One of the older employees who had, or was reputed to have, a "long stocking" was asked into the boardroom, sworn to secrecy and cards were put on the table. Could he see his way to lending the firm this week's wage bill? The firm was owed a large cheque from a dealer for the cars he had sold but it hadn't arrived. It is a mark of the man's loyalty and trust that he could and did, and heartening to record that he got it back, for there was no security on offer. It was a long way from

today's industry.

But suddenly things were looking up at Lagonda. The M45 was the car to have and attracted enormous publicity, aided by Woodwright's skilful handling of the press fleet. It looked to be a bargain to everyone. Its only real competitors were the Alvis Speed Twenty, £100 cheaper but with nowhere near the performance, and the equally new Bentley 3½ Litre, just as quick but nearly £600 more expensive and not available with a works body; you still had to negotiate with a coachbuilder before you could drive off. So M45s began to sell as quickly as the factory could turn them out. They became fashionable in a way that no Lagonda before ever had. Sir Malcolm Campbell bought one (AYU 1, chassis Z10993) painted "Blue, to customer's pattern", and of the 17 Lagondas

entered in the 1934 RAC Rally, eight were M45s accompanied by three 16/80s, two 3 Litres, three 2 Litres and a Rapier prototype. The Mann family had swapped their blown 2 Litre for an M45, which is still in the family, and Lord de Clifford was in that Rapier. Of the 400 entrants, virtually everyone got to the Bournemouth finish without loss of marks, and the results depended on split-second timing in the wiggle-woggle tests on the seafront. Here the bulky Lagondas were at their worst and the best of them was Roland Gardner (2 Litre), who came 10th overall.

It was not surprising that Lagonda production was dominated by the M45 in the first half of 1934, with 16/80s in small batches and 3 Litres in ones and twos. Then from May onwards Rapiers begin to dominate, at first in small batches but then in 10s, 12s and 20s.

With space at the front of the chassis at a premium, the headlamp support tubes were tucked behind the radiator. 3½ Litres were originally supplied with Lucas "Projector" dipping headlamps but many, like Bryan Hyett's, have been converted to P100s.

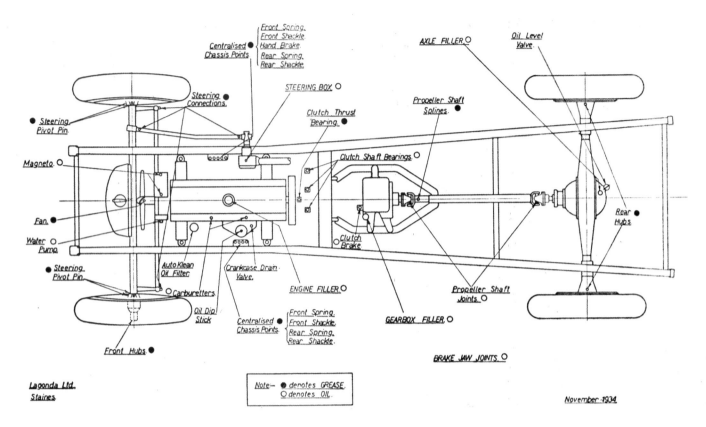

Centralised ● Chassis Points

Front Spring.
Front Shackle.
Hand Brake.
Rear Spring.
Rear Shackle.

AXLE FILLER ○

Oil Level
Valve.

Steering ●
Connections.

STEERING BOX ○

Propeller Shaft
Splines. ●

● Steering.
Pivot Pin.

Clutch Thrust
Bearing. ○

Magneto. ○

Clutch Shaft Bearings ○

Fan. ●

Rear ●
Hubs

Water ○
Pump

Clutch ●
Brake

● Steering.
Pivot Pin.

Auto Klean
Oil Filter

Crankcase Drain
Valve.

ENGINE FILLER ○

Propeller Shaft
Joints. ○

○ Carburetters.

GEARBOX FILLER. ○

Oil Dip
Stick

Centralised ●
Chassis Points.

Front Spring.
Front Shackle.
Rear Spring.
Rear Shackle.

Front Hubs ●

BRAKE JAW JOINTS. ○

Lagonda Ltd.
Staines.

Note— ● denotes GREASE.
○ denotes OIL.

November 1934

Having adapted the ZM Maybach chassis to accept the Meadows engine for the M45, Lagonda built a totally new design for the Rapide and then had to adapt it, with a gearbox sub-frame, for the 3½ Litre.

The Rapier was an assembly job with very little made in the factory. Engines came from Coventry Climax, gearboxes and rear axles from ENV and front axles from Alford & Alder. From time to time, when demand unexpectedly dried up, the whole place was swamped in chassis awaiting being driven to the body builders generally Abbott's of Farnham.

In the autumn of 1934 Lagonda gained enormous publicity from their performance in the Ulster Tourist Trophy. Fox & Nicholl had returned to the make and three special short-wheelbase 4½-litre chassis had been bought by Warwick Wright, although there was almost certainly factory support, since Fox was given the use of the Staines test beds to tune the special engines. The whole story is recounted in the author's 4½ Litre book in this series. The shorter 10ft 3in (3124mm) chassis featured the newly introduced Girling braking system, which aimed to have all its rods in pure tension and was thus a great deal lighter than any design using cross-shafts in torsion. The shorter chassis was designed for the new Rapide model of 4½ Litre which was introduced at the 1934 Motor Show. This "top of the range" car used a more highly tuned

Meadows engine and the gearbox had a free-wheel. It boasted built-in jacks, hydraulic dampers and a new tourer body, the T9, with only vestigial elbow cut-outs and a concealed hood. Alongside it, on the same chassis but with some of the trimmings omitted, was a new model, the 3½ Litre. This had a new engine, directly descended from the 75mm 3 Litre but bored out to 80mm, giving 3619cc, and for once Lagonda quoted a power output, 88bhp at 3000rpm. At the outset only a tourer body was offered, virtually identical to the Rapide's and coded the same as T9. The missing T8, meanwhile, had appeared on the ordinary M45 and had two huge doors, one each side, instead of the one and a half doors of the T7. The T9 body, perceptibly more modern looking, was the first Lagonda touring body to have wheel arches, all previous ones since the Speed Model having bodies which fitted within the rear wheels. The new larger doors permitted the sidescreens to be stored within them, avoiding the muddle sometimes found earlier when they all went behind the rear seat squab. Semaphore traffic indicators were fitted, and in fact appeared on all models. The

A 3½ Litre saloon, still Silent Travel and pillarless, coded ST44. The upper hinge of the front doors takes up all of the waist moulding as far as the bonnet edge. This enables the two hinges to be vertically above each other.

windscreen was top-hinged as on the 3 Litre and not the Rapide's fold-flat version.

At the front of the car the shorter wheelbase led to some re-arrangement of the headlamp supporting structure, the "goalpost"-like frame being replaced by streamlined vertical struts, braced to the wings and radiator. The headlamps themselves flanked the radiator instead of being in front of it. Inside the body the elliptical metal dash panel first found in 1929 was finally pensioned off and the 3½ Litre dash was very nearly the same as the Rapide one, complete with little grooves in the surrounding woodwork for the tails of the lighting and ignition switches to operate in.

A saloon body for the new model was not initially on offer but it arrived during the winter of 1934, almost exactly the same in appearance as the Rapide saloon but coded differently, ST44 to the Rapide's ST54, perhaps to reflect that the cheaper car was not so well equipped; it had no built-in jacking system, for example. This was in contrast to the tourers, where both 3½ and Rapide were coded T9. There was a clear family resemblance to the earlier ST34 but the body was less angular, more rounded and with a greater curvature to the roof. On this body a solution was found for the first time to the vexing problem of how to reconcile a raked hinge line with the pillarless construction, which necessitated trailing front doors.

Earlier pillarless cars had had to make the hinge line vertical, which affronted the designers who wanted this line to be an extension of the raked windscreen. The solution was to outrig the upper hinge and make it, when closed, part of the waist moulding. In this way the door could be wider at the bottom than at the top, easing access, but still have a vertical hinge line. It sounds a small point, but had a surprisingly large effect on the appearance. As did narrowing the roof so that it was no longer the widest part of the body. All the official literature suggested that the 3½ would be offered as well as the 3 Litre in its latest form, but the fact is that no 3 Litres were made after the introduction of the more modern car.

Although the 3½ Litre engine looked exactly

Rear view of 3½ Litre saloon. Rear windows were beginning to grow again after the letter-box-like slots of the early 1930s.

Near side of the 3½ Litre engine. Outwardly at least very similar to the 75mm 3 Litre engine.

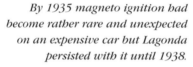

By 1935 magneto ignition had become rather rare and unexpected on an expensive car but Lagonda persisted with it until 1938.

the same as the 75mm 3 Litre one, it is doubtful that the existing design could accommodate a further 5mm overbore and one suspects it was a new casting. The slender steel connecting rods were replaced by much stouter aluminium alloy ones with stouter gudgeon pins (1-inch instead of $^{11}/_{16}$th-inch, 25.4mm instead of 18mm). The new pistons which ensued gave a raised compression ratio of 7:1, high for the period but viable now that leaded fuel was freely available. An SU electric fuel pump replaced the mechanical one, probably as a starting aid, but the lobe on the camshaft was still there if an owner wanted to revert. The Autoklean oil filter continued to be operated by the throttle pedal, despite the more popular alternative arrangement found on the 16/80 where the clutch pedal worked it. Possibly it was felt that 3½ Litre drivers would never change gear. The only objection to the throttle method of operation was that as the discs turned they changed the feel of the pedal, which could be disconcerting.

The gearbox was the "silent third" version of the Z type unit, which sported double-helical gears. It was indeed much quieter but had the unfortunate effect of making a tricky gearchange even trickier. The shifting yoke worked on the layshaft, while the engaging dogs were on the mainshaft, so a bad gearchange would put a great side thrust on the double helicals, and if it damaged them they were very expensive to replace (and to cut in the first place, of course).

As this car had the Rapide's Girling brakes, inevitably it had similar axles, 3.67:1 at the rear, but without the built-in jacks, Telecontrols and Luvax dampers. A standard 3 Litre radiator was another distinguishing feature, compared with the Rapide's new tapered design, wider at the top and fitted with a streamlined filler cap.

Lagonda had Stand 143 at the Motor Show, and with such an array of models there must have been quite some heart-searching as to which to omit. Naturally the new models predominated and there were two Rapides,

Offside of the 3½ Litre engine. Asbestos string wound round the exhaust pipes was an attempt to keep some of the heat out of the cockpit.

The retention of the 3 Litre radiator on the 3½ Litre was one of the few external differences from the M45 Rapide, whose differently shaped shell carried a "streamlined" filler cap.

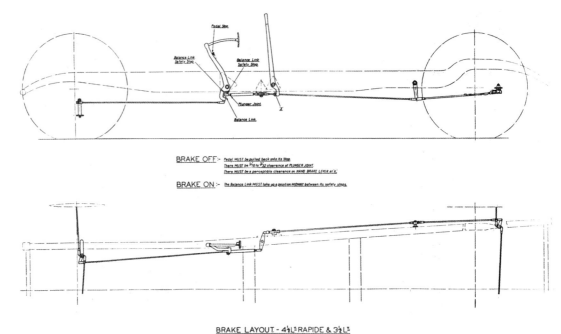

BRAKE OFF :- *Pedal MUST be pulled back onto its Stop.*
There MUST be ³⁄₁₆ to ³⁄₃₂ clearance at PLUNGER JOINT.
There MUST be a perceptible clearance on HAND BRAKE LEVER at 'X'.

BRAKE ON :- *The Balance Link MUST take up a position MIDWAY between its safety stops.*

BRAKE LAYOUT - 4½L. RAPIDE & 3½L.

The 3½ Litre inherited the M45 Rapide's Girling brake system, even simpler and lighter than the ZM version. Its only disadvantage comes after very high mileage or in racing, when wear in the pivots reduces braking efficiency far more than with earlier designs with longer movements.

These rear lamps on stalks were the result of new regulations laying down how far from the back of a car the lamps could be. Lagonda didn't make their own, they used ones from a contemporary Buick. The amber flasher is a recent addition, recognising modern drivers' ignorance of "flipper" indicators.

the saloon by Gurney Nutting and the factory tourer; a brace of 3½s, a normal M45 pillarless saloon, a 16/80 tourer and a Rapier chassis. It was as well that the company had booked one of the larger stands. It was dominated by an outsize replica of the winged radiator badge, from the wingtips of which were suspended huge lamps. To avoid wear and tear, all the cars had transparent bonnet sides, kept locked so that the sporting lines were never spoilt by folded bonnets, which could

also scratch the beautiful chromium plating on the special headlamps. In addition, Olympia was crawling with Lagondas on the coachbuilders' stands, adding 12 more cars to the seven on the Lagonda stand. Eleven of these were either 4½ Litres or Rapiers, but Carlton showed a drophead coupé on the 3½ Litre chassis. Its unique point was a hood which folded out of sight, very rare in those days when folded hoods tended to be an untidy heap destroying rear vision.

At the end of November the first of the new models to be road tested was the 3½ Litre in *The Autocar*. The car was a tourer and the testers declared themselves delighted with what was in effect a slower Rapide, with a top speed over 84mph. There was a slight qualification about the gearbox but otherwise the test was a eulogy. The figures were respectable but no great advance on the 3 Litre's, since the new car was 2cwt (101kg) heavier and had higher gears. The acceleration figures were almost identical and the 3½ used more fuel, giving 18mpg instead of 20. When *The Motor* came to test BPK 742 in their turn, they made it faster, going from rest to 60mph in 25 seconds against their rival's 27.2 seconds, but this reflects as much as anything else the differing policies of the two magazines. *The Motor* reckoned to test a car to its utmost, whereas *The Autocar*'s testers drove

as they fancied an owner would, conscious of repair costs. *The Motor*'s more forceful driving increased fuel consumption to 16mpg, exactly the same as the M45, but without the top speed.

You would expect a new numbering system for the 3½ Litre. Hitherto all 10ft 9in chassis had been coded with a Z prefix and this was extended to the 10ft 3in cars, both Rapide and 3½ Litre. To begin with the latter were coded 3.5 on their identity plate but quite soon this was changed to M35R, a thoroughly illogical idea since the car didn't have the "M" chassis, nor was it a Rapide, although it shared that chassis. The engines themselves were stamped 35Z/xxx, apparently starting at 100. In later years 3 Litre owners able to get hold of 3½ Litre engines have fitted them with no trouble at all, and the extra power in the lighter earlier car is very noticeable. But as the 3½ had such a short production run the supply of surplus engines is very small.

Lagonda entries for the 1935 Monte Carlo Rally were confined to 4½ Litres, plus Lord de Clifford in a Rapier, the latter performing best of them, taking 24th place overall. The motoring papers were busy testing Rapides,

recognised as the fastest unsupercharged car on the market in the UK, but behind the scenes the Lagonda company was in serious financial trouble and the final blow was to come in March with the introduction of the 30mph speed limit in built-up areas. Before that, in February, it had been announced that the company's future had been secured by an agreement with a syndicate of financiers, but no more was heard of this and it must have fallen through.

Lagonda were very good at designing hoods that didn't spoil the looks of the car. But getting into the back seats with it up could be something of a struggle.

The large 20 gallon (91 litre) petrol tank made the boot rather shallow but sturdy stays allowed the lid to carry extra luggage.

This rear view shows the extra width found by using wheel arches. Most T9 tourers mounted the spare wheel on the bootlid, but a sidemount was an option.

The RAC Rally was now attracting the large numbers of entries hitherto found on the Exeter and Land's End Trials, with nine Lagondas in the 1935 event, which finished at Eastbourne. Two were Rapides, two normal M45s, two 16/80s, two 2 Litres and Lord Walpole in a solitary Rapier. Eileen Ellison was driving the works demonstrator Rapide tourer, gaining a silver, and announced an entry in the Mille Miglia with it. Gold medals went to A E Dobell (M45R), C Dodd (16/80),

D G Silcock (16/80), T C Mann (M45). Silvers went to Miss Ellison, Denis Flather (2 Litre) and Lord Walpole.

Although in retrospect the 30mph limit was a necessary measure, given the anarchy and spiralling accident figures that no limits had produced, there was the expected reaction of a collapse of the sports car market. This market is illogical and emotional by definition, so one cannot complain if it behaves illogically. By the middle of April the whole

For years the sidescreens of a tourer lived behind the rear seat squab. The big doors of the 3½ Litre enabled a storage compartment to be provided on each side. And here they are in place.

By 1935 Lagonda finally allowed the driver of a tourer to have his own door.

Legroom for rear passengers suffered a little from the growing size of luggage boots, but is still generous by today's standards. This was Lagonda's first tourer body to have wheel arches instead of fitting between the wheels.

Above: The dashboard layout was almost exactly the same as the more expensive Rapide. Only missing are gauges for the Telecontrol dampers, not fitted to the 3½ Litre.

Left: Handbrake and gear lever still rather obstruct the driver's door. The catch on the gear lever guards reverse.

Right: One always feels that the grooves cut out of the dash for the tails of the ignition and lighting switches smacks of an oversight at design stage. The earlier M45 had the panel the other way up with no problem. 3½ Litre ignition switches are either on or off and do not have the intermediate positions of 4½ Litre models.

After 1933 Lagonda started to mark a red line on rev. counters, coinciding with larger diameter instruments.

"A" and "R" stand for "advance" and "retard" of the ignition, so "O" and "S" must mean "open" and "shut" for the hand throttle.

The 3½ Litre's 6-inch shorter wheelbase than its predecessor meant a little squeeze to get the sort of accommodation Lagonda customers expected but the result was a very handsome car.

The Vokes family's array of Lagondas included this 3½ Litre T9 tourer. It stayed in the family through several generations. Photo Tony Vokes.

factory was awash with unsold Rapier chassis, so many that they were parked in gangways and were a serious hazard to shins everywhere. On 18 April the bank panicked and brought in a Receiver. This was Maundy Thursday, so there was little effect until after the holiday, when the Receiver's first action was to stop production, stock-take and give notice to 125 employees. Ironically, that week's copy of *The Autocar* carried the long-delayed road test of the Rapide and the same magazine was preparing to carry a test of a fixed-head coupé Rapier, which never did appear. Sir Edgar Holberton issued a statement excusing the bank's behaviour, claiming that they had shown great forbearance for

eight years. The Receiver then un-froze the stocks but would give no authority for new production, so the cars that emerged for the next month or so were all built up from parts already manufactured. Lagonda was never noted for consistency in its production but the cars emerging during the "bankruptcy" period defy description. A Maybach gearbox lurking in the stores was bolted into a 3½ Litre chassis, there were 10ft 9in Rapides, ordinary M45s with Rapide engines - the list is endless. A J A Wallace Barr, the owner of Cellon Ltd, who supplied Lagonda's paint, was persuaded to accept a car in lieu of settling his bill. A big splash of advertising in the Silver Jubilee editions of early May could not be stopped, but after that all advertising ceased and Woodwright was discharged. Alvis had scented the coming storm and had increased its capitalisation at the end of 1934 with an eye to buying up Lagonda, and they were first in the queue with an offer of £35,000, which the Receiver rejected as not enough. On 16 May he announced that the whole company would be auctioned by tender, which had to be returned on 18 June, the day after Le Mans. Before long, production was down to the odd car and staff were down to 25. Frank Feeley left and went to Newns, where his first jobs were a special Eagle 2-seater for Sir Malcolm Campbell on the Rapier and the second the Light Tourer Railton.

The unexpected win by Hindmarsh and Fontes in the 1935 Le Mans focused even more attention on Lagonda than anticipated and Alan Good's success in buying the company and rejuvenating it is outside the scope of this book. The first decision of the new company was to hive off the Rapier to Rapier Cars Ltd and drop all models apart from the 4½ Litre. This was undoubtedly the right thing to do at the time. But the new company reassured existing customers with the smaller cars that the warranties would be honoured. This was a public relations master-

A 3½ Litre tourer being carried overland to Nepal in the mid-1930s, before there was a road link to India. The owner must have had money to pay for this and not be impatient. He was probably a member of the ruling family.
Photo John Anderson.

The 3½ Litre had a very short production run, less than a year, so is quite rare now.

stroke, especially as they did indeed honour them.

So 1935 saw the last of the 2 litre and 3 Litre models and their derivatives. They had carried the company successfully through the turbulent years of the Depression which had destroyed many worthy rivals. Their sturdy construction means that a very high propor-tion of the output survives to give pleasure and satisfaction to owners 70 to 80 years after they were built. The numbers manufactured are difficult to arrive at, but my best estimate is around 2470 from 1925 to 1935. The 3½ Litre had a very short production run of about 5 months, and all 16/65s have disappeared except one, and that has a 3 Litre engine.

3½ LITRE SUMMARY STATISTICS

Engine

As 3 Litre except

Capacity	3619cc
Bore & stroke	80 x 120mm
RAC rating	23.8hp
Compression ratio	7:1
Valve timing	io 6° ATDC,
	ic 48° ABDC,
	eo 40° BBDC,
	ec 5° ATDC
	Inlet open 222°,
	exhaust open 225°
Brake horsepower	88 at 3000rpm
Water capacity	3.75 gallons (17 litres)
Fuel supply	SU type L electric pump.

Chassis

As 75mm 3 Litre except

Wheelbase	10ft 3in (3124mm)
Track	4ft 10in (1473mm)
Overall length	15ft 7in (4750mm)
Turning circle	42ft (12.8m)

Rear Axle

Type	Spiral bevel by Lagonda
Ratios	3.67:1 (tourer), 4.1:1 (saloon)

BRAKES	Girling pattern by New Hudson
	16in (406mm) drums
WEIGHTS	
Tourer	32cwt (1626kg)
Saloon	Never published

Prices

Chassis	£550
Tourer	£695
Saloon	£795

Chapter Eleven

On The Road Today

Listed at the end of this book are the published contemporary road tests of the 2, 3, 3 ½ Litre and 16/80 cars. Most are full of praise, since these were expensive and desirable cars and even if the testers were disappointed when a car failed, sometimes by a long way, to return the performance claimed by the maker, they emphasised the good points and tended to ignore or excuse the others. Most road tests of the period were like that, but I have to single out Edgar Duffield, writing in *The Automotor Journal*, for a much more stringent regime. He alone of the motoring press was prepared to say when a car was not properly prepared or broke down on test. Unfortunately the magazine went under in 1931 and one hopes Duffield's outspokenness was not the cause. There was a case in 1935 when Lagonda lent a Rapier fixed-head coupé to *The Autocar* which was running so badly that the paper sent it back and never published the test.

One of the aspects always remarked upon then was the lowest practical speed on top gear. By this they meant the lowest speed from which it was possible to accelerate in top gear without snatching or stalling. This reflected the public's horror of changing gear. The makers of the Invicta car, for example, boasted of its ability to start from rest in top. Buyers of these expensive cars could be presumed to be middle-aged and likely to have learned to drive before or in the

First World War. The difficult transmissions of such early vehicles meant that their drivers strove to reduce the number of gear changes that they made, especially downwards ones – always the more difficult. So, even with a four speed 'box there was a tendency to start in second, get into top as soon as possible and try to stay there, fiddling with the ignition advance/retard lever if necessary. Over time, the gear ratios provided came to fit in with this style of driving, with a stump-pulling first gear, never used; a lowish second, used for starting from rest; a top gear about right and a very high third which the driver could drop into to tackle a hill without slowing down too much. Modern drivers expect to use all the gears provided and may find Lagonda's choice of ratios a touch eccentric, although you soon get used to them.

Over the ten years of production which we are considering, the cars changed very considerably. An early 14/60 saloon today feels like a very over-bodied affair and you need to use the gearbox frequently to get any reasonably brisk progress. The five-bearing crankshaft does mean that compared to other four-cylinder 2-litres of its era the engine is smooth, but there isn't the low-speed torque you might expect from such a long-stroke engine. The OH gearbox takes a little getting used to, partly because the gate is laid out in the reverse pattern to today's norm, with first and second to the right of third and top.

There is no synchromesh or any aid to quiet changes and the clutch stop may help or hinder, according to how it is set. This device, in effect a disc brake on the shaft joining engine to gearbox, can be adjusted as to when it comes in and how hard. In the 1920s and particularly with the Speed Model, the hotshoes of the day would set it both fierce and early, with the result that they could pull the lever straight through for lightning upward changes, at the price of a much more awkward downward change. These settings are very much a matter of personal taste and the author's choice is to slacken the clutch stop right off so that it has no effect and rely on sound to judge downward, double-declutched, changes. But not everyone will agree.

Moving to the Speed Model, virtually always a tourer nowadays as restorers have baulked at the cost of rebuilding a saloon, the increased power, lighter bodywork and taller gearing transform the car. Excellent handling and the splendid brakes make the driving process much more enjoyable. One of the

hidden aspects of the chassis design, a hold-over from the 12/24, is that in a real emergency grabbing the handbrake gives extra stopping power as it works on a separate set of brake shoes in the rear drums and the fly-off action means there is no danger of it sticking on.

The driver of a Speed Model tourer was not allowed a door and the gear lever and handbrake lever are perfectly situated to go up his trouser leg as he climbs in over the side. To add confusion, if a high chassis car is still fitted with its original Barker headlamp dipping system, there is a third lever, distressingly similar to the gear lever and next to it. This, when moved, physically tilts the entire headlamp assembly downwards and is just as effective at going up trouser legs. Plus Fours or riding breeches were commonly worn by rally drivers in the 1920s and now you know why.

Although the only seat adjustment is fore and aft, most people find the seats very comfortable, and since the Lagonda company specialised in very tall executives there is

High chassis Speed Model dashboard. This car has been converted to a right hand throttle pedal, but is otherwise standard.

The knob for the Ki-gass petrol priming pump. It must be screwed shut once the engine is running steadily.

brake pedal in an emergency since the right hand pedal is straight in front of the leg and not biased to the left. Many Lagonda Club owners have been driving their cars with this pedal set-up for 50-plus years and we have yet to hear of an accident caused by the layout.

With the car open, the all-round visibility is perfect, with the top of the nearside front wing visible if the car has the long Speed Model wings. With cycle wings and a low chassis car this last may not apply since the crew sit lower in the car and the sidelamp will have removed itself to the scuttle. If the car was built now, scuttle sidelamps would be illegal, but fortunately "grandfather's rights" prevail for some aspects of car lighting. The low chassis windscreen was cut down in height to aid the sporty look and a very tall driver may find his head out in the slipstream. Lord de Clifford was very tall indeed and fitted a larger, non-standard, windscreen to each of his cars that subsequent owners have usually removed. With hood up and sidescreens in place the situation changes, and tourers and saloons both suffer very restricted view to the rear, with the tiny rear windows of the saloons and letter-box-like openings in the original hoods. Wing or door mirrors become essential. This wasn't a problem when the cars were new as few cars were fast enough to overtake a Lagonda and reversing was rare, except out of the motor house in the morning. After the Second World War, when the cars were generally in daily use, there was a trend to fit large plastic rear windows in hoods. Certainly practical, this did little to help the appearance and most modern restorers attempt to reproduce the original designs.

always ample leg room in front and rear. This is especially so in the early saloons, where the absence of a boot gives enormous space in the back. In fact 14/60s offered fold-up occasional seats here if a division was fitted, without any changes anywhere else and certainly without lengthening the wheelbase. The author once navigated in a rally in a 14/60 saloon and, the day warming up, found he had to throw his discarded hat to place it on the back seat. You couldn't just place it there, it was too far away.

The open tourers are very open, and suitable clothing is vital; it has to be very hot indeed before thinking of driving in shirt sleeves. In the back seats this applies in spades and the option of a separate windscreen for the rear passengers was very popular with the 14/60. In its absence a flying helmet begins to look very desirable.

Lagonda, right up to the introduction of hydraulic brakes, resolutely made the brake pedal the right hand one, with the throttle in the centre. This arrangement tends to frighten newcomers but one soon gets used to it. It was done to get simple and thus better performing braking systems and has the advantage of making "heel and toe" braking, whereby the driver brakes and changes gear simultaneously, a very much more natural action. It also assists a really hard push on the

The 2 Litre low chassis cars differ a great deal in appearance but feel very little different on the road. The crew sit lower in a perceptibly lower car, but accommodation is much the same. In theory, cornering should be better with a lower centre of gravity, but this is arguable and anyone asserting this at a club gathering is assured of a noisy dispute. For no very obvious reason the low chassis car is heavier, even though there seems to be less of it. It is probably due to the increased number of accessories, although the massive cast alloy bulkhead looks heavier than the high chassis flat one. The more steeply dropped front axle of the low chassis car is more prone to axle tramp under braking. Over the years the club magazine has carried learned articles about why this should be and offered a variety of ways of overcoming it.

There is a great similarity in appearance between the 2 Litre and 3 Litre and when stationary they feel very similar. The accommodation is nearly identical. But once on the move the differences appear. The 3 Litre engine was originally designed to haul around ponderous, heavy saloons and limousines with great smoothness and with a minimum of gear-changing. Which it did admirably. Later, when Lagonda produced the sporting versions, the Special was in many ways a Speed Model which you didn't have to row along with the gear lever. The engine in its original form had very conservative valve timing and a tiny updraught carburettor. When the Special came along and then the twin SU versions, the top speed was little different to a Speed Model's but the increased torque is very noticeable on the road and if the driver is prepared to adjust the ignition timing it is very much a top gear car. Which is just as well, because the heavier Z type gearbox can be tricky. They do seem to vary immensely and the author has had experience in other people's 3 Litres of Z 'boxes that

varied from the delightful to the absolute pigs. Mind you, the owner will usually get the hang of it after a bit.

The added weight of the Maybach gearbox forced the company to fit larger brakes to the ZM 75mm 3 Litres. On the road this doesn't seem to make any appreciable difference, since the extra braking effort just about balances the extra weight, but you no longer have the possibility of yanking on the handbrake to get more retardation. In the newer design the hand lever operated the same linkage as the footbrake, with a slotted link which in theory confines its influence to the rear shoes only. In practice, after a while this stops sliding and works all four.

There is only one Maybach-equipped Selector known to be on the road and its owner finds that for practical purposes he has a 5-speed gearbox, with one split shift between low and high ratio. It works well but whether it was worth importing all that weight and complexity is arguable. One is always surprised how long it took British manufacturers to adopt synchromesh. It may be that General Motors wanted an extortionate amount for a licence to use it to begin with.

The 16/80 was to all intents and purposes a low chassis 2 Litre fitted with the Crossley six-cylinder engine. The extra revs available give

All Lagondas with mechanical brakes have the throttle pedal as the central one. You soon get used to it.

it a performance bonus compared with the four-cylinder car but at the price of fussier cruising, since there are 50 per cent more bangs per mile. The ribbed brake drums are much longer-lasting and may resist fade better, but actual stopping power feels much the same. All these Lagonda models have excellent brakes anyway and in their heyday the 14/60s used to carry little warning triangles on the rear to alert following drivers to the phenomenal retardation potential. Later 16/80s had the Wilson epicyclic gearbox, as manufactured by ENV. There was a debate at the time about whether you also needed a clutch with this gearbox. Lagonda decided you didn't, with the result that there can be a problem with rapid wear on the first gear band as this acts as a clutch in taking up the drive from rest. There was also a problem with creep while the oil was cold, so that the car had to be held on the footbrake to stop it inching forward, even in neutral. The gear lever looks conventional but only moves in the fore-and-aft plane and only selects a gear, engagement being by the left pedal. Later, with the Rapier, the company changed its mind and not only added a plate clutch but also a natty little catch that held the clutch out in neutral. This not only killed the creep but also stopped the gears growling, an annoying habit of early epicyclics. The ENV 'box cars were heavier than the manual ones and lower geared, but gear-changing was so much simpler that most buyers would put up with that.

Dashboard design from 1925 took on three separate phases. The 14/60 had the free-standing arrangement where the central metal part of the dash was outrigged from the bulkhead and could be installed before any bodywork was added. Thus a bare chassis could be driven legally to an outside coachbuilder. This metal panel contained a smaller rectangular one by CAV with the ignition and other electrics, plus the ammeter. Flanking this were the large rev-counter on the left and a matching clock in front of the driver. Underneath the CAV panel was the speedometer, reading to 80mph and flanked by the oil pressure gauge and water temperature gauge. Ergonomics had not been invented then and the presumption that the driver was more interested in the time of day than what speed

he was doing or what speed the engine was turning at gives us a reasonable idea of the type of customer the car was aimed at. With the Speed Model an entirely new dash layout arrived, with the rev-counter immediately in front of the driver and mounted directly in the wooden part. The central metal panel was smaller and still had the electrics, but also the speedometer and clock. The newly invented Hobson Telegauge for the first time indicated fuel contents without a walk to the rear of the car, but the water temperature gauge vanished, replaced by the Boyce Motometer fixed to the radiator cap. The high chassis 3 Litre Special introduced yet another layout that eventually found its way on to all low chassis cars and the 16/80. This had a much larger, elliptical, metal panel set in the wooden dash and containing all the instruments except the rev-counter, still directly in front of the driver. The quick-release clip-type radiator cap meant that the water temperature gauge returned to the dashboard. Throughout all these changes the ignition advance lever and the hand throttle lever stayed in place on the steering column.

The 3½ Litre had a very short production run and is quite a rare animal now. It is believed only one saloon survives, but there are a handful of dropheads with bodies provided by outside coachbuilders. The majority of surviving cars have Lagonda's T9 tourer body. With its shorter chassis and Girling brakes the 3½ drives very like a slow M45 Rapide. As remarked in earlier chapters, the extra power almost exactly balanced the extra weight and the overall performance is pretty well indistinguishable from a 3 Litre's. The 3½-litre engine fits easily into a 3 Litre and there the extra power does tell, but spare 3½ engines are pretty thin on the ground so this is a rare combination. The handling is a little on the heavy side owing to the more concentrated weight at the front end and a greater tendency to understeer.

The 3½ Litre had the final version of the Z gearbox, the "silent third" type which used double helical gears. The purpose of these was to eliminate side thrust in the main cogs, which was done as much in the search for silence as for longevity. Unfortunately the design led to an even trickier gearchange and the added disadvantage that any damage caused by mishandling would be even more expensive to put right. It is a good job you don't need to use it much.

Now we have to start the engine. Early 14/60s and 16/65s had a strangler to enrich the mixture for a cold start but from the introduction of the Ki-gass pump about 1927 Lagonda fitted this device, which is a small pump to inject a dose of neat petrol into the inlet manifold, where it forms a pool and evaporates. It can usually be screwed home within a few seconds of a cold start as it is bad practice to leave it out. Engines that start without it are probably running over-rich. From contemporary accounts, a few cars at the change-over period had both a strangler and Ki-gass, but it is doubtful that any survive like this. Early SU carburettors had fixed jets and thus the Ki-gass was still required. Only about 1935 did adjustable jets appear, with an ability to lower them for starting. The ignition switch may or may not have a key. Originally there was a distinction between coil-ignition cars with a key and magneto ones without, but after 80 years and countless rebuilds this has long been blurred. Supercharged 2 Litres, as built, had both, with a changeover switch. The owner was expected to start on coil and switch to magneto once running. This proved to be unreliable – not intrinsically, but because owners forgot to change and burned out the starting coil, which was incorporated in the magneto.

The supercharged 2 Litre, now that it has been mentioned, is very much faster than the unblown car and has a great deal more low-speed torque. In the 1930s many owners experienced loads of trouble with them and most have at one time or another been running unblown, but modern lubricants solve most of the problems and increasingly the blowers are returning. However, they do require more attention than the unblown cars and it can be argued that the transmission is just a bit marginal for the extra power produced. If contemplating the purchase of a blown 2 Litre, do make absolutely sure the engine is a genuine supercharged one, coded 2B on the nearside of the timing case. There have been cases of unscrupulous owners adding a blower to an unblown engine, coded OHL2. Without the strengthened bottom end, such a mongrel will wear very

rapidly at best and might go bang if maltreated.

Both 2 Litre and 3 Litre engines run quite cool in normal use and overheating is not normally a problem. If a car does overheat, the likely culprit is a choked radiator. Lagonda always advised, correctly, that only rain water should be used in the cooling system. Tap water, in many parts of the country, contains enough dissolved lime to quickly deposit in the fine passages of the radiator and block them. Oil pressure is modest, around 20psi (1.4 bar) at running speeds when warm, and

The driver of a saloon could see behind him better than on the tourer with the hood up, but external mirrors were still vital. Even more so today.

will drop to virtually zero at idle. This is of no significance. The warm-up period is very prolonged compared to modern cars, as a result of the huge water and oil capacity related to the size of engine. While modern practice is to move off at once, cars of the 1920s and '30s were expected to warm up while stationary until some heat had got into everything, and this is still good practice.

Once warmed up and on the move all these cars prove to have great charm, addictive almost, and it is no great surprise to find many members of the Lagonda Club who have owned their cars for 30 years or more. The 3 Litre is, and feels, perceptibly heavier than the 2 Litre, but still handles well, and all models have positive, direct steering that will come as a revelation to anyone brought up on power assistance and squidgy radial tyres. The reason for the large steering wheel and its proximity to the driver's chest will soon become apparent, since the steering is very high geared, but you will find that on a straight road the car has admirable self-centering and only the lightest grip is needed.

Driving at night will show up the fact that Lucas P100s or P80s were designed for long straight roads, since the beam is powerful but very narrow. The foot dipswitch can prove elusive if the car is only occasionally used after dark and vintage dynamos aren't too keen on driving with the headlamps on for long periods. Earlier cars give the driver a choice of battery charging rate, important in those days of three-brush dynamos which could easily overcharge a battery on a long daylight trip. Switching on the lamps automatically increased the charging rate to the "winter" position. Even so, it is not uncommon to see the ammeter showing a discharge when headlamps are in use. A good battery is essential and probably a trickle charger in the garage if much night driving is contemplated. The lighting systems fitted changed several times over the ten years in question. Early 14/60s had a "dimmer", which was literally that; a switch introduced a resistance into the headlamp circuit, dropping the output available and hence dimming the lamps. With the Speed Model came the Barker dipper, which physically tilted both headlamps downward. Simple and reliable. Lagonda adopted Lucas P100s as soon as they

appeared in 1929 and the first kind had a second out-of-focus bulb in each lamp which came on when the dipswitch extinguished the main beam. By 1932 another system came in, now illegal, where both headlamps went out and a single central "pass lamp" came on, this having a flat-topped beam giving less dazzle. This would appear to be retrograde, but the thinking at the time was that the second bulb in the P100 compromised the shape of the beam, so the second bulb vanished and the desired main beam pattern was restored. All cars with this system should by now have been altered, as the law now demands all headlamps to be illuminated in pairs. In the same way, the original single offside rear lamp must by now have a second one added on the nearside. Finally, with the 3½ Litre, yet another system was adopted, largely because the shortened front end left too little room for the centre lamp, a rather bulky item. The P100s were replaced by Lucas "Projector" lamps which had tilting reflectors. Switches were provided which gave a choice of three modes; full beam on both; dipped right lamp plus full beam left lamp and dipped on both. Again, this is illegal now. But the tilting reflectors proved unreliable and virtually all 3½s seem to have been rebuilt with either P100s or P80s.

One thing an owner only accustomed to modern cars will find strange is the lack of luggage accommodation. If travelling two-up, the rear seats and footwells get conscripted to take the picnic and the waterproofs but there is more of a problem when three or four are aboard. One supposes that in the 1920s either people didn't carry that much kit about or that the owner sent the bulky stuff ahead by rail. Or perhaps the servants brought it. An external luggage rack was a common accessory, to which sturdy cabin trunks could be lashed. In extreme cases, owners have been known to attach cases to the running boards.

Although Lagonda was unique among up-market manufacturers in offering factory-built bodies, quite a few owners wanted something more distinctive. In some cases *outré* is the better word. Sadly, few of these cars have survived unchanged, and when the time has come for major rebuilds most restorers opt for a standard Lagonda design which they can measure and reproduce.

Chapter Twelve

Ownership Today

One hopes that some readers of this book will be contemplating buying a Lagonda. They may never have owned a pre-war car or, if they have, one of another make. Lagondas have the common characteristics of most pre-1939 cars, plus a few specific to the make, such as the centre throttle pedal, covered in the last chapter. The first piece of advice one can give is to join the Lagonda Club. It is not necessary to own a Lagonda to do this, and when cars come on the market members are encouraged, not least by the minimal advertising rates, to first offer their cars through the club's monthly newsletter.

By joining, one can take advantage of the accumulated experience of over 800 members worldwide and have access to the "Workshop Manuals" produced by expert club members. Then there is the club's spares service, which manufactures virtually all components to either the original design or, where appropriate, in improved modern materials if there was a problem with longevity. An example of the latter is the various aluminium water pipes found on the engines, which are prone to corrosion from the inside. The replacements are made in a modern alloy which resists such corrosion well. As well as the club's official Spares Scheme, a number of keen members produce parts or provide services to members and some traders specialise in the repair and maintenance of the make.

First of all, the prospective owner faces the choice of model and body type. It is a sad fact that open cars fetch about twice the price of closed ones, so that when a saloon needs bodywork attention it has been very common for an owner of the philistine persuasion to scrap the body, replace it with a tourer or even a primitive boy's racer and then sell on at a profit. As a result, good saloons have become very scarce. The author's view is that the saloons, which changed annually, are more interesting than the tourers, all much of a muchness, and carry a lot more period charm in their fittings. It will, of course, depend on what is available on the market and how long the buyer is prepared to wait for the right car. A good car, of any of the Lagondas covered in this book, will be quite expensive. The cheap "barn find" may not be such a good buy if it requires expensive professional attention, but might attract a person able to do it him/herself. It is not uncommon to find such a vehicle semi-dismantled and you then have the nagging doubt – have I got all the missing bits? On one famous occasion a member bought not only the car in a dismantled state but also the top six inches of the earth floor of the garage, which was accommodating scores of small components which had got trodden in.

The first requirement will be a set of Whitworth/BSF spanners. These are no longer stocked by mainstream tool merchants but are

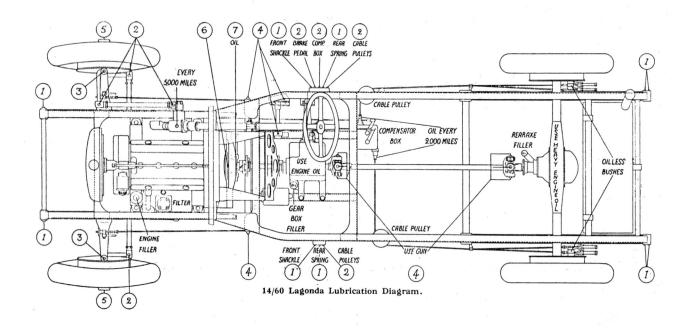

14/60 Lagonda Lubrication Diagram.

Lubrication chart from the Instruction Book for a very early 14/60, showing the roller bearing propeller shaft universal joints, which do not seem to have a splined coupling to accommodate changes in length.

available at the larger autojumbles. The open-ended variety will do most jobs on the Lagonda but there are one or two places where a tubular spanner, rare nowadays, was originally employed. Mostly a modern socket set will replace it. For all the models covered in this book you will require an 18mm plug spanner, now very hard to find. The 18mm size is a trap for the unwary as it refers to the size of the hole in the cylinder head. The actual hexagon size is nine-sixteenths Whitworth. The Lagonda Club supplies special NGK sparking plugs which have the 18mm thread but also the 14mm size hexagon, which most modern plug spanners fit. For dealing with the electrical side, should you feel competent to do so, you will also need a set of BA spanners, chiefly the even number sizes, 2BA, 4BA and 6BA. Imperial feeler gauges for setting valve clearances are still easy to find and it is safer to use these than to attempt to convert to the nearest metric equivalent, which is not near enough when dealing with these tiny dimensions. It scarcely needs stating that you will also need a substantial supply of sticking plasters for grazed knuckles and industrial sized pots of Swarfega, but then that applies to all old cars.

Where should your car come from?

Undoubtedly the best source is a fellow club member. He will have the history of the car in his ownership and will of course let you drive it to sample its performance and listen for unwanted noises at the same time. Most Lagonda engines are renowned for being easy to start from cold, so I would be a bit alarmed if the car is nicely warmed through when you arrive. The starting handle will enable you to check if all the compressions are there; if two are missing and they are adjacent cylinders, suspect gasket failure. The easy check here is to see if there is water in the oil. As it is heavier than the oil it will be on the very bottom of the dipstick. If you are unsure, it is prudent to take with you an experienced club member who is familiar with the model, but buy him a decent lunch for his trouble. As most owners are hoarders of one kind or another, the chances are that he will have a stock of spare parts, some useless, others less so. This is your chance to do a favourable deal about these.

Buying from a dealer can be a more high-pressure experience, but you may be able to screw some sort of guarantee from him to justify the higher price. Again, a test drive is vital and possibly an RAC or AA inspection, although expertise on old cars in their ranks

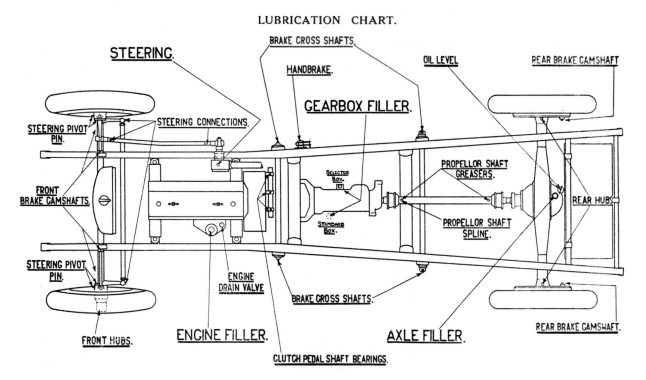

LUBRICATION CHART.

must be getting rare now. Auction prices are the lowest, but you rarely get much chance to drive the car. Remember, the auctioneer is acting for the vendor and only knows, officially, what the vendor tells him. Unfortunately, not all vendors are strictly truthful.

Having bought your Lagonda, some choices regarding maintenance become immediate. If leaded petrol is available locally, use it as the cars were designed for it. If not, the unleaded plus additive route is recommended, provided the additive is one approved by the Federation of British Historic Vehicle Clubs, who test them at regular intervals to make sure the formulation hasn't changed. The choice of oil is very subjective and depends on engine history. The old "straight" oils, ie non-detergent, tended to deposit carbon in all sorts of nooks in the engine, which is why pre-war motorists decarbonised so regularly. When detergent oil came in, it dissolved this carbon, carried it round the engine and, if you were lucky, deposited it in the filter. But Lagonda engines of this era don't have much in the way of filtration, only enough to keep out the larger rocks, and those of us who converted to detergent oils found them turning jet black after only a few miles. Several changes later, it

all sorted itself out, but the conversion was messy and expensive in oil. You need to know the engine history before deciding on which oil to use. If in doubt use what was originally recommended. Synthetic and semi-synthetic oils are very expensive and a waste of money in a Lagonda.

Chassis lubrication is another debatable issue. The 14/60 and its successors all had grouped nipples which actually used a product called "solid oil", now no longer available. It was a kind of halfway house between oil and grease. The nipples require quite frequent attention, as the lubrication diagram shows. As owners became richer or less inclined to employ a chauffeur attempts were made to simplify this chore and the Selector model 3 Litre used the newly introduced Silentbloc rubber bushes in profusion. One suspects that there were problems as the subsequent Rapide chassis, used for the 3½ Litre, reverted to grouped nipples. There is always bound to be a need to establish that the little pipes are not blocked and some owners have substituted ordinary greasers, leaving the grouped nipples for authentic appearance but not actually functioning.

Access to the working parts was always a Lagonda priority. In the days of the 16/65

By adopting Silentbloc rubber bushes throughout the suspension, Lagonda reduced the amount of greasing required for the ZM chassis, but there still remained quite a formidable list.

great play was made of the fact that the oil filler held a quart, so the owner could open a tin, dump it in and go off and do something else while it drained. The following cars, within limits, follow this philosophy and most operations can be carried out without access problems, although the new owner must learn to beware of the weight of the bigger components A selection of jacks that fold up really small will be a good investment.

One striking feature of Lagondas which will be immediately noticed by someone with experience only of modern cars is the quality of the materials and engineering. Rust is very rarely a problem. Wings, even steel ones, were rolled around wire on their edges and welded up, and much of the bodywork was aluminium. Mind you, there may be a problem with woodworm or moth. On the engineering side, consider the fit of the brake drums. Having removed the road wheel and the eight bolts that fasten a brake drum to its hub, one still cannot move it by hand. Two holes tapped ⁵⁄₁₆in BSF are provided in the base of the drum and two matching bolts in the tool kit. Screwing the bolts into the holes forces the drum off. Putting it back only involves a soft-faced hammer, also in the toolkit.

It is quite likely that the car you have acquired will need some attention. There has to be a reason why the vendor parted with it. He may have died, of course, and the widow may not be able to be much help. As a general rule, mechanical work is much quicker and cheaper than bodywork repairs. What tends to happen is that the new owner, keen to get the thing on the road, gets the engine overhauled and back in the car so that he can drive it and then either neglects the bodywork or, at the other extreme, spends so long on the bodywork that the engine goes all rusty. The council of perfection, which nobody follows, is to restore the body first and then tackle the mechanics.

The choice of model to buy obviously depends on what is on offer at any given time. There are very few saloons left on the earlier models for reasons already set out, but for the 16/80 and later 75mm 3 Litres there is a wider choice. They have a distinct period charm compared with the slightly spartan tourers. In the author's 4½ Litre book, he was able to say that the big Lagondas can easily keep up with modern traffic. This is not so with these earlier cars, but sheer speed is not the reason for wanting to own one. One hesitates to try to explain the attraction, but to quote a famous trumpeter, "If you got to ask, you ain't never going to know".

Lagonda didn't rely on the instruction book for lubrication instructions. On the high chassis tourer this plate was mounted next to the oil filler. Most cars have now been converted to mineral oil in the gearbox and back axle from the original castor-based vegetable oil. It is vital a new owner checks what is actually there before topping up.

APPENDIX 1. SUMMARY OF ROAD TESTS

Magazine	Date	Model	Weight cwt	Mpg	Max. speed mph	0-50 in gears	0-60 in gears	0-70 in gears	10-50 in third	10-60 in top	10-70 in top
14/60											
*The Autocar	30.10.25	Saloon									
*Automotor Journal	28.1.26	Saloon									
The Motor	20.7.26	Semi-sports		25	65					18.0	44.0
*AMJ	13.1.27	Semi-sports									
The Autocar	11.2.27	Semi-sports	26	28	67					Ice and snow	
16/65											
The Motor	26.7.27	Saloon (65mm)	33.75		65					33	54.6
*AMJ	10.5.28	Tourer (69mm)	23.5 (ch)								
2L HC Speed Model											
The Autocar	16.12.27	Tourer	26	23	70+						
The Motor	31.1.28	Tourer	21(ch)		c75					27	50
*Motor Sport	1/2.28	Tourer									
AMJ	31.5.28	Saloon			c78						
Supercharged 2 Litre											
The Motor	29.7.30	Tourer	28.75	c20	90					15	32
The Autocar	12.9.30	Tourer	29	18	88.2						
Motor Sport	10.30	Tourer			92	12	18				
*The Field	23.5.31	Tourer									
The Autocar	20.11.31	Saloon	30.75	19	80						
Country Life	6.2.32	Tourer									
3 Litre High Chassis											
The Motor	11.12.28	Saloon			64				22.5	30	
*AMJ	3.1.29	Saloon									
The Motor	24.9.29	Tourer	31.75		80				20	35	50
The Autocar	15.11.29	Tourer	30.5	20							
*The Tatler	16.10.29	Tourer									
3 Litre low chassis											
*AMJ	11.4.30	Tourer	30								
The Autocar	25.4.30	Saloon	32	20	75.3						
The Autocar	8.5.31	Tourer	30.25	20	83						
Motor Sport	3.32	Tourer			70					20	
(Lord de Clifford's rally car)											
3 Litre Selector											
The Motor	6.10.31	Tourer	32		82 (high ratio)			20.8	15	22	
The Autocar	11.12.31	Saloon	35.75	20	73.2						
The Autocar	18.11.32	Saloon	33	17							
The Autocar	5.6.36	Saloon (used)			69.2	21.4	27				
16/80											
The Autocar	16.9.32	Tourer	28.5	20	80						
The Motor	20.9.32	Tourer	28	20			19.2		18	35	50
Motor Sport	1.33	Tourer			78	16	22				
The Autocar	14.7.33	Tourer (ENV)	30	20	77.6	17.2	26.2				
The Autocar	22.6.34	Saloon	30	21	74	20.6	33.6				
3 1/2 Litre											
The Autocar	23.11.34	Tourer	32	18	84.1	17.6	27.2				
The Motor	8.1.35	Tourer	36.5 (loaded)	17.5	82	16	25			20	35

* No figures published.

The Lagonda Club

The Lagonda Club was formed in 1951 by the amalgamation of the Lagonda Car Club, itself a reformed pre-war club, and the Two Litre Register. It has three main objectives.

First, to preserve and develop interest in all types of Lagonda vehicles from the motorcycles to the latest models. Second, to promote the sport and pastime of using Lagonda cars by by various activities - social, sporting or just fun. The club publishes a monthly newsletter, a high quality colour magazine and a worldwide register of members and their cars. The club also reprints and publishes the original instruction books for each model, plus amplified "Workshop Manuals" prepared by club experts on most models.

Thirdlly, the club operates a comprehensive "in-house" spares section, which holds and manufactures virtually a complete range of spares for the pre-war cars. Also, there is a range of high quailty regalia, ties, badges, etc.

For the new member, the club can provide a wide range of general, technical and historical information from the club's archives. It offers the opportunity to meet like-minded people and make new firends. We pride ourselves on being non-stuffy and approachable. For those seeking a car, advertisements are published monthly in the newsletter.

For more information, please contact the Hon. Secretary, Colin Bugler, at Wintney House, London Road, Hartley Wintney, Hants RG27 8RN. Tel/fax: 01252 845451. Email: lagclub@tiscali.co.uk

The Lagonda Club AGM weekend is always well attended and is the big social event of the club year, held each September.